DATE DUE

JUN 0 2 1996	

The Human Services

The Human Services

edited by

Ronald J. Kase

AMS PRESS, INC.
New York, N.Y.

HV
11
H83

Library of Congress Cataloging in Publication Data
Main entry under title:

The Human services.

1. Social work education—United States—Addresses,
essays, lectures. 2. Medical social work—United
States—Addresses, essays, lectures. 3. Social service
—United States—Addresses, essays, lectures.
4. Medical care—United States—Addresses, essays,
lectures. 5. Mental health services—United States—
Addresses, essays, lectures. I. Kase, Ronald J.
NV11.H83   361'.973   79-2341
ISBN 0-404-16048-4

International Standard Book Number:
(cloth) 0-404-16048-4
(paper) 0-404-16049-2

MANUFACTURED IN THE UNITED STATES OF AMERICA

Dedication

To Bleakney Benedict
and, to Leo McLaughlin . . .
my teachers and friends.

Foreword

The Human Services is a unique collection of both new and reprinted material. Each article was selected for its relevance to those who are embarking on a study of the human service field.

New authors along with well known social theorists have contributed their work in order to make this book available to undergraduate college students, and to those who are involved in training programs at social and health agencies. I appreciate the contributors' willingness to share their work with social service students.

Original articles in this book concerned with social work process, aging, drug and alcohol abuse have been developed particularly for student readers. Classic articles by Riessman, Gans, Morris, Greer, and Harrington are of interest to everyone concerned with the helping professions. This mixture of new and traditional material is what makes *The Human Services* a special tool with many applications for the education and training of human service practitioners.

The Source Book section provides important information for those who need to know about graduate programs in human service, professional associations and national organizations dedicated to research and information gathering. It is as up to date as possible, but not every program can be listed, and new programs are always starting. By using the listed resources it is possible to gather enough information to make career and educational decisions.

It is my hope that *The Human Services* will provide information and education to all who read it.

Acknowledgments

I would like to thank Marvin A. Karp for his persistence and support. Without him this project would never have been realized.

I also want to thank Madeline Trezza for applying her considerable organizational and technical skills to this book, and a special thank you to Michael Rein for his assistance with the research.

"The Place of Social Work in the Human Services" appeared in *Social Work*, September 1974, and is reprinted with permission of the publisher, National Assoc. of Social Workers, Inc.

"Human Service on the Road to Social Progress" appeared in *The New York Times*, July 20, 1972, and is reprinted with the permission of the author.

"The Revolution in Mental-Health Care — A Bold 'New Approach'?" appeared in *Transaction*, April 1968, and is reprinted with permission of the publisher.

"Neighborhood Psychiatry: New Community Approach" appeared in the *Community Mental Health Journal*, Vol. 10 (1), 1974, and is reprinted with permission of the publisher.

"The 'Helper' Therapy Principle" appeared in *Social Work*, April 1965, and is reprinted with permission of the author.

"Delivery of Health Care" appeared in *Nursing Concepts for Health Promotion* (Prentice-Hall, 1975) and is reprinted with permission of the publisher.

"The Invisible Land" appeared as a chapter in *The Other America* (Macmillan, 1962) and is reprinted with permission of the publisher.

"The Positive Functions of Poverty" appeared as a chapter in *More Equality* (Random House, 1973) and is reprinted with permission of the publisher.

"Implementing the Objectives of Family Planning Programs" appeared in *Social Casework*, Vol. 50, No. 4, April 1969, and is reprinted with permission of the Family Service Association of America and the author.

"How to Look at Day-Care Programs" appeared in *Social Policy*, July/August 1972, and is reprinted with permission of the author.

"Battered Children" appeared in *Transaction*, Vol. 8, Nos. 9/10, 1971, and is reprinted with permission of the publisher.

"Battered Women and Their Assailants" appeared in *Social Work*, November 1977, and is reprinted with permission of the publisher.

"Critical Needs of Older People" appears in "Redirection of Services for the Elderly" and is printed here with permission of the author.

"Aging" is a chapter in "Alternatives" and is reprinted with permission of the author.

Contributors

RONALD J. KASE (editor) is a member of the Human Services faculty of New York City Community College of the City University of New York, and is consultant to the Graduate Program in Human Services at the University of Sarasota.

BONNIE E. CARLSON is a member of the faculty of the School of Social Work, University of Michigan, Ann Arbor.

ANN GLENANE FLYNN is Associate Professor of Gerontology, Graduate School of Management and Urban Professions, New School for Social Research.

HERBERT J. GANS is Professor of Sociology at Columbia University, and author of many books and articles concerned with poverty and other social problems.

COLIN GREER is Executive Editor of *Social Policy*, and Core Professor at the Union Graduate School.

MICHAEL HARRINGTON is Professor of Political Science, Queens College of the City University of New York, and is the author of *The Other America* (Macmillan) and other books dealing with social issues.

LEO McLAUGHLIN is the former President and Chancellor of Fordham University, and is currently Professor of Literature at Ramapo College of New Jersey.

GITTA MEIER is a consultant, and has written extensively in the fields of family planning, mental health, and social welfare.

ROBERT MORRIS is Kirstein Professor of Social Planning, Florence Heller Graduate School for Advanced Studies in Social Welfare, Brandeis University.

RUTH MURRAY is Associate Professor of Nursing, School of Nursing, St. Louis University.

LILLIAN OXTOBY is Associate Professor and Coordinator of the Early Childhood Education Program of New York City Community College of the City University of New York.

FRANK RIESSMAN is Editor of *Social Policy*, and Co-Director of the New Careers Development Center, and the New Human Services Institute of the Graduate Center, City University of New York.

PAMELA ROBY is Professor of Sociology, Kresge College, University of California, Santa Cruz, and is the editor of *Child Care . . . Who Cares?* (Basic Books).

ROSE M. WALKER ROSS is Assistant Professor and Coordinator of the Social Work Program at Medgar Evers College of the City University of New York.

STEVEN S. SHARFSTEIN is Special Assistant to the Acting Director, Office of Program Planning and Evaluation, Alcoholism, Drug Abuse and Mental Health Administration, U.S. Department of Health, Education and Welfare.

ROGER SHIPLEY is Assistant Professor in the Department of Health and Safety Studies, California State University, Los Angeles, and is the author of articles and textbooks relating to health, sex, alcohol and drug education.

M. BREWSTER SMITH is Professor of Psychology and Director of the Institute of Human Development at the University of California, Berkeley.

PAULA L. ZAJAN is Professor and Director of the Early Childhood Education Program at Hostos Community College of the City University of New York.

SERAPIO R. ZALBA was Professor and Chairman, Department of Urban Studies and Applied Social Sciences, Case Western Reserve University, and at present is Executive Director of the Geauga Alliance of Human Service Agencies in Ohio.

JUDITH ZENTNER is co-author of *Nursing Concepts for Health Promotion* (Prentice-Hall).

Contents

Introduction to the Human Services

RONALD J. KASE

The human services are a collection of activities which provide aid, comfort and contribute to the development of individuals, families, and groups. Generally the human services include the fields of health, social welfare, and parts of the educational establishment. It is significant that the Department of Health, Education, and Welfare of the United States has spent some ten million dollars on studies to define the terms and areas associated with human services.

Human services programs are found in urban, suburban, and rural areas, and are available to the poor, the middle class, and the wealthy. Staffs of human service programs are composed of professional and non-professional workers who perform a variety of tasks.

The origin of the human services in the United States like other parts of our culture stem from the traditions of England which were brought to us by the founding colonists. In the seventeenth century a series of laws were enacted in England which were designed to benefit the poor. Known as the Elizabethan Poor Laws, they were developed to prevent starvation through neglect.[1] The laws were hardly a give-away program, and provided no more than the basic necessities such as food and shelter, and then only after family resources and neighborly assistance were exhausted. The aged, the handicapped, and the sick were allowed to live in workhouses and were fed. The stronger poor known as sturdy beggars had to work hard for their keep, as did children.

The remarkable thing about the Poor Laws is that they marked the beginning of government accepting some responsibility for the welfare of the ordinary citizen. This concept of government responsibility has been carried forth from the limited Poor Laws to complicated social welfare systems in the United States, England, Sweden, and other nations.

The Poor Law mentality was brought to the United States by English colonists who provided the basics needed for survival for those in need. As American society developed it became obvious that informal programs of social welfare were not adequate to meet the needs of all who required assistance in the new dynamic society. Specialized programs began including: the first mental hospital (1769), the first orphanage (1729), schools for the deaf (1817), and the blind (1829).[2] States also began to establish departments to oversee social welfare programs.[3] Mostly concerned with hospitals and prisons, the states left services to individuals to be provided by voluntary organizations set up for that purpose by religious groups and concerned citizens. The Charity Organization Society founded in 1877 formalized many of the procedures carried out by volunteers. The Society employed the first paid caseworkers, developed the case history, and provided training and consultation to groups in other cities desiring to set up a local Charity Organization Society. From these roots of social work casework developed along with the casework agencies which dominated social welfare until the 1960s.

The Human Services Revolution

Like social welfare the health and education fields at one time accepted only professionally trained persons into their ranks as practitioners. Health personnel included only physicians, nurses and a small amount of non-professional orderlies and aides who had no chance for advancement. Similarly the public education field employed only teachers who held baccalaureate and masters degrees, and social caseworkers and social workers all were degree-holding professionals.

Thus the human services resembled a closed shop in that they were open only to those who could afford to attend college prior to gaining employment. As a result the segment of the population most in need of human services was excluded from entry into this field of employment, diminishing even further any chance of recipient participation in formulating policy which directly affected their lives and well being.

The passage of the Community Mental Health Act of 1961 and the Economic Opportunity Act of 1964 created the paraprofessional human service worker. The concept of employing and consulting those who are most affected by social programs was spelled out in the Economic Opportunity Act. The Act called for "the maximum feasible participation of the poor." This meant that persons from proverty areas served on the boards of directors of anti-poverty agencies along with professionals and political appointees, and that indigenous people were hired by community-oriented health, education, and social agencies in both the public and voluntary sectors.

Most important was the fact that many aide positions formally considered dead-end jobs were eliminated. Now for the first time entry level persons could aspire to professional level jobs by climbing a career ladder.[4] The career ladder combined in-service training with community and four-year college programs. Many of the college programs gave credit for life experience and employment activities. Through this carefully developed combination of work, training, high school equivalency diploma preparation, and higher education, a large number of indigenous human service workers moved from aide positions to professional careers.

Another important aspect of infusing the human services with new kinds of workers was that a certain amount of institutional change took place. All too often our social welfare, health, and educational organizations have been unresponsive and hostile to the requests and rights of clients, patients, and students, and their families. With the influx of new paraprofessionals who, as family workers, teacher's assistants, and mental health workers, could identify with clients from particular ethnic and socio-economic groups, traditional staff members had to become more aware of their attitudes. Community groups were consulted before embarking on new programs. Clinic hours were made more convenient to the patients rather than the institution, and the paraprofessional slowly became accepted as a full fledged member of the treatment and educational team. The human service fields had undergone a peaceful revolution which brought about sweeping changes in a rather short time.

Human Service Practitioners

Today we see numerous career titles in the human service field. Students of the human services should be familiar with these titles, and with the roles of persons who work in various positions in social and health agencies.

The following career titles represent most of the positions considered part of human service practice. Titles and requirements will vary according to location, but the list can serve as a guide to the human service student.

Mental Health Field

Psychiatrist — A licensed physician who treats patients with emotional problems and mental disorders. Psychiatrists work in mental hospitals, community mental health centers, special mental health programs (alcohol and drug abuse, family crises programs, etc.) and private practice. *Requirements:* M.D. degree, state certification, completion of an approved residency in psychiatry.

Psychiatric Nurse — A registered nurse working in various mental health settings with individuals and groups. The psychiatric nurse supervises and participates in therapy programs for patients with emotional problems and mental disorders. *Requirements:* Registered Nurse, M.S. degree in Psychiatric Nursing, experience in mental health settings.

Psychiatric Social Worker — A social worker who provides social work and theraputic services to patients in mental health programs. Psychiatric social workers are members of the staffs of mental hospitals, community mental health centers, drug abuse and alcoholism programs, and are in private practice. *Requirements:* Master's Degree in Social Work (MSW), and supervised experience in mental health settings.

Psychologist — A mental health professional involved with the evaluation and treatment of emotional problems and mental disorders. Psychologists work in all mental health and many social welfare and educational programs. *Requirements:* State certification, doctorate in an area of psychology from a university program approved by the American Psychological Association.

Mental Health Worker — A member of the mental health team who provides: follow up, home visits, coordination of services. Mental health workers are employed by community mental health centers, and by special mental health programs. *Requirements:* Knowlege of the community, Associate Degree in Community or Human Services.

Health Field

Family Physician — A physician who treats all members of a family for a variety of health problems. Family physicians practice in family health centers, and are in private practice. *Requirements:* M.D. degree, state certification, approved residency in family medicine.

Nurse Practitioner — A registered nurse who provides primary care to individuals and families through hospital and health center programs or through private practice. *Requirements:* Registered nurse, M.S. degree in a nurse practitioner specialty area.

Family Health Worker — One who provides follow up, home visits, escort, and coordination of health services to families and individuals. The family health worker is usually employed by community based health programs. *Requirements:* Knowledge of the community, Associate Degree in Community or Human Services.

Discharge Planner — A registered nurse employed by a hospital to coordinate the discharging of patients with home care services, medicaid, long term care facilities, and other out of hospital services. *Requirements:* Registered nurse.

Social Welfare Field

Social Worker — A human service professional who works in a variety of areas including: public assistance, children's services, mental health, hospital social service, and school social work. Social workers are also found in supervisory positions in social agencies, and many work as therapists in mental health programs and in private practice. *Requirements:* Master's Degree in Social Work (MSW). (In some states certification is available.)

Caseworker — One who provides direct casework services to individuals, families, and groups. Caseworkers are employed by public and voluntary social agencies. Caseworkers comprise the largest single group of human service practitioners. *Requirements:* Baccalaureate degree in an area of human service or social science, and experience as required by local civil service or voluntary agencies.

Rehabilitation Counselor — A human service professional who provides counseling services to those who are in need of rehabilitation because of physical, emotional, or social problems. *Requirements:* A Master's Degree in Rehabilitation Counseling, supervised experience in rehabilitation settings.

Assistant Caseworker — A member of the human service team who provides: out-reach service, escort service, referral, and casework services. The assistant caseworker may be employed by public assistance programs, and by voluntary social agencies. *Requirements:* Knowledge of the community, Associate Degree in Community or Human Services.

Education Field

Special Education Teacher — One who works with children who are physically or mentally disabled. Special education teachers are employed by school districts and special schools. *Requirements:* M.S. Degree in Special Education, state certification in special education.

Guidance Counselor — A counselor working for a school system who provides academic advice and personal counseling usually to junior and senior high school students. *Requirements:* M.S. Degree in counseling and guidance, state certification as a guidance counselor.

School Psychologist — A psychologist employed by a school district who does diagnostic testing and counseling of students at the request of teachers and school officials. *Requirements:* M.S. Degree in School Psychology and state certification as a school psychologist.

Teacher Associate — One who provides individual teaching to students who require special attention. Teacher associates work along with and under the supervision of classroom teachers. *Requirements:* An Associate Degree.

Notes

1. The Elizabethan Poor Law enacted by the English Parliament in 1603 established the early pattern of social welfare in the future United States. The Poor Law authorized governmental intervention so that no one would starve through neglect.
2. In 1769 the legislature of Virginia established the first mental hospital in the colonies. The Ursuline Sisters in 1729 set up an orphanage to care for children who were survivors of a small pox epidemic in New Orleans. Schools for the deaf were established in 1817 in Connecticut, and in Kentucky in 1824. Perkins Institute for the Blind was established in Boston in 1829.
3. The first state board of charities was established in Massachusetts in 1863.
4. Pearl, A. and F. Riessman, *New Careers for the Poor*, New York, 1965.

Suggested Readings

Bloom, R.H., *Community Mental Health — A General Introduction*, Belmont, California, Brooks/Cole, 1975.

Dugger, J., *The New Professional: Introduction for the Human Service/Mental Health Worker*, Monterey, California, Brooks/Cole, 1975.

Gartner, A., *Paraprofessionals and their Performance*, New York, Praeger, 1971.

Haveman, R.H., (ed.) *A Decade of Federal Antipoverty Programs*, New York, Academic Press, 1977.

Mills, C.W., *The Power Elite*, New York, Oxford University Press, 1959.

Pearl, A. and F. Riessman, *New Careers for the Poor*, New York, Free Press, 1965.

Waxman, C.I., (ed.) *Poverty: Power and Politics*, New York, Grosset and Dunlap, 1968.

Wilensky, H.L. and C.N. Lebeaux, *Industrial Society and Social Welfare*, New York, Free Press, 1965.

Selected Knowledge Areas in Social Work Intervention

ROSE M. WALKER ROSS

Ideally, reflection about the social worker's relation to the entire pattern of civilization will reveal a practitioner who is committed to the development of heightened understanding and sensitivity for humanitarian purposes. This commitment and purpose should functionally reflect the knowledge and skills required for professional practice. The humanitarian purpose and intellectual functions are not incompatible concepts since they are most often intertwined. However, the relationship between the humanitarian purpose and intellectual function must be clearly perceived for effective practice. Recognizing that there are patterns of civilization, the range of learning should be broadly drawn to encompass the changing functions and purposes of the society. The range should also deal with individual to societal problems associated with a computer-age with unresolved ecological, economic, and political survival issues.

Reports from the Council on Social Work Education[1] have conveyed the importance of the role and growing number of Associate degree (pre-professional) and Baccalaureate level (beginning professional) practitioners in Social Work intervention.

These undergraduate social work students and practitioners may be aware of the vast knowledge and evergrowing research in the

9

social work field. A rationale for this contribution is, therefore, in order. First, basic attitudes and values are examined. Second, variables have been selected from the 1978 graduate program offerings to help the undergraduate student and practitioner synthesize and understand existing trends and set realistic social work career goals and training needs. Third, social work is approached from an ecological-systemic framework in preparing the undergraduate social worker for a more dynamic and transactional view of multi-system intervention. This analysis should also serve as a guide for study in areas where the undergraduate seeks professional knowledge and skills. Fourth, specific competencies and knowledge areas will be juxtaposed for the undergraduate to identify specific disciplines, their interdisciplinary relationship, and continuity for practical relevance.

Because of the above, the purpose of this article is to assist the undergraduate student in his efforts to clarify this humanitarian and functional relationship by analyzing basic attitudes, and by placing selected knowledge and skill areas into an organized approach and framework as a guide for professional growth.

In order to avoid treating social work knowledge in a disconnected way, the organizing procedure for the presentation will inquire into comprehensive patterns and interconnections.

Empirically, this article relies heavily on secondary data with original analysis and comparisons.

Basic Attitudes and Values

In order to meet today's challenges, the social worker or any human service practitioner must acquire a set of attitudes, knowledge, and skills which are indispensable to carry out an egalitarian role. This role advocates the doctrine of equal political, economic, and legal rights for all people. The role of advocate and broker for the increasing number of the exploited and oppressed must be incorporated within the professional practitioner's value system.

This egalitarian role is the pre-requisite from which knowledge and skills evolve. Humanization of science and technology, social justice and social responsibility are the values embedded in this role.

These values prevail irrespective of the level of social work practice and should *precede* any decision to enter the human service field.

Professionally, the limited, but important "calling" of social workers should emanate from this attitudinal base of humanitarian and egalitarian values. Entering the profession with these values, the social worker begins the lifelong task of understanding himself. The goal is self-awareness, self-acceptance, and self-understanding. The assumption is that an acceptable attitude towards oneself and an understanding of oneself are necessary in order to understand others and diagnose problems more objectively. The practitioner attempts to recognize, understand and communicate empathy, sensitivity, genuine concern, and respect for the client's individuality and difference in feeling, experiences, and patterns of response.

The focus is on facilitating the client's strengths in decision making, problem-solving and social functioning. A professional role is neither elitist nor over-identified with the client in differentiation. The limit or range of the professional role is based on humanitarian and egalitarian values, a diagnosis of individual client needs, and basic principles of the social work profession which form the attitudinal framework for practice. Armed with this attitudinal framework, what are the areas of training, and careers for the undergraduate?

According to Siegel's *Social Manpower Needs:*

> Increasingly, professionally trained social workers (MSW) will be called upon to perform managerial functions including financial management, developing and managing information systems, and evaluating program performances. In direct client service, social workers (Associate degree and Baccalaureate level social workers) will be more involved in programs and techniques of community-based prevention areas such as mental health, corrections, abuse, and economic dependency.[2]

What are the present professional managerial and direct service program offerings that prepare the Associate degree and Baccalaureate student and practitioner for better present and future task performances? In examining the 1978 graduate program offerings over 50 different program concentrations or substantive areas were noted. The author placed these descriptions into seven categories for more careful examination (Table 1).

TABLE 1. CLASSIFICATION OF THE 1978 CONCENTRATIONS AND

Planning, Development, and Administration	Physical and Mental Health	Criminal Justice System
Agency planning and administration	Family mental health	Juvenile justice system
Social planning, development and adm.	Physical health	Juvenile and adult criminal
Social service management	Health systems	justice
Program planning and admin..	Mental retardation	Social work and the law
Program development	Maternal and child health	Juvenile justice and correction
Organization of human service	Medical care delivery	
Social welfare and federation	Alcoholism	
Social welfare administration	Community mental health	
Social development	Human sexuality	
Community and neighborhood development	Comprehensive health	
Institutional development	Health services	
Social health	Mental health	
Social development/ alternative futures		
Youth and community		

SUBSTANTIVE AREAS IN GRADUATE SCHOOLS OF SOCIAL WORK

Direct Micro-Intervention	Egalitarian Foci	Policy, Research and Evaluation	Joint Programs
Interpersonal practice	Family service and welfare system	Policy research and development	Social work and law (MSSA/JD)
Social strategy	Social justice	Research	Social work and library science (MSSA/MS)
Family development	Poverty and associated problems	Program evaluation	
Maternal security and education			Social work and business management
Children and their families	Social and economic inequalities		Social work and urban planning
Family and child education & development	Public welfare		Social work and public health
Clinical social work practice	Women's issues		Social work and Jewish studies
Older adolescent and adult	International cross cultural		
Autonomous social work practice	Income maintenance		
School social work	Afro-centric communal service		
Aging	Humanistic values		
Child and family advocacy	World of work		
	Protection and social service		

Although the first year of graduate study focuses on generic social work practice, a more comprehensive framework is indicated for decision-making in selecting a concentration in advanced study. The terms micro, mezzo, and macro are used by a few graduate schools in describing their areas of concentration (e.g. Fordham University). Although there is consistency in describing the micro areas (i.e. practice with individuals, small groups, and families), some graduate schools omit the term mezzo entirely, while others use the term macro to describe different and conflicting substantive areas. Myers provides the analysis and framework that the prospective graduate student can find useful in understanding these concentrations.[3]

Table 2 more clearly delineates the terms micro, mezzo, and macro and their primary units of attention. It is important to note that all units are interdependent and transactional.

The value of this beginning knowledge can be enhanced by an understanding of social work relationships with other disciplines. The distinctive features of social work can be best comprehended in the light of its similarities, interconnections, and contrasts with other knowledge areas.

Realms of Meaning: Symbolics, Empirics, Esthetics, Synnoetics, Ethics and Synoptics

Realms of meaning is a critical examination of a coherent system of ideas by which all the constituent parts of intervention are identified and ordered. It identifies the complete pattern of the social worker's learning experience and character emerging from a philosophy of man and his ways of knowing. Each realm (symbolics, empirics, esthetics, synnoetics, ethics, and synoptics) will be explained under individual headings. Each realm will be explored in the context of its correlation and nature of meaning to social work. These six fundamental patterns were conceptualized by Phenix.[4]

Symbolics

Phenix explained that symbolics comprise ordinary language, mathematics, and various types of nondiscursive symbolic forms

TABLE 2. SYSTEMS INTERVENTION CONTINUUM MATRIX SHOWING LEVELS OF ANALYSIS

Interfacing variables	Microsystem	Mezzosystem	Macrosystem
Problems (psychosocial, socio-economic, political)	Mental disabilities Physical disabilities Drug abuse & other crimes Educational inadequacy Housing inadequacy Employment inadequacy	Neighborhoods Communities Localized, organizational structures	Institutional racism Social policy inadequacy Economic policy inadequacy Political policy inadequacy Inequities of legal-judicial system
Targets (units of attention)	Individuals Small groups Family units	Neighborhoods Communities Localized, organizational structures	Large-scaled, complex systems (scattered populations: Metropolitan, regional, national
Goals (preventive & corrective)	Individual behavioral changes Small group cohesiveness Family unit effectiveness	Neighborhood & community development Organizational effectiveness (intra- & inter-) Service program effectiveness	Large-scaled systems change Responsive & proactive social policy Comprehensive social plans Metropolitan, regional & national General welfare
Methods (tools)	Clinical & counseling Services—individuals Family therapy Group work Organizational development Experiential learning techniques [etc.]	Community organization Community needs assessment Organizational development Management development Urban planning	Social planning Social policy: Analysis, planning, evaluation, development Legislation: municipal, regional, state, federal Executive orders

such as gestures, rituals, rhythmic patterns, and the like. These symbolic systems in one respect constitute the most fundamental of all the realms of meaning in that they must be employed to express the meanings in each of the other realms. It is the most fundamental realm in social work.

As an applied intervention technique and a helping process, social work makes use of ordinary language for verbal communications and nondiscursive symbolic forms as non-verbal communication. Communication is basic to the helping relationship. The building of trust and rapport is the basic medium or tool in social work.

Verbal communications and non-discursive symbolic form are also used in mutual assessment in the helping process. In casework, the worker is attempting to establish rapport with a client in a one to one (dyadic) relationship or with the family as the unit of attention.

In group work, individual members, the group as a whole, and the worker are the medium and agents of change. Both intervention methods are attempts to modify some aspect of the client's social functioning. The client and the worker use symbolics as their basic instrument of interaction.

Caseworkers may choose or combine one of several interactional models or approaches to direct practice. They include client-centered therapy, behavior modification, the functional model, problem-solving approach, rational approach, and the psychosocial method (see Roberts and Nee; also Turner).[5] The psychosocial method is the predominant training focus in social work training. The basic assumption of this model is that a structured approach is not incompatible to humanistic concern. The psychosocial model makes use of verbal and nonverbal communication in the following interactional process (see Hollis for an excellent presentation of this model).[6]

(1) The social worker makes an initial assessment or study of the presenting problem by gathering objective and subjective data.
(2) The gathered data (study) are used to assess the client's functioning and patterns of coping and the worker's competency in assessment.
(3) The diagnosis is used to evaluate the client's strengths and weaknesses as to resources in the area of personal

motivation, capacity, and opportunities in his social environment.

(4) The treatment plan is based upon all of the above and is focused and narrowed down to the most useful and feasible treatment for the client.

In the above summary of the study, diagnosis, evaluation, and treatment plan, the verbal and non-discursive symbolic forms play an important role. Associations of ideas, concealed meanings, gaps and consistencies, shifts in conversation, recurrent preferences, are all important diagnostic clues (see Garrett and Schubert for interviewing techniques).[7]

Casework also makes use of professional techniques expressed in representative ideas as clichés. The clichés include "starting where the client is . . .," "in the client's best interest," or "how did you feel about that?"

These casework techniques are client/worker interactional measures used to facilitate the helping relationship. They are sustainment (sympathetic listening reassurance, and acceptance of difference), direct influence (suggestion and advice), reflective consideration (patterns and insights), description, ventilation, and exploration (fact-building), confrontation and clarification (reality focus). These communication procedures, along with the indirect technique of environmental manipulation, are all semantic ideas describing communications.

In group work, the approach and type of group is determined and distinguished by the method, goal, function, knowledge base, and core competencies required. The type of groups include recreational groups, task-oriented groups, group counselling, group therapy, social group work, T-group, sensitivity training, and encounter groups.

In each type of group, verbal and nonverbal communication are essential to the helping process. Treatment considerations in group work are based on verbal and non-verbal diagnostic clues. These symbolic interactions provide the data to assist the worker and client in determining the goal of the individual members and the groups as a whole.

The treatment sequence in group work begins with initial assessment, and follows with diagnosis and formulation of individual and group treatment goals, treatment planning, group composition and formulation, group development and treatment, evaluation and termination. Verbal and non-verbal interactions are the direct means of intervention and influence in the group session itself with worker, individual members, and in contacts outside of the group.

The role of the group worker as an intervener is a theoretical controversy that should be explored by the group work practitioner. Klein makes an analysis in this area.[8] This controversy could be called the quantitative and qualitative role of the worker in symbolic group interaction.

Group development and problem levels of individuals and groups can be viewed as stages of progress in verbal and non-verbal communications among worker, clients, and peer relationships. Bernstein's stages of group development underscore this focus:[9]

As noted in Bernstein's model (Table 3), the communication procedures or techniques used in group work are an integral part of the dynamic characteristics and stages of group development. These techniques are exploration, clarification, support, permissiveness, confrontation, and facilitation. Communication procedures are used when diagnostically indicated and are not necessarily sequential.

The casework and group work techniques, as tools in verbal and non-verbal communication, are also used in supervisory conferences and recordings for training and assessment of worker activity and client progress.

In summary, symbolic data are based upon the client's feelings (subjective) as expressed verbally, but also non-verbally. Gestures, eye level, facial expressions, body movements, etc., constitute important silent communication data. A discrepancy between non-verbal and verbal language represents important diagnostic clues.

The use of symbolics, as mathematics, is discussed by Ferguson:

> All public welfare bureaucracies involve the computation of budgets. Day sheets, monthly reports, mileage accounts, and similar routine processes demand accuracy and ease in simple arithmetic procedures. As social work is becoming more research oriented, social workers need to develop some sophistication about statistics and computers, as well. They may never be asked to carry out the technical procedures involved, but they should be able to present accurate data for statistical analysis and be able to read research reports critically and with understanding.[10]

Knowledge of human communications can be extracted from the fields of linguistics, phonetics, communication theory, semantics, psychology and mathematics.

Non-verbal communication draws largely from biology and knowledge of cultural groups (Stansfeld and Williamson; Eichorn; Montagu, provide a discussion of these areas).[11]

Empirics

Empirics include the sciences of the physical world, of living things and man. Social work makes use of empirics in the pure and applied forms as its knowledge base in professional training and practice. To adequately assess objective and subjective data, diagnose, evaluate, and make effective treatment plans, social workers must understand the patterns of meaning emerging from the analysis of empirics, the applied social work curriculum foci, and the core competencies derived from them. The author has, therefore, organized this data by the following analytic clarification, evaluation, and synthetic coordination with empirics as its base:

Table 4 interrelates program concentration, selected knowledge areas, and competency goals by using empirics as the knowledge base.

Esthetics

Esthetics contain the various arts, visual arts, performing arts and literature. Ferguson provides an interesting application of esthetics to social work intervention:

> Study and enjoyment of literature and the arts both enrich the social worker's understanding of the infinite ways in which people respond to inner and outer stimuli and enlarge the possible avenues of communication between social workers and their clients. Whether it is the finger painting of a troubled child or the brilliant "flight of ideas" of a manic patient, the arts are ways of expressing inner feelings. Creative artists in all fields are often peculiarly sensitive to the world about them and illuminate, for the less articulate, feelings that are widely known. Psychonalysts have found infinite riches for their study in

TABLE 3. BERNSTEIN'S MODEL FOR STAGE OF GROUP DEVELOPMENT

Stage	Dynamic Characteristic	Frame of Reference	Program	Worker Focus
1. Pre-affiliation	Exploration	SOCIETAL "The Crafts Class"	Quick satisfaction important	Allowing and supporting distance
	Approach-avoidance dilemma	"Teacher"	Parallel individual play	Inviting trust gently
	Stereotypic activity	"Coach"	Exploring ambivalence between cooperation & cleanup vs. hit & run	Facilitating exploration
	Trust, preliminary commitment	"Hey Kid"		Providing program structure & initiation
			Ambivalence over accepting material	
			Non-giving to group	
2. Power & control	Locking horns with the reality of the group	TRANSITIONAL "How come you let him get away with that?"	Program breakdown at times, low planning	Permitting rebellion
	Status Jockeying		Aggressive competition	Protecting safety of individuals and property
	Power struggles among members and with worker		Testing strength and authority	Providing activities for mastery
	Autonomy, individual and group		Attempts at formalizing relationships through dues, rules	Clarification of power struggle
	Drop out danger high			
	Normative & membership crises begin			

Stage			Activity	Worker role
3. Intimacy	Normative & membership crises continue; Mutual Revelation; Dependency; Intensified interpersonal involvement, transference; Facing "What this club is for"	FAMILIAL "You're a good club Mama" "You're worse than my little sister"	Activity openly emotion-laden, struggles for attention & material; Growing ability to plan, carry out group projects, but often with emotional turmoil	Consistent giving in face of turmoil; Flexible assumption or giving of responsibility as group vacillates; Clarification of feelings, positive & negative
4. Differentiation	Cohesion; Free expression; Mutual support; High communication; Few power problems; Identity	GROUP-INTERNAL "Our social worker" "This club is different"	Freer mutual giving; Club traditions & customs around activities; Cooperative activity planned, sustained; Projects, etc., in relationship to community, other groups; Outside interests start	Helping group to run itself; Facilitating opportunities to act as a unit in relation to other groups and community; Facilitating evaluation process
5. Separation	Denial, regression, and recapitulation; Review and evaluation; Moving apart, nihilistic and positive flight	GROUP (carried to other social situations, new groups)	High mobility travel; Problem of activity routine becoming stale; Re-enacting stage one activities; Outside interests—vocational in older groups; Reunion	Letting go; Concentrating on group and individual mobility; Facilitating evaluation; Facilitating post-group meeting of needs via other resources

TABLE 4. SELECTED KNOWLEDGE AREAS AND COMPETENCIES IN SOCIAL WORK INTERVENTION

Social Work Concentrations	Selected Knowledge Base (disciplines and concepts)	Selected Competency Goals in Undergraduate Education
Direct Micro Intervention	*Human Growth and Development* (family and individual dynamics)	*Casework/Group Work Competencies* [12]
(Casework)	Psychology: • Psycho-social development; life cycles and identity stages (Erikson). • Motivation and personality; hierarchical needs (Maslow). • Intellectual processes (Piaget). Ego psychology: • Defense mechanisms (A. Freud). • Ego development (Hartmann). Psychoanalysis: • Personality structure; transference and countertransference (S. Freud). Anthropology and sociology: • Symbolic communication (White; Leach; Hall; Cooley; Mead).	The professional context of practice. The ability to identify the effects of one's own attitudes, values, and characteristic patterns of behavior upon one's own practice. The ability to relate one's own activities to a reasonable definition of social work as a profession; the ability to distinguish the orientation, role, and activities of social workers from those of other professions; the ability to establish personal and role limits in dealing with clients that are consistent with good judgement and social work ethics. The ability to use available resources to improve knowledge and skills and show capacity for and interest in keeping abreast of current literature and developments within the field. Problem identification and assessment: The ability to perceive and articulate the relevant factors surrounding the initial request for service, the ability to obtain thorough yet relevant information via interviews and other data collection techniques, and the ability to conceptualize the problem situation and delineate its critical dimensions.

in cooperation with the client, specific objectives for the change effort; the ability to derive a cogent intervention plan and specify the model or theory that underlies the plan; and the ability to specify a rationale for the chosen plan.

Implementation of the intervention plan: The ability to engage and maintain the active participation of all parties involved, the ability to carry out the plan in a cogent and purposeful fashion, and flexibility in dealing with obstacles to progress and other process issues.

(Social work theories and inter-disciplinary approaches)

The psycho-social process (Hollis).
- Family therapy (Munichin; Ackerman; Satir).
- Problem-solving (Perlman).
- Helping (Mahoney).
- Crisis intervention (Parad; Rapoport; Lendemann; Caplan).
- Interviewing (Garrett; Schubert).
- Common human needs (Towle).

Biology:
- Gestation and infancy; heredity (Eichorn; Montagu).

(Casework and Group Work)

Sociology:
- Personality and socialization; the social system and cultural influences (Mead; Cooley; Simmel).
- Pattern of suicide (Durkheim).
- Social structure (Merton).
- Role socialization (Parsons; Merton; Linton).
- Agents of socialization and general personality structure (Reisman).
- Systems theory (Bales; Parsons; Hoamans; Bertalanffly).

Social psychology:
- Field theory (group dynamics) (K. Lewin; Deutsch).

(continued)

TABLE 4. (Continued)

Social Work Concentrations	Selected Knowledge Base (disciplines and concepts)	Selected Competency Goals in Undergraduate Education
	Group work theory and group analysis: • Group theory development (Bernstein; Bennis; Shepard; Olmstead). • Group methodology (Vinter; Schwartz; Grosser; Warren; Brager).	
Direct Mezzo Intervention (community planning, development, and action; agency development)	*Organizational Theory and Management* (Blau; Etzioni; Weber; Argyris) Administration of social service (Billingsley; Piven; Handler; Cloward; Hanlan). Political science: Urban communities; public and private influences (Warren; Dye; Taeuber; Bernard). Community organization theory and methodology (Rothman; Brager; Specht; Ross; Grosser). Social change (Piven; Brager).	*Mezzo Competencies*[12] The B.A. social worker should be able to meet the following expectations: 1. He is able to recognize and work within the purpose and structure of an agency or the goals and constraints of a particular setting and will hold himself accountable for completion of particular assignments within his own competence. 2. He should be able to establish a rapport with clients from various cultures, with varying needs, dispositions, levels of emotional stability, and intellectual levels. 3. He will have the ability to communicate with people in a way which will enable them to identify their needs, concerns, situational realities, distortions, and identify alternatives of behavior which are available to them. He will be able to help clients to see that they both influence and are influenced by their environment.

4. He is able to facilitate clients and community groups to mobilize their own resources which will enable them effectively to cope with, overcome, and prevent problems, through use of the supporting relationship, the provision of information, and clarification of the problem.

5. He is able to involve and work with significant other people in service provision as indicated.

6. He is able to consider the effectiveness of the services provided in relation to client needs and their effect on client situations, in order to recognize when the agency program and operation is not sufficiently effective. He knows how to bring this appropriately to the attention of the agency in order to begin the process of change and improvement of the program. This involves the ability to relate to the respective agency staff in a facilitating manner.

7. He has the ability to consult with peers and supervisors as well as with staff with less education on understanding client situations and modifying his mode of intervention as appropriate alternatives are developed.

8. He is able to impart information and instruct in certain areas, especially those having to do with the provision of concrete services, identification and use of resources, and means of negotiating and/or confronting complicated systems.

9. He has the capacity to synthesize related experience and arrive at meaningful generalities which will enable him to participate in the development of strategies of intervention.

(continued)

TABLE 4. (Continued)

Social Work Concentrations	Selected Knowledge Base (disciplines and concepts)	Selected Competency Goals in Undergraduate Education
Direct Mezzo Intervention (continued)		*Mezzo Competencies*[12] (continued) 10. He is able to function within an interdisciplinary framework entailing a knowledge of the role and appreciation of the functions of disciplines other than social work.
		11. He will generally make use of direct consultation with a social worker with a master's degree in order to establish a social diagnosis and to make decisions of a critical nature and in determining appropriate modes of treatment.
Macro Intervention (policy, research, and evaluation)	Social work history: Residual and institutional services (Wilensky and Lebeau).	12. Except in those agency situation where the program of the agency has been so structured that the whole service delivery system for that particular program does not require functions which he is not prepared to perform independently, he will work as a member of a service team or function under the general direction of and with regular consultation from an MSW social worker.
	Impact on institutional racism (Clark; Grier and Cobbs; Fanon; Knowles and Prewitt; Glasgow; Mills; Brown; Little; Reissman).	
	Statistics, social research, and research methods: the conduct of inquiry (Greenwald; Goode; Kaplan).	13. Understanding of the organizational context of practice. Knowledge of the purpose and goals of the agency and the services provided, knowledge of the limitations of agency service, knowledge of agency policies and procedures and the ability to operate effectively within them.
	Industrial psychology—personality assessment (Mishel).	
	Agency evaluation (Mager; Goldstein).	
	Social policies and public policy making (Gilbert and Specht; Kahn).	

Macro Intervention Competencies[12]

Assessment of social policy and social issues. To appreciate the influence of social issues and social policy upon the problems of the individuals the student serving, ability to identify areas where existing policies and programs are not adequate, and to suggest policies that could remedy the inadequacy.

Evaluation and feedback

The ability to assess the extent to which the objectives of the intervention were accomplished, the ability to assess the general effectiveness of the change effort, the ability to learn from experience, and the ability to use outcome data to refine one's commitment to specific models of change.

Ability to use outcome data and experience to provide feedback to the community and to social policy.

Shakespeare; it has been said that Hamlet has been analyzed more carefully than any living man has ever been. While it is obviously impossible to expect all social workers to be expert critics and performers in every field, the more sensitive they are to any of these fields, the more likely they will be to pick up allusions to grasp what clients are struggling to say, and to appreciate the depths and the subtleties of their clients expression.[12]

Esthetics can be used as a method of establishing a supportive relationship with an extremely withdrawn or less articulate client as indicated above.

Synnoetics

Synnoetics signify personal or relational knowledge in a concrete, direct, and existential way.

Social work is a helping process that is contingent upon *selfawareness,* as understanding or personal insight by way of introspection, and *reflective consideration,* as past to present interrelational understanding, are both synnoetic concepts. The interrational understanding and self-awareness reflect the quality of personal meaning. Synnoetic knowledge is learned from intimate and early identification and/or direct concrete association with the client's or the worker's primary group (the relationship with the respective extended family or significant others), and from personal and existential awareness and direct experiences in human associations in the respective social environments.

The most important application of the quality of personal meaning consummates in the concrete experience of the evolving casework relationship between the worker and the client. The quality and range begin with the impact of the first contact through termination as the concrete experience reflects relational understanding in future human encounters. The aim of social work is to make this concrete experience one in which the long range effects will assist the client towards more effective social functioning and with a higher degree of satisfaction to him or herself.

Ethics

Ethics include moral meanings that express obligation based upon free deliberate decisions.

Ethics in social work is basic to the professional practice of social work. Selected principles and codes of ethics are used as standards or grounds for moral/professional decisions. These basic principles and codes are deliberate but are not "free" since the obligations to abide by these principles are uniformly used in professional training, professional organization membership, and certification to develop and maintain a professional and ethical level of practice.

The professional social worker's morality reflect both humanistic and egalitarian qualities. Membership in the two leading professional social work organizations carries subscription to their Code of Ethics. The spirit and intent of NASW's Code of Ethics are as follows:

> Social work is based on humanitarian and democratic ideals. Professional social workers are dedicated to service for the welfare of mankind, to the disciplined use of a recognized body of knowledge about human beings and their interactions, and to the marshaling of community resources to promote the well-being of all without descrimination.
> Social work practice is a public trust that requires of its practitioners integrity, compassion, belief in the dignity and worth of human beings, respect for individual differences, a commitment to service, and a dedication to trust. It requires mastery of a body of knowledge and skill gained through professional education and experience. It requires also recognition of the limitations of present knowledge and skill and of the services we are now equipped to give. The end sought is the performance of a service with integrity and competence.
> Each member of the profession carries responsibility to maintain and improve social work service; constantly to examine, use and increase the knowledge upon which practice and social policy are based; and to develop further the philosophy and skill of the profession.
> This Code of Ethics embodies certain standards of behavior for the social worker in his professional relationships with those he serves, with his colleagues, with his employing agency, with other professions, and with the community. In abiding by it, the social worker views his obligations in as wide a context as the situation requires, takes all the principles into consideration, and chooses a course of action consistent with the code's spirit and intent.[13]

The National Association of Social Workers (NASW) adopted their Code in 1960 and amended it in 1967.

The National Association of Black Social Workers (NABSW) adopted the following Code of Ethics in 1968:

> In America today, no Black person, except the selfish or irrational, can claim neutrality in the quest for Black liberation nor fail to consider the implications of the events taking place in our society. Given the necessity for committing ourselves to the struggle for freedom, we as Black Americans practicing in the field of social welfare set forth this statement of ideals and guiding principles.
>
> If a sense of community awareness is a precondition to humanitarian acts, then we as Black social workers must use our knowledge of the Black Community, our commitments to its self-determination and our helping skills for the benefit of Black people as we marshal our expertise to improve the quality of life of Black people. Our activities will be guided by our Black consciousness, our determination to protect the security of the Black community and to serve as advocates to relieve suffering of Black people by any means necessary.
>
> Therefore, as Black social workers we commit ourselves, collectively, to the interests of our Black brethren and as individuals subscribe to the following statements:
>
> I regard as my primary obligation the welfare of the Black individual, Black family and Black community and will engage in action for improving social conditions.
>
> I give precedence to this mission over my personal interest.
>
> I adopt the concept of a Black extended family and embrace all Black people as my brothers and sisters, making no distinction between their destiny and my own.
>
> I hold myself responsible for the quality and extent of service I perform and the quality and extent of service performed by the agency or organization in which I am employed, as it relates to the Black Community.
>
> I accept the responsibility to protect the Black community against unethical and hypocritical practice by any individuals or organizations engaged in social welfare activities.
>
> I stand ready to supplement my paid or professional advocacy with voluntary service in the Black public interest.
>
> I will consciously use my skills, and my whole being, as an instrument for social change, with particular attention directed to the establishment of Black social institutions."[14]

Both NASW and NABSW recognize confidentiality (i.e. the communication between the social worker and clients as privileged information) although records may be and have been subject to court subpoena. The egalitarian and humanistic focus by NABSW is an ethical attempt to manipulate the systemic impact on the potential of the exploited and oppressed.

Synoptics

Synoptics refer to meanings that are comprehensively integrative. They include history, religion, and philosophy.

The questions of value are illuminated by philosophy because philosophy challenges social work to examine, interpret, and organize critically its goals and method from a more integrated outlook and with conceptual patterns from all human experiences.

Social work uses history to help in its understanding of the events in social work eras as reflected in present day social work practice. Wilensky and Lebeaux discuss residual and institutional attitudes and concepts.[15]

In summary, the human service practitioner must acquire the freedom to develop himself through basic attitudes and values. These values begin with a humanistic and egalitarian framework for practice. Training and integrated knowledge can be better analyzed and learned as a comprehensive view of man's human nature and the patterns of meaning related to human understanding. The author has attempted to guide the undergraduate social worker toward a more purposeful, enlightened and humanistic view of knowledge in social work intervention.

Notes

1. See *Colleges and Universities with Accredited Baccalaureate Social Work Programs* (New York: CSWE Publication, 1978) and Edward J. Mullen, *Evaluating Student Learning* (New York: CSWE Publication, 1976).

2. Sheldon Siegel, *Service Manpower Needs: An Overview to 1980* (New York: CSWE Publication, 1975).

3. Ernest R. Myers, *The Community Psychology Concept* (Washington, D.C.: University Press of America, 1977).

4. Philip H. Phenix, *Realms of Meaning.* (New York: McGraw-Hill, 1964).

5. Robert W. Roberts and Robert H. Nee (eds.), *Theories of Social Casework* (Chicago: University of Chicago Press, 1970) and Francis J. Turner (ed.), *Social Work Treatment* (New York: Macmillian Publishing Co., Inc., 1974).

6. Florence Hollis, *Casework*, 2nd ed., rev. (New York: Random House, 1972).

7. Annette Garrett, *Interviewing* (New York: Family Service Association of America, 1942) and Margaret Schubert, *Interviewing in Social Work Practice* (New York: Council on Social Work Education, 1971).
8. Alan F. Klein, *Social Work Through Group Process* (Albany: School of Social Welfare, 1970).
9. Saul Bernstein (ed.), *Charting Group Progress* (New York: Association Press 1949).
10. Elizabeth A. Ferguson, *Social Work* (Philadelphia: J.B. Lippincott Company, 1975), p. 44.
11. Sargent Stansfeld and Robert C. Williamson, *Social Psychology*, 3rd ed. (New York: The Ronald Press Company, 1966), pp. 191–192. D.H. Eichorn, "Biology of Gestation and Infancy," *Quarterly of Behavior and Development*, 14 (1968). A. Montagu, *Heredity* (New York: Harcourt, Brace and World, 1959).
12. Ferguson, *Social Work*, op. cit., p. 44.
13. "Code of Ethics," *National Association of Social Workers* (New York: 1969).
14. "Code of Ethics," *National Association of Black Social Workers* (New York: 1969).
15. Harold L. Wilensky and Charles N. Lebeaux, *Industrial Society and Social Welfare* (New York: Free Press, 1965).

Suggested Readings

Ackerman, Nathan W. *The Psychodynamics of Family Life.* New York: Basic Books, 1958.

Argyris, C. *Interpersonal Competence and Organizational Effectiveness.* Homewood, Ill.: Dorsey Press, 1962.

Bales, Robert F. *Interaction Process Analysis.* Cambridge, Mass.: Addison-Wesley, 1950; Talcott Parsons, Robert F. Bales, and Edward A. Shils, *Working Papers in the Theory of Action.* Glencoe, Ill.: Free Press, 1953.

Bernard, Jessie. *The Sociology of Community.* Glenview, Ill.: Scott, Foresman & Company, 1973.

Bertalanffy, L. Von. *General Systems Theory.* New York: Braziller, 1968.

Bennis, Warren G., Kenneth D. Beene, and Robert Chin (eds.) *The Planning of Change.* New York: Harper and Row, 1961.

Billingsley, Andrew. "Bureaucratic and Professional Orientation Patterns in Social Casework", *Social Service Review*, vol. 38 December 1964.

Blau, Peter M. *Bureaucracy in Modern Society.* New York: Random House, 1966.

Brager, George A. "Advocacy and Political Behavior", *Social Work*, vol. 13, No. 2, April 1968.

Brager, George and Harry Specht. *Community Organizing*. New York: Columbia University Press, 1973.
Brager, George. "Institutional Change: Perimeters of the Possible", *Social Work*, vol. 12, No. 1, January 1967.
Brager, George and Valerie Jorrin. "Bargaining: A Method in Community Change", *Social Work*, vol. 14, No. 4, October 1969, pp. 73–83.
"Bread and Butter Programs: Sewing Co-op, Food-buying Club, Rehab Beats Nothing!" *Communities in Action*, vol. 2, No. 4, August-September 1967.
Brown, Claude. *Manchild in the Promised Land*. New York: Macmillan, 1965.
Caplan, Gerald. *Principles of Preventive Psychiatry*. New York: Basic Books, 1964.
Clark, Kenneth B. and Jeannette Hopkins. *A Relevant War Against Poverty*. New York: Harper & Row, 1969.
Clark, Kenneth B. *Dark Ghetto: Dilemmas of Social Power*. New York: Harper Torchbooks, 1965.
Cloward, Richard A. and Frances Fox Piven. "A Strategy to End Poverty", *The Nation*, vol. 202, No. 17, 2 May 1966, pp. 123–137.
Cloward, Richard A. and Frances Fox Piven. "Finessing the Poor", *The Nation*, 7 October 1968.
Cooley, Charles Horton. *Human Nature and the Social Order*. New York: Schocken Books, Inc., 1964.
Cooley, Charles H. *Social Organization*. New York: Charles Scribner's Sons, 1929.
Deutsch, Morton. "Field Theory in Social Psychology", in Gardner Lindzey, *Handbook of Social Psychology*, vol. I. Cambridge, Mass.: Addison-Wesley, 1954, pp. 181–222.
Durkheim, Emile. *Suicide: A Study in Sociology*. Trans. John A. Spauling, George Simpson, ed. George Simpson. New York: The Free Press, 1951.
Dye, Thomas R. *Politics in State and Communities*. 1st ed. Englewood Cliffs, New Jersey: Prentice-Hall, 1969.
Eichorn, D.H. *Biology of Gestation and Infancy: Fatherland and Frontier*. Quarterly of Behavior and Development, 14. Merrill-Palmer (1968).
Erikson, Erik. *Childhood and Society*. New York: Norton, 1950.

Erikson, Erik. *Identity and the Life Cycle: Monograph 1.* New York: International Universities Press, 1959.

Erikson, Erik. *Identity, Youth and Crisis.* New York: Norton, 1968.

Etzioni, Amitai. *Modern Organizations.* Englewood Cliffs, New Jersey: Prentice-Hall, Inc. 1968.

Fanon, Frantz. *Black Skin White Masks.* New York: Grove Press, Inc., 1967.

Freud, Anna. *The Ego and Mechanisms of Defense.* New York: International Universities Press, 1946.

Freud, Sigmund. *The Ego and the Id.* Standard ed. London: Ilgarth, 1961.

Freud, Sigmund. *An Outline of Psychoanalysis.* trans. James Strachey. New York: W.W. Norton & Co., Inc., 1949.

Garrett, Annette. *Interviewing.* New York: Family Service Association of America, 1942.

Gilbert, Neil and Specht, Harry, *Dimensions of Social Welfare Policy.* Englewood Cliffs, New Jersey: Prentice-Hall, 1974.

Glasgow, Douglas. "Black Power Through Community Control," *Social Work,* Vol. 17, No. 3, May 1972, pp. 59–64.

Grier, William H. and Price M. Cobbs, *Black Rage.* New York: Basic Books, Inc., 1968.

Grosser, Charles F. "Community Organization and the Grass Roots," *Social Work,* Vol. 12, No. 4, October 1967, pp. 61–67.

Grosser, Charles F. "Changing Theory and Changing Practice," *Social Casework,* Vol. 50, No. 1, January 1969.

Grosser, Charles. *New Directions in Community Organization.* New York: Praeger, 1973.

Grosser, Charles and Gertrude S. Goldberg, eds. *Dilemmas of Social Work Leadership: Issues in Social Policy, Planning and Organizing.* New York: Council on Social Work Education, 1974.

Hall, Edward. *The Silent Language.* Greenwich, Conn.: Fawcett Publication, Inc., 1959.

Handler, Joel F. and E.J. Hollingsworth. "The Administration of Social Services and the Structure of Dependency: The Views of AFDC Recipients," *Social Service Review,* Vol. 43, December 1969.

Hanlan, Archie. "Counteracting Problems of Bureaucracy in Public Welfare," *Social Work,* Vol. 12, No. 3, July 1967, pp. 88–94.

Hartmann, Heinz. *Ego Psychology and the Problems of Adaptation.* New York: International Universities Press, 1958.

Hollis, Florence. *Casework: A Psychosocial Therapy.* 2nd ed., rev. New York: Random House, 1972.

Kahn, Alfred, ed. *Shaping the New Social Work.* New York: Columbia University School of Social Work, 1973.

Kahn, Alfred J. *Social Policy Issues.* New York: Random House-Alfred A. Knopf, 1973.

Kaplan, Abraham. *The Conduct of Inquiry.* San Francisco: Chandler, 1964.

Kaplan, David. "A Concept of Acute Situational Disorders," *Social Work*, 7. 2. April 1962, pp. 15–23.

Knowles, L. and K. Prewitt, eds. *Institutional Racism in America.* New Jersey: Prentice-Hall, 1969.

Leach, Edmund R. "Anthropological Aspects of Language: Animal Categories and Verbal Abuse." *New Directions in the Study of Language*, 1964. WM R368.

Lewin, Kurt. *Resolving Social Conflicts.* ed., Gertrud Weiss Lewin. New York: Harper, 1948.

Lindemann, Erich. "Symptomatology and Management of Acute Grief," *American Journal of Psychiatry*, 101, 2 September 1944. Reprinted in Parad (ed.), *Crisis Intervention*, 1965, pp. 7–21.

Lindemann, Erich and Donald C. Klein, "Preventive Intervention in Individual and Family Crisis Situations," in G. Caplan (ed.) *Prevention of Medical Disorders.* New York: Basic Books, 1961.

Linton, Ralph. *The Study of Man: An Introduction.* New York: Appleton-Century-Crofts, Inc., 1936.

Little, Malcom. *The Autobiography of Malcolm X.* New York: Grove Press, 1965.

Mahoney, Stanley C. *The Art of Helping People Effectively.* New York: Association Press, 1967.

Mead, George H. *Mind, Self and Society.* ed., Charles W. Morns. Chicago, Ill.: The University of Chicago Press, 1934.

Merton, Robert. *Social Theory and Social Structure.* Glencoe, Ill.: Free Press, 1954.

Mills, C. Wright. *The Power Elite.* Fairlawn, New Jersey: Oxford University Press, 1956.

Minuchin, S.B., G.G. Montavlo, B.L. Guerney, Rosman and F. Schumer. *Families of the Slums.* New York: Basic Books, 1967.

Montague, Ashley. *Man's Most Dangerous Myth: The Fallacy of Race.* 5th ed. New Jersey: Oxford University Press, 1974.

Olmsted, Michael S. *The Small Group*. New York: Random House, 1959.

Parad, Howard J., ed. *Crisis Intervention: Selected Readings*. New York: Family Service Association of America, 1965.

Perlman, Helen Harris. *Social Casework—A Problem-solving Process*. Chicago: The University of Chicago Press, 1957.

Piaget, Jean. *The Child's Conception of the World*. London: Routledge and Kegan, Paul, 1951.

Piaget, Jean. *The Child's Conception of Numbers*. New York: Humanities Press, 1952.

Piaget, Jean. *The Language and Thought of the Child*. London: Routledge and Kegan, Paul, 1952.

Piaget, Jean. *The Construction of Reality in the Child*. New York: Basic Books, 1954.

Piven, Frances. "Participation of Residents in Neighborhood Community Action Programs," *Social Work*, Vol. 11, No. 1, January 1966.

Rappaport, Lydia. "The State of Crisis: Some Theoretical Consideration," *Social Service Review*, 36, 2, June 1962. Reprinted in Parad (ed.) *Crisis Intervention*, 1965, pp. 22–31.

Rappaport, Lydia. "Working with Families in Crisis: An Exploration in Preventive Intervention," *Social Work*, 7, 3, July 1962, pp. 48–56.

Rappaport, Lydia. "Crisis-Oriented Short-Term Casework," *Social Service Review*, 41, 1 March 1967, pp. 31–42.

Rappaport, Lydia. "Crisis Intervention as a Mode of Brief Treatment," In Robert W. Roberts and Robert H. Nee, eds. *Theories of Social Casework*. Chicago: University of Chicago Press, 1970, pp. 267–311.

Reissman, Leonard. *Inequality in American Society: Social Stratification*. Glenview, Ill.: Scott, Foresman and Company, 1973.

Riesman, David. *The Lonely Crowd*. Garden City, New York: Doubleday and Company, Inc., 1953.

Ross, Murray. *Community Organization: Theory, Principles, and Practice*. New York: Harper and Brothers, 1967.

Rothman, Jack. "An Analysis of Goals and Roles in Community Organization Practice," *Social Work*, Vol. 9, No. 2, April 1964, pp. 24–31.

Satir, Virginia M. *Conjoint Family Therapy.* Palo Alto, Calif.: Science and Behavior Books, 1964.

Schwartz, William. "The Social Worker in the Group," *Social Welfare Forum.* New York: Columbia University Press, 1961, pp. 159–172.

Simmel, Georg, *Conflict and the Web of Group Affiliations.* trans., Reinhardt Bendix. New York: The Free Press, 1955.

Simmel, Georg. "The Poor" (trans. Claire Jacobson). *Social Problems,* Vol. 13, No. 2, 1965.

Specht, Harry. "Disruptive Tactics," *Social Work,* Vol. 14, No. 2, April 1969.

Taeuber, Karl and Alma F. Taeuber. *Negroes in Cities: Residential Segregation and Neighborhood Change.* Chicago: Aldine, 1967.

Vinter, Robert D. ed., *Readings in Group Work Practice.* Ann Arbor: Campus Publishers, 1967.

Vinter, Robert D. "Small Group Theory and Research: Implications for Group Work Practice, Theory and Research," *Social Science Theory and Social Work Research.* Kogan, ed., National Association of Social Work, 1960.

Warren, Roland L. ed. *Community Development and Social Work Practice.* New York: National Association of Social Workers, 1962.

Warren, Roland L., "The Impact of New Designs of Community Organization," *Child Welfare,* Vol. 44, No. 9, November, 1965.

Warren, Ronald L. *Studying Your Community.* New York: Russell Sage Foundation, 1955.

Warren, Roland L. *The Community in America.* Chicago: Rand McNally and Company, 1963.

White, L.A. "The Symbol: The Origin and Basis of Human Behavior," eds. J. Hennings and A. Hoebel. *Readings in Anthropology.* New York: McGraw-Hill, 1966.

Wilensky, Harold L. and Charles N. Lebeaux. *Industrial Society and Social Welfare.* New York: Free Press, 1965.

The Place of Social Work in the Human Services

ROBERT MORRIS

Many of the forces that will shape the role of social work in the human services in ten years cannot be clearly defined, nor can their effect be predicted with uncertainty. Some assumptions are made about more general phenomena, however: (1) there will be no major wars, (2) the economy will continue to move by fits and starts, but there will be no major depression or runaway inflation, (3) the population will continue to grow at the rate of approximately .8–1.0 percent per year, even though the long-term trend is for slower growth, (4) there will be no major redistribution of income or wealth in the population, and (5) the base of income for the lowest 10 percent of the population will rise slightly, but the gap between that group and higher income groups will remain the same or will increase. Further, minority groups will continue their slow penetration of professional, technical, and higher-income activities without producing a dramatic redistribution or universal equalization of income or position.

The people's uncertainty about the value of scientific changes and skepticism about the reliability and trustworthiness of government will make it difficult to develop any grand national plan or significantly reduce their level of anxiety. Moreover, national values and attitudes will remain about what they are today: a high premium will still be placed on the private acquisition of material goods and people will continue to try to satisfy their private desires with little regard to the adverse effect this may have on the common well-being. Generous, idealistic movements will persist, but society will not be radically altered.

Definitions

And what will be the place of social work in the human services in ten years? This question contains ambiguity because social workers have not agreed on the exact meaning of the terms "social work" or "human services." Thus before continuing his discussion, the author proposes the following definitions, which should be kept in mind when reading this article.

Social work refers to all the interpersonal and social tasks and the roles performed by persons holding either a bachelor's or master's degree in social work. Not all persons who happen to be employed in social welfare activities are social workers.

The term *human services* covers several subsystems of the social welfare system that employ social workers in either a dominant or peripheral position. These subsystems include health and medical care, law and justice, education, income security, and the reinforcement of personal growth and family cohesiveness (family services, character-building, and the like).

The *place* of social work refers to the relative statuses of social workers in these human service subsystems—that is, how important they are to the subsystems.

The author recognizes that these definitions leave the boundaries of the subject overlarge. In many states the human services, thus interpreted, include as much as 50 percent of state government employees and account for between 50 and 65 percent of state governmental expenditures. The human services have room for the most varied activities: protecting society against destructive members; punishing deviance according to current mores; safeguarding and sheltering the helpless and vulnerable, be they children, the disabled, or the aged; correcting economic inequities through income maintenance programs; and reinforcing social and personal strength or integrity through a variety of family or community services. And social workers must find their place in relation to a variety of other professional, quasi-professional, and nonprofessional persons also involved in similar activities—physicians, nurses, teachers, psychologists, college graduates in the humanities, and paraprofessional personnel without college degrees.

This article will consider three perspectives from which to anticipate the shape of social work in the 1980s. And it does so within the larger context of national change, which is also ambiguous. The three perspectives are: (1) an estimate of the forces for change and the forces against change, (2) the roles to be filled in the various human service subsystems, and (3) the functions of the professional practices to be performed in the systems.

Forces for Change

The two most significant forces in the direction of change seem to be demographic trends and the erosion of public confidence in the national government.

Demography. Although no significant alteration in population growth is expected in so short a time, the effect of population shifts in the past twenty years will begin to impose an inexorable force for change. Since World War II the proportion of persons in the work force aged 25–45 has decreased from 30.1 percent to 23.7 percent and of those aged 45–65 has increased from 18.8 to 20.5 percent. During the same period persons aged 65 and older have grown from 6.8 percent to 9.9 percent, while those over age 75 have increased at the rate of nearly 50 percent.[1]

In addition, the number of severely disabled persons continues to grow, although the percentage increase has not been dramatic. In this group are children born of genetic anomalies as well as those with a variety of birth defects, including mental retardation and the whole range of difficulties that comprise the term "developmental disabilities." Medical and technical means permit the survival of an infinitely diverse group of persons, young and old alike, with disabilities severe enough to require not only therapeutic intervention but continuing personal care from others. For example, the survival rate of young adults with spinal cord injury has grown from 10 percent to 84 percent since 1946.[2] The startling increase in survival beyond age 75, when the demand for both medical and personal-care services is four times the average demand of the population, has and will continue to enlarge the group of disabled confronting society.

Medical technologies, such as renal dialysis, suddenly make possible the long-term survival of thousands of persons each year with kidney diseases. At the same time, the tide of revulsion against warehousing large numbers of law violators, addicts, and mentally ill persons in vast institutions will continue to swell. Taken together, these factors will force attention to the alternatives of institutional versus community care and the balance to be struck between short-term therapeutic intervention and the long-term requirements of maintenance.

Public confidence. A second major force for change is the public's shifting and eroding confidence in the national government as an instrument with which to shape specific remedies for distressing human situations. Although the national government still is recognized as the primary financial resource, a marked decline in confidence is evident about the national government's ability to organize programs that will satisfy both the recipient of service and the voting citizen.

Although some citizens and even political figures hope that the problems can just be ignored, most are trying to find some approach that will join the collection of taxes at the national level with decision-making at the local level about how the tax moneys are to be spent. Sometimes the hope is expressed that the capacity of local governments to deal with the citizens' social needs will be revived; more often, it is a nostalgic wish that voluntary associations will be restored with enough strength to assume social responsibilities, even if this must be done with extensive tax support.

These two forces (demography and the erosion of public confidence) create a tension that will continue into the 1980s—a groping for ways to shape life, given the prevailing conditions in society. In such an environment, experimentation and the generation of new ideas will be encouraged, although widespread support for any clear course is unlikely to emerge.

Forces Against Change

Against the forces for change can be posited several forces in the direction of stability and maintenance of the status quo.

Institutionalized opinions. The professions and the government have institutionalized their opinions, which are therefore frozen and not subject to rapid change. Civil service at all levels embodies a set of practices that argue against a rapid shift in the nature of personnel employed or in their tenure.

In general, the adult labor force has been educated and therefore conditioned by old ways of thinking. It adopts new ideas slowly, if not reluctantly. This conservative tendency is reinforced by the fact that key policy- and decision-makers are likely to be older than the average worker. In addition, civil service regulations, union contracts, and agency personnel practices often link the rewards of promotion and the security of tenure to years of service, which further strengthens the proclivity toward maintaining the status quo.

Social work education. Professional training and the standards of professional associations also change slowly. For example, graduate education for social work has had a distinctive character for at least twenty years, and this character has shaped the thinking and activities of virtually all persons now employed. And these social workers are primarily responsible for shaping whatever programs will exist in ten years. If the imprinting of professional education does exist, the influence of the past ten years will govern the shape of practice during the next ten years. The major shift—recognition of the bachelor's degree in social work (BSW)—cannot yet be tested, but it is reasonable to assume that much of the BSW education will draw heavily on the curriculum of the master's degree (MSW) and will rely heavily on persons who received an MSW in the past.

The bias in favor of the MSW will certainly be moderated by persistent efforts to create an educational base that will produce more qualified generic personnel. At the same time, the opportunities for experimentation in state and local governments will grow because of pressure to produce better results in services. In addition, there will be stronger and more widespread objections to increases in taxes and governmental spending. These two factors should increase the influence of major specialized service agencies in shaping the staffs they will employ for both specialized and specific positions. The outcome of this war between the efforts of educators to generalize and the tendency of employers to specialize is not easy to predict, but it is likely that there will be an increase in short-term post-BSW training by schools and employers alike, while the MSW progams will experiment with the development of advanced forms of specialized skills.

Public expenditures. Although overall public expenditures in the social sector will continue to increase despite cuts in some specific areas, it is doubtful that the rate will be as high as it was in the years 1959–69 (141 percent),[3] or that the rate of MSW social workers employed will grow as rapidly (125 percent).[4]

Even if the policies of the Nixon Administration are reversed, it is doubtful that the number of direct service personnel will again increase so fast. Rather, cash benefits through social security will grow at a more rapid rate than expenditures for services. In 1970, cash benefits, housing, and education represented at least 80 percent of all governmental social welfare expenditures, and it is unlikely that social services will ever dominate the rest of welfare expenditures.[5] If these forces are operative, as the author believes them to be, then the period of the 1980s is likely to see a redistribution of roles and functions rather than a dramatic alteration in the shape of social work.

Most analyses of professional efforts have been based on the educational qualifications for social work practice rather than on the place of social workers in the major welfare systems. However, the author believes that social work should be examined in the context of the social organization or social structure of which it is a part. If one takes this approach, it is possible to borrow a framework from census studies. Census studies identify employment categories (e.g., professional, technical, and kindred workers), and it should be possible to examine the place of social work according to the proportion of social workers found in these categories in the various human service subsystems.

Social workers are distributed throughout four types of human service subsystems: (1) those that are controlled by social work and in which 75 percent or more of all professional and technical personnel are social workers (voluntary family service agencies and children's programs), (2) those in which social work is recognized as an important ancillary function, but social workers represent only a small proportion of the professional and technical personnel (medical care, mental health services, and income security programs), (3) those in which social workers are found in small numbers and their function is not universally accepted and may be considered peripheral or experimental (school social work and corrections), and (4) private practice.

Family and Child Welfare

Social work will control only a small sector of the human service system—the subsystem made up of family and child welfare agencies. Although there are no adequate figures on the proportion of the total system devoted to this area of practice, it is clearly minor. In the 1980s, social workers will continue to perform their functions much as they do today. The professional hierarchy will be weighted in favor of employing MSWs, and a limited number of BSWs will be hired as social work aides. The functions performed by these agencies will be as diverse as in the past, but such agencies will continue to be much like those in the 1970s. Self-selected caseloads, small-scale penetration of target populations (accounted for by limited support for such agencies), and reliance on one-to-one relationships or family or small-group therapy will be buttressed by practice that is primarily psychotherapeutic.

However, in the 1980s there will be more experiments to supplement counseling with a variety of more tangible services, often funded under contract with third parties or public purchasers. For example, foster care and the development of small group residences for children displaying serious adjustment problems will more and more be supported by contracts from public agencies. The expansion of homemaker services for the chronically lonely elderly may likewise be paid for through public third-party payments. Day care for children will continue to grow, but it is still moot whether its leadership will be from the profession of education or social work. As of now, it seems that social work will concentrate on day care for children with special behavioral problems, while education will lead in general child development programs.

The family and child welfare agencies and their staffs will continue to experiment with trying to reach trouble spots in urban areas—the urban ghettos, the centers of high delinquency rates and high dependency. However, these experiments, given the characteristics just noted, are not expected to lay the foundation for a massive approach so that penetration of the at-risk population will continue to be insignificant.

Mental Health

The greatest changes that social work can anticipate in the next ten years will be in the second human service subsystem—agencies in which social work is recognized as an important ancillary function. The mental health subsystem is the one in which social workers are now most firmly embedded. For example, in 1968, 14,427 social work positions were identified in various psychiatric facilities. And 11,000 of over 50,000 members of the National Association of Social Workers were employed in psychiatric settings in 1969.[6] Approximately one-quarter of all full-time professional personnel in community mental health centers were social workers in that year. More social workers will be accepted as administrators of such psychiatric facilities as the shortage of physicians and psychiatrists becomes more pronounced and the demand for administrators grows.

The use of large state hospitals will continue to decline, and treatment will increase in psychiatric wards of acute general hospitals, in community mental health centers, or through community-care treatment that combines chemotherapy and psychotherapy. Greater attention will be given to community living and community care for the mentally ill, with or without treatment, and this will also increase demands on social workers to arrange for facilities for community care, such as halfway houses. Individualized treatment and mobilization of a variety of community resources to buoy up disturbed, mentally ill, or distracted individuals will become increasingly important adjuncts to chemotherapy and psychotherapy. Thus instead of concentrating on rehabilitation, social treatment, and "cure," social workers will be involved more and more in activities designed to help the mentally ill maintain themselves for long periods with their illness or limitations only partially reduced.

Social work will rediscover the close association between the individual psyche and the social environment. It will realize that social vulnerability is as significant as psychic vulnerability and that long-term modification of the living environment is essential. In fact, environmental modification will become a key rationale. It is the blend of psychological insight and readiness to take social responsibility for the living arrangements of others that is expected to make social workers more important in maintaining the mental health system.

Health Care

Health care represents the second major arena for the development of social work. The congressional debate on national health insurance has stimulated a massive reappraisal of the organization of health services. Whatever the outcome of the debate, it is clear that the investment in health services will not decline. Moreover, numerous experiments, both large and small, will be undertaken to reorganize the system for delivering health care and the personnel to provide the care, as well as to bring about slowly an equitable redistribution of health services to the poor, whose social needs complicate their health needs.

The attempt to minimize or control the phase of acute care in hospitals will continue, and this will place an increasing demand on health-based services to move patients from one to another of the various kinds of health facilities (e.g., hospitals, nursing homes, extended care facilities, hospitals for chronic illness, protected environments, and home care) so that the interface between medical services and social welfare services will become more significant. Medical institutions will become dependent on those persons responsible for making appropriate arrangements for transferring to community facilities those patients with acute conditions during periods of convalescence and those with long-continuing disabilities.

The unresolved question facing the health subsystem is this: How much responsibility should health agencies assume in caring for as well as treating persons with long-term conditions? A simple listing of such conditions indicates the scope of this problem: children born with severe genetic or birth defects; degenerative neurological conditions of cerebral palsy, multiple sclerosis, Parkinson's disease, and the like; severe traumatic injury resulting in spinal cord severance or loss of limbs; and the wasting diseases—including cancer—as well as the accumulating burden of long-term conditions of older adults, including hypertension, heart disease, and the crippling form of arthritis.

The position of social workers in the health subsystem will be similar to their position in the mental health subsystem. That is, they will be required to handle the enlarged set of relationships between the intricate network of health services and social services in the community that the long-term conditions require. In addition, they will be called on to manage and coordinate complexes of such services on behalf of individual patients. Although social workers will continue to help physically ill and emotionally disturbed persons face the realities of their health conditions and to use the health care system adequately, they will be expected to assume the much wider responsibilities involved in managing the liaison between health care and social services in the community.

The proposed new requirements of the Joint Commission on Accreditation of Hospitals signal this future role.[7] If they are adopted, all hospitals, to be accredited, will be required either to have a social work department of their own or to arrange for appropriate social work services from other sources. Another indication of what is to come is the fact that group health practices and health maintenance organizations are beginning to employ social workers in addition to the usual clinical complement of physicians, nurses, and the like. Numerous proprietary institutions, such as nursing homes, are also starting to hire social workers and to respond to mounting pressures to improve the quality of care by individualizing the treatment of patients.

Role in the Community

Although medical social workers have up to now worked primarily in hospitals, it is likely that with experimentation, they will expand their role in the community to encompass more than doing referrals and acting as liaisons to community agencies. Whether hospital and health facilities will assume responsibility for developing supportive out-of-hospital social work services (such as providing home helps or home health aides) depends on whether health insurance companies will reimburse them for such services. While reimbursement for home health aides is already well established, the current narrow definitions of home health aides may be broadened to include duties not limited to completing treatment of an acute episode of illness. Social work can assume responsibility for these functions if they become part of the health care continuum.

Social workers have the pertinent experience to manage such out-of-hospital and hospital-community services, although public health nurses and nurse's aides also perform these functions in many places. Social workers have no monopoly on this aspect of medical care today, but the demand for such services can be expected to increase in the next decade. And if the profession recognizes this opportunity it can become *the profession* responsible for this dimension of medical care. If social work is recognized as being responsible for such community roles, social workers at both the bachelor's degree and master's degree levels will be in great demand. A recognizable hierarchy based on promotion from one level to the next will develop, encompassing management, social assessment, and provision of both tangible (home help) and intangible (casework) services.

It is likely that in this area social workers will be recognized as the professionals who perform a range of specialized activities for which they will have requisite professional authority to exercise judgment. Today physicians overburdened by their clinical tasks rely on the opinions of social workers but make the final judgment themselves. In the future, the social worker's decision about the social conditions appropriate for a patient's discharge from an institution will be comparable to the physician's clinical judgment about the patient's physical condition. The social worker of the future will decide, for instance, whether the available residential, family, and community environment is suitable for a specific patient and will try to provide such an environment if it does not exist.

In addition, social workers might assume authority in determining whether patients are entitled to various social benefits—a function now performed by physicians. For example, they might decide when a patient with a complicated illness is to be judged disabled according to the definition in the Social Security Act or in a specific program for the permanently and totally disabled. In the field of mental health, it is possible that the clinical diagnosis of whether the patient is ready for medical discharge from a mental hospital may be accompanied by the social worker's decision about whether the patient is capable of adapting to society or the community environment is ready to receive him. Such an enlargement of authority as well as responsibility has already occurred in the United Kingdom, where physicians are required to consult social workers in all cases of involuntary commitment to a mental hospital on the grounds that a social worker's judgment about the suitability of an alternative environment is vital.

These expectations for social workers in the health field are buttressed by the extent to which social work has become professionalized in this field. Fifty-five percent of the medical social workers and 12 percent of the psychiatric social workers have had two years of professional education, the definition of a professional until recently.[8] This base of professionals provides an excellent springboard from which the field can be further extended; additional manpower for expanded functions can be provided by professionally trained personnel at both the bachelor's degree and master's degree levels.

Income Security Programs

Income security programs are the bedrock on which the human service system rests, but social work's role in this subsystem, especially in public assistance and social security, has been marginal in the past and probably will be even more so in the future. Although professional social workers constitute a fraction of all public assistance employees, they are frequently supervisors or administrators. Nonetheless, it is difficult to assert with any confidence that throughout the country the social work profession is in a position to administer the vast public assistance program. Now that the separation of income and social services under the Social Security Act is becoming a reality, social workers in public welfare are likely to become even further removed from the provision of income.

How does one reconcile these facts with the general public's identification of social work with public assistance? The answer, of course, may be found in the use of the term "social worker" to apply to *all* public assistance employees. However, in a 1972 survey of NASW members, only 8.2 percent with a professional education indicated that they were employed in public assistance agencies.[9]

There has been a long-term, steady trend toward the development of a standardized flat-grant system for handling income security, recognized first through the Old Age, Survivors, Disability, and Health Insurance Program, and more recently in the federalization of the adult categories in public assistance. This has been paralleled by attempts to develop Allied Services legislation to deal with social work services for recipients of assistance that are independent of income.[10]

This trend toward a separation of the management of financial security and the provision of services to recipients of assistance is expected to continue. The separation will be confused by the fact that the public tax fund will support only those social services directed primarily to recipients of assistance, although changing regulations of the Department of Health, Education, and Welfare permit limited public funds for persons recently on relief or likely to become eligible for relief. Despite the current limitation, this author predicts that by the middle 1980s there will be a network of comprehensive tax-supported social service agencies throughout the United States, as part of state and local governments, that will offer some services directly to clients and not be responsible for income security programs. These agencies will represent a small splintering off of public welfare social services from the antecedent public assistance program, but will have the potential for greater development in the future.

A small group of social workers with advanced degrees will be responsible for administering a large staff with diverse qualifications (BAs and paraprofessionals). It is expected that persons with bachelor's degrees will constitute the majority of personnel, and persons with advanced training will be involved mainly in administration, research, and the development of policy.

The direct-service agencies will be responsible initially for handling cases of persons who are and some who are likely to become eligible for public financial aid. They will eventually carry out many activities previously handled only by voluntary family and children's agencies for nonrecipients of relief. They can be expected to perform the following functions: placing dependent and neglected children in foster homes; attempting to manage predelinquent youths; and providing day care services for poor families and working mothers, home helps and homemakers, and counseling services for a variety of other public programs, such as those dealing with alcoholics, addicts, the aged, and the severely disabled.

By the 1980s, these agencies will still be concerned primarily with rehabilitation, counseling, and the provision of those concrete services such as day care and homemaker services that enable persons with physical or mental handicaps or social disabilities (unmarried mothers with small children) to seek employment and economic independence to the extent of their abilities. When economic independence is not possible, functional independence for the severely handicapped in lieu of institutional placement will emerge as a secondary goal. Functional independence is the ability of a handicapped person to manage the requirements of daily living despite his handicap. Many persons with severe physical handicaps can maintain functional independence with supplemental personal care assistance, while remaining in charge of their life decisions. Recent revisions in the legislation on rehabilitation, passed by both houses of Congress but vetoed by President Nixon, have provided for just such a development.

It is doubtful that services in this network of agencies will be based solely on the conventional skills of casework or individual counseling. Rather, sensitivity to human beings and assessment of individual needs will be buttressed by responsibility for managing and administering a variety of concrete services (e.g., those previously mentioned), which will constitute the public responsibility for strengthening family life and personal adjustment. The concept of managing or administering social services is used to distinguish this function from the more prevalent idea that professional social workers refer clients to others who provide concrete services. In this case "management" implies that the professional social worker is to be responsible for delivering concrete services, directing a variety of staff workers, deciding who shall be served and when, choosing which services take priority over others, making a budget, and being accountable to the supporting community.

One may ask: Why choose social workers for such a function? The answer is simple: No other profession, except perhaps community nursing, has shown the slightest interest in looking after troubled people day after day by becoming responsible for their basic living conditions. Others may move in a crisis, e.g., law and medicine, but few are prepared to live for long with the unpleasant aspects of living.

A strong basis for such a network already exists in local communities. Departments of public welfare already offer child care services through which neglected children are frequently placed in foster homes by public agency staffs. In addition, several departments of public welfare maintain or purchase from private sources a variety of home-health-aide and homemaker services for the disabled. It is likely that there will be different forms of organization throughout the country, but whether programs of child care, day care, foster home, child guardianship, and home help are developed through separate public agencies or become the consolidated function of one comprehensive public social service agency need not obscure the growth of this sector.

The British Experience

Such a program would represent the beginning in this country of the remarkable chain of events that took place twenty-five years ago in the United Kingdom, when income payments were separated from social services. In the current United Kingdom pattern, which was mandated by Parliament, each local jurisdiction is required to have a local public personal social services department staffed both by qualified social workers and by a large complement of persons providing a variety of concrete services. The department's responsibility is not limited to assistance recipients but is extended to all vulnerable persons in the defined geographic area. In a typical area, perhaps 100,000 to 250,000 persons are served by area teams of social workers who reach out to the community, are up to date about the people in their area, and construct means whereby persons in need are brought to the staff's attention. The staff then assesses these persons' needs and orders and manages a complex variety of concrete services available in each jurisdiction. Varying from community to community, these concrete services include some or all of the following: home health services provided for varying periods of time and at various levels of skill; day centers that train persons released from mental hospitals and the severely disabled either in employment or in socialization, that provide retarded children and adults with educational, occupational, and social programs, and the elderly with rehabilitation and social activities; foster care and small institutional programs for dependent children; small training institutions for delinquent youths; and day care centers for children.

In the United Kingdom the local department is strong because it is responsible for assessing the needs of individuals, case counseling, and managing a complex of concrete services. It is no longer wholly dependent on services provided or controlled by other independent agencies, but instead controls its own network of tangible services, which does much to enhance the morale and self-confidence of the staff. In many jurisdictions, the department is also able to purchase some supplementary services from willing, cooperating voluntary agencies to fill out the public services. Payment for such services is controlled by judgments made by the staff of the public personal social services department.

It is remarkable how decentralized the United Kingdom program is. Local departments are not required to distribute cash payments. Instead, staffs are assessed primarily on their ability to reach out and be receptive to people with a variety of needs. They are responsible for a population in a geographic area, *not* for a caseload screened and sifted by regulations that are barriers to eligibility. Responsibility decentralized to small area teams has encouraged an atmosphere of helpfulness rather than rejection, since meeting the needs of the population is the criterion of success. Decentralization is extended to include case authority, which means that area teams are free to determine how to use their personnel and budgetary resources according to the unique needs of their immediate population as long as they stay within the broad policy guidelines. This situation is in sharp contrast to that in the United States, where the national government and state governments superimpose their detailed standards on local jurisdictions.

It has also been possible in the United Kingdom to use only a small cadre of professional social workers (perhaps 10 to 15 percent in any department). The remaining personnel comprise persons with varied backgrounds who are chosen because of their interest in helping people and their personal qualifications rather than their educational credentials. Although it is expected that in time a common educational base will be established for this diverse group, at present it has been possible to launch a varied program without awaiting the development of standardized training for personnel. As a result, young people with only a high school diploma or some college education, college graduates with concentrations in the social sciences but no social work training, mature adults dissatisfied with routine tasks who want to help other human beings, and middle-aged housewives seeking to supplement their income through part-time work are blended together around the core of a trained cadre of social workers.

Although the experience in the United Kingdom cannot be simulated exactly in the United States, it does seem reasonable to expect that there will be a practical evolution in this country, by which local public social services will be separated from the provision of income, that it will start in the 1980s, and that it might well evolve along the same lines over a longer time span, as it has in England.

Work in Other Systems

Social workers will continue to be employed in a variety of other human welfare systems such as corrections, probation, and the public schools. Although they will perform important functions, they are not expected to assume significant positions in these systems for a variety of reasons. Schools are heavily influenced by the training that teachers receive, and the philosophy and methodology of the corrections system differ from those of social work too much; these factors will discourage widespread employment of social workers in positions of primary responsibility.

What about the private practice of social work? In 1967, 8–10 percent of practicing social workers were engaged in private practice at least on a part-time basis.[11] However, private practice is expected to expand and to become more attractive to those persons with exceptional skills and interests in psychotherapy and social counseling. Most private practice has been some form of therapy, and the almost inexhaustible American demand for such counseling indicates that social workers will have an increased opportunity to practice, along with psychologists, psychiatrists, rehabilitation counselors, and the like. Private practice is likely to fit into the mainstream of the development of social work in much the same way as the private practice of medicine has fitted into the growth of the institutionalized practice of medicine and such phenomena as third-part payments and hospital systems.

The most important functions of social work in the human services have already been discussed. There are two other parallel functions that will be significant in the 1980s—research and social action and planning.

Research

Advanced social work training at the doctoral level will slowly produce a sufficient cadre of systematic investigators to make possible the application of modern scientific approaches to human resources. Until recently, basic research into the functioning of the social service systems and the human services has been left to researchers from the fields of sociology, economics, and public administration. Social work researchers have been concerned mainly with practice with individuals or groups. By the mid-1980s, doctoral-level and master's-level training in social planning and research should have proceeded far enough for trained investigators to make useful contributions to the assessment of the fundamental operations of the major human service systems; their focus will be on improving the responsiveness of these systems to human needs as well as trying to validate social work case methods.

Research into the effectiveness and suitability of social work methods will become more critical. It will lead to the development of more effective forms of practice by all social workers. Such research should finally bridge the gap that has separated work with individuals from an assessment of the ability of service systems to meet the needs of large populations of vulnerable persons. This research capability will be carried forward by small numbers of persons employed in key positions in major human service systems. It will not become exclusive to social work, but rather will be shared by researchers drawn from other fields. The major contribution of the social work researcher will be to create a balance between individual needs and a rigorous, critical evaluation of institutional approaches to meeting those needs, whether through the practice of individuals or through the structuring of service delivery systems.

Social Action and Planning

The traditional social action and social planning functions of social work are not expected to change materially in the next ten years. The demand for coordination and linkage among a variety of services will continue, and the function of managing resources in various systems, such as income maintenance, medical care, and mental health, will continue to be supplemented by formalized mechanisms devoted to various types of coordination and planning. Examples of such mechanisms may already be found in comprehensive health planning agencies, agencies for the aged, community mental health centers, and in the attempts to improve general-purpose governmental planning at state, local-regional, and metropolitan levels.

United Way of America will continue to operate, but this

association probably will concentrate more and more on the links between voluntary agencies and will represent the interests of voluntary agencies in various contractual relationships with governmental bodies seeking to purchase services mandated by law. At the same time, a variety of governmental coordinating mechanisms will expand to join together public organizations. These will draw on the traditional social work skills of coordination and community organization, notably in state and area planning agencies for mental health, comprehensive health planning, work with the aging, and the like.

Other forms of social action will provide scattered opportunities for employment. Organizations representing minority groups and some community action organizations will continue to provide career opportunities that will probably be dominated by bachelor's degree social workers and a few committed social workers with master's and doctoral degrees. However, employment opportunities will be as limited as they are now. Workers in this area of social action will continue to act as public consciences, to bear witness against injustice and inequality, and to prod society to move faster toward improving conditions.

It is doubtful whether most social workers will have an opportunity to be paid to engage in what has been conventionally defined as social action. However, it is possible and even expected that most professional membership associations will find their most acceptable function to be the expression of the social conscience of its members. However, the conversion of the membership associations of social workers primarily into social action bodies remains fraught with uncertainty. In the past social workers at the master's and doctoral levels first acquired a sufficient professional security and then sought additional outlets for their concern with social injustice. They asked their membership associations to engage in the expression of such concern in various ways. However, bachelor's degree social workers, who have not as yet been overwhelmingly attracted to professional or association membership, may require primary attention to their economic and status positions in a changing employment and professional scene. It is not clear whether any one national organization can adequately represent the status needs of this much larger base of the profession and simultaneously give attention to social action and legislative change. It can be expected that the next ten years will see a competition among professional organizations comparable to that which took place in the late 1930s and early 1940s among such associations as the American Association of Social Workers, the American Association of Medical Social Workers, and the American Association of Psychiatric Social Workers on one hand and the various unions representing the economic interests of employees in public and private agencies on the other hand.

Conclusion

In the 1980s, social work will continue to find its greatest strength in using the interests, concerns, and skills of its members, at both the bachelor's and master's degree levels, to come to grips with the problems of living encountered by the disadvantaged. The uncertainties of life will broaden the definition of "disadvantaged populations," and the interpersonal skills of social workers will be much expanded. Regardless of economic class, the problems of addiction, injury, mental and physical illness, retirement, family disorganization, and other hazards of daily living will continue to exist and perhaps even increase. These conditions will stimulate the demand for social work skills.

The strength of the profession will continue to be its readiness to go into the homes of the persons it serves and to look clearly at the problems they confront. However, in the future the profession will be stronger in its readiness to combine assessment and counseling with management of other more tangible services. It is expected that control of new resources will gravitate to social work, and the effective management of such resources will become the hallmark of the profession, humanized as it will be by insight into human needs to moderate the impersonality of large-scale programs.

None of this can be accomplished with the current focus of professional social work education. However, it is expected that schools of social work will respond to the predicted developments by enriching their basic curricula. BSW programs will supplement their courses in the concepts of human development with training in techniques of providing a variety of tangible services, such as home health, home maker, home help, day care, institutional, or residential care. On the MSW and Ph.D. levels there will be increased attention to the management side of administering such services and to complexities of team leadership, especially when such leadership includes administrative responsibilities. Advanced training in interpersonal treatment skills will be offered by some schools of social work, but will also be sought by social workers in other educational institutions as well. New patterns of study and work—and challenging opportunities—may come out of the interweaving of the various levels of practice. It is clear that the newly defined manpower needs of the field will play a crucial role in shaping future professional education.

Notes

1. *Statistical Abstract of the United States, 1972* (Washington, D.C.: U.S. Department of Commerce, Bureau of the Census, 1972), Table 37: "Population by Age, 1940–1970."

2. Data refer to veterans surviving for one year in 1946 and in 1958. *See Mortality Report on Spinal Cord Injury* (Washington, D.C.: Veterans Administration, November 13, 1958).

3. Annual Statistical Supplement, *Social Security Bulletin*, 1969. Tables 1 and 3. The increase in terms of the gross national product is 32 percent.

4. Derived from *Encyclopedia of Social Work* (New York: National Association of Social Workers, 1971), Table 52, p. 1612.

5. Annual Statistical Supplement, *Social Security Bulletin*, 1971, Table 3.

6. *See* Martin Nacman, "Mental Health Services, Social Workers in," *Encyclopedia of Social Work* (New York: National Association of Social Workers, 1971), p. 823.

7. *Accreditation Manual for Hospitals* (Chicago: Joint Commission on Accreditation of Hospitals, December 1970), pp. 139–142.

8. *See* Arnold Gurin, "Education for the Profession of Social Work," in Everett C. Hughes, ed., *Education for Changing Practice*, to be published by McGraw-Hill Book Co.

9. "NASW Manpower Data Bank Survey" (Washington, D.C.: National Association of Social Workers, 1972).

10. The adult categories include income for the aged, permanently and totally disabled, and the blind. "Allied Services" is the term coined in legislation to cover federal grants to the states for those social services previously administered in state public assistance programs—an uneven mixture of services such as casework, homemaker, employment, day care, child care, protective, and family services.

11. *See* Margaret A. Golton, "Private Practice in Social Work," *Encyclopedia of Social Work* (New York: National Association of Social Workers, 1971), p. 952.

Human Service on the Road to Social Progress

COLIN GREER

More and more college graduates (and many among those who never complete college) are entering what is now engagingly called the human-service professions. Because this coincides with the social rhetoric of recent decades, we tend to assume that large expansion in the number of health, education and welfare professionals means the improvement of the quality of life for the millions of Americans who are the clientele of these workers. The fact is, however, that the social-reform rhetoric has done more to expand the employment opportunities in the service sector of our economy than it has to solve any of the problems it has addressed.

The number of jobs in human-service fields has been expanding at an unprecedented rate. Someday soon, Daniel Bell points out, "the proportion of factory workers in the labor force may be as small as the proportion of farmers today." And what Herbert Gans called the equality revolution of the sixties, the New Deal between the Depression and World War II, and the so-called Progressive Era in the early twentieth century, have all been powerful forces contributing to the development of the service sector. It is almost as if the social rhetoric behind these reform thrusts was a public-relations campaign for the job expansion from which so many in the so-called helping professions have benefited.

But even if the social rhetoric did function in this way in the last decade, its most important effect may be found in the way it has been teaching us to view society. It has served as a prepatory public socialization process, an anticipatory rhetoric for service-state consciousness. Indeed, we often forget that shifts in economic emphases require a new public outlook, a new conventional wisdom about personal and social life.

Since World War II (following the sudden growth of about 60 per cent in service employment at that time) the theme of service has emerged at the core of an emerging national ideology, an ideology favoring group cohesion which prizes self-evaluation through introspection and sensitivity rather than competitive success.

The sixties mood, in which applied social consciousness and social service are the criteria for "relevance," the mood so forcefully expressed at Berkeley, Columbia and Yale, has been filtering into the public colleges, now increasingly populated by the working-class students recently admitted to higher education. As a result, this version of relevance has become synonymous with what is superficially observable as an increasingly homogeneous student culture. It seems to be a culture which can best be characterized by its often rhetorical, sometimes intense concern with self; its general devotion to the ideas of peace and brotherhood; and its embarrassment and awkwardness in asserting personal ambition. It is a culture to which students are drawn even, or perhaps especially, when schools and colleges fail them academically.

It is this cultural antagonism to what are perceived and experienced as maliciously competitive norms which is, I believe, the major substance behind what Charles Reich refers to as Consciousness III. Yet I know of no evidence to support Reich's claim that this spirit has been or can be the source of the structural reorganizations on which significant social change depends. It is rather the spirit, as Michael Novak describes, where Consciousness I and Consciousness II were heading all along: "a synthesis of WASP individualism and corporate teamwork, with a sensuous mobility. . . ." A person will no longer be defined by what he does, actualizing himself by acting on the world; he will be defined instead by how he gives and receives.

Apparently the old rat race will no longer make Sammy run. It cannot be ruled out that this change could be a step toward actually dealing with the problems and miseries of millions of Americans.

But we may be doing little more than slightly, just slightly, enlarging the middle class.

It is, however, by no means certain that we will finally have more than a slightly different race, with new criteria for privilege and new categories for explaining away those who lose. We are seriously diverted from analyzing how we are really doing and what we might be doing to solve our social problems by our persistent and erroneous desire to regard the expansion of the human service professions as synonymous with the social progress our social rhetoric talks about. It isn't.

The Revolution in Mental-Health Care—A "Bold New Approach"?

M. BREWSTER SMITH

American society is now well launched into a third mental-health revolution—a revolution that promises to end the isolation of the mentally disturbed and bring them back into the community as fully accredited human beings. And yet this revolution is in great danger of faltering, of being prevented from ever realizing its magnificent potential.

The first mental-health revolution unshackled the insane. By calling them sick, it managed to treat them as human. Its monuments and symbols are the great, usually isolated, state mental hospitals. The second revolution came from the spread of dynamic psychiatry (mainly Freud's) and was characterized by individual, one-to-one psychotherapy. Now the third revolution throws off the constraints of the doctor-patient medical model—the idea that mental disorder is a *private* misery—and relates the trouble, and the cure, to the entire web of social and personal relationships in which the individual is caught.

Perhaps the depth and significance of this new revolution are not so obvious as they should be. The first two revolutions were great steps forward, but they could not come to grips with the problems that afflict most of the disturbed, and they brought in a number of unintended evils. The new revolution offers new solutions to old and unsolved problems, and seeks also to cope with urgent new problems of our seething urban society.

The first revolution goes back to the birth of institutional psychiatry in the 19th century. It was a progressive movement then, under medical auspices. What it offered to insane people was *asylum*—a humane alternative to almshouses and jails. This revolution respected their humanity, accepted some responsibility for their care, and offered at least some hope for cure. The state hospitals that came into being gave psychotic people at least a modicum of care. At the beginning, there was a hopeful—and surprisingly modern—emphasis on moral treatment.

This system, we now know, became by and large a bad one. It served mainly to ease the public conscience by putting crazy people out of sight and mind—in hospitals, typically built out in the country, in the district of some powerful legislator. There a large number of chronic patients were trained, in effect, to be nothing but patients for life.

The second mental-health revolution occurred in the wake of Freud's insights and discoveries. The forefront of innovation was the consulting room of the private practitioner; the method, treatment by talk. And the patients were limited almost entirely to those who could afford this expensive new treatment.

Furthermore, the medical language of illness and health, disease and cure, had to be stretched beyond comfortable limits. In the beginning the patients Freud saw were mainly hysterics—troubled people whose difficulties mimicked organic disease, and who therefore tended to turn up in the offices of physicians. But in recent years the problems that middle-class patients bring to therapy are increasingly those of the sick soul—malaise, meaninglessness, a vague sense of missing out on the satisfactions of life. The language of health and illness doesn't really fit such complaints.

This second revolution brought mostly sorrow to the big state mental hospitals. It could not give them much help. There was simply no real possibility of extending individual psychotherapy to the great mass of inmates—though some attempt was made. Hospital psychiatry had to rely on the organic therapies (like lobotomy and electric shock) and fell into even lower repute. Private practice, with its well-heeled and sophisticated patients, is what attracted the bright young psychiatrists and clinical psychologists—even if, now, they are trained largely at public expense.

Yet the doctor-patient medical model, as embodied in the first two revolutions, got attached to mental disorder more for historical reasons than for intrinsic reasons. Why should medicine, more than religion or education, provide the framework for helping disturbed people cope with their problems? "Mental illness" *is* very different from physical illness, even if some physical illnesses produce disturbed behavior. It is not just somebody's private misery. Mental illness usually grows out of—and contributes to—the breakdown of a person's normal sources of support and understanding, especially in his family. It is part of a vicious circle. Not only has he himself faltered, but the social systems on which he depends have failed to sustain him—family, school, job, church, friendship, and the like. The task is not to cure an ailment inside his skin, but to strengthen him to the point where he can once again participate in the interactions that make up the warp and woof of life. It is also one of helping those subsystems function in ways that promote the well-being and effectiveness of all people who take part in them. Of course, genetic and other organic factors may contribute to a troubled person's difficulties. But primarily, as the new community approach sees it, his troubles amount to malfunctions of ordinary social participation.

Creating a Therapeutic Community

In the great mental hospitals, the hours of therapy—whether individual or group—are few and far apart, if the patient is lucky enough to get *any*. It is therefore obvious, according to the new approach, that the day-in and day-out routine of ward life has more effect on a patient's progress—or lack of it—than all formal therapy. Moreover, the discovery of tranquilizing drugs has ushered in a whole new revolution of its own, making possible an entirely new role for the hospital as well as new concepts of therapy. Thus was born the idea of remaking the mental hospital into a *therapeutic community*, rather than a mere treatment center.

Next, the enormous gap between the state mental hospital and the patient's home and community had to be bridged. As this idea gained general acceptance (aided considerably by the report of the Joint Commission on Mental Illness, *Action for Mental Health*, 1961), the third mental-health revolution was under way.

The first big step in the third mental-health revolution has been to bring the treatment of the seriously disturbed back from the remote state hospital into the community. That means, among other things, taking patients away from the dehumanizing damage done by the old state hospitals with their isolation, their locked doors and back wards. We must keep patients in their home communities even if they go to hospitals there—this first of all.

It follows that we must:

—Leave the hospital doors unlocked—if people are *expected* to act crazy, most of them will.

—Make it easy to enter the hospital voluntarily, and depart voluntarily; make it easy for the individual to return and feel free to return in times of stress and extra need. The "open door" and the "revolving door" help to lower the barriers that stand between mental hospital and community life.

—Integrate in-patient and out-patient services so that there is continuity of care within the mental-health system. Provide intermediate way-stations between complete hospitalization and out-patient status—night hospitals for those able to work during the day, day hospitals for those who can more profitably spend nights and weekends at home.

—Cut down the waiting, so help is provided when it is needed. To those in crisis, make emergency help immediately and conspiciously available.

All this constitutes the essential, giant first step. But it is still not enough, and I predict that this new revolution will peter out in disillusionment unless we quickly go beyond it.

This first stage is inadequate for several reasons:

—Present models of "treatment" generally do not reach or help those with the most serious problems.

—If we use only the mental-health professionals we use now, the expanded programs will be impossible to staff.

—The importance of the community for bad or for good—for sustaining vicious circles of human misery and ineffectiveness, or for helping people achieve satisfying lives—is not yet grasped in the hospital-clinic-centered program. (See "Worlds That Fail," by Dorothy Miller, *Trans-action* Dec. 1966.)

Let me elaborate on these points:

Present methods don't reach those who need help most. The second, Freudian, mental-health revolution set the standard for the most prestigious technique of treatment: intensive individual therapy, the more like psychoanalysis, and the longer, the better. This is what most psychiatrists and clinical psychologists are trained to do, and get most satisfaction from. They are themselves middle-class; and they work best with relatively sophisticated patients, who can both appreciate them and what they are doing.

But it is the poor, the dispossessed, the uneducated—the "poor treatment risks"—who have the really serious mental-health problems. And these people—less verbal, less subjective—tend not to understand dynamic psychotherapy, or want it, or benefit from it. They don't see their troubles in psychological terms, and don't believe that talk can be a treatment. The modern professional, with his fixation on psychotherapy, is a little like the drunk who kept looking for his keys under the streetlight, not because he had lost them there but because it was easier to look there.

Radical departures are needed. And there are promising new models. Some draw on the behavior therapies. They try, unabashedly, to use learning principles to remove troublesome symptoms directly rather than concentrating on remote, "un-derlying causes." A variety of promising therapies emphasize ac-tion—such as roleplaying—rather than talk, and explore the real problems of people in their real lives, rather than in their subjective fantasies.

Expanded programs cannot conceivably be staffed on present patterns. The federal program for community mental-health centers began with a appropriation for bricks and mortar. This was a big mistake. Buildings are *not* the strategic ingredient of a com-munity mental-health center. The key ingredient is services—and services mean professional people. There are not enough of them to go around, and there won't be in the foreseeable future. The lack of mental-health manpower is on the verge of becoming a national disaster.

Clearly, to cling to the model of one-to-one individual psychotherapy, even if there were no doubt about its effectiveness, is downright irresponsible. We need to employ scarce professional resources in ways that *multiply* their effectiveness. Community mental-health programs need to make more use of very carefully selected and briefly trained nonprofessionals. In working with unsophisticated, poor people, carefully selected "indigenous" nonprofessionals may achieve better communication than the scarce middle-class professional ever can. It would be better to employ his scarce talents in selection, training, and supervision of non-professionals.

The potential of the community for bad or good isn't recognized in the hospital-clinic-centered program. We are not dealing with isolated disease processes, but with vicious circles of human misery and ineffectiveness, with patterns of self-defeating behavior that are hard to break because they are embedded in the very texture of people's lives. We need to invest more in working on the social contexts in which troubled people are involved, and to count less upon the effectiveness of the isolated therapeutic hour.

Project Re-Ed

In this connection, I think of my colleague Nick Hobb's very important Project Re-Ed, centered at Peabody College in Tennessee. This was a boldly innovative demonstration project that is now ready for export. Project Re-Ed is a residential-school program. It seeks not to "cure" the "sick" child but to give him sufficient strength and resources so that—when he is reintroduced into family and school—constructive, benign circles of causation replace the earlier, vicious ones. When you think about it, investment in working with the child's normal environment is just as essential as investment in re-education itself. The child is not released as "cured," but reintroduced into his everyday life in such a way that he is more likely to gain progressively in competence and satisfaction.

The teacher-counselors—the frontline staff of these residential schools—are recruited from the large pool of would-be teachers, rather than from the highly restricted one of indentified mental-health professionals. The job attracts the same sort of dedicated people as those who join the Peace Corps.

The Re-Ed program recognizes that learning takes place 24 hours a day. For continuity, night-teacher-counselors plan programs and activities together with day-teacher-counselors. The teacher-counselors are backed up by expert psychiatric and psychological help; they accept and support the children without setting themselves up as junior psychotherapists. Hobbs has found that the *liaison teacher* is the crucial link between the residential school and the child's real school in the community he will return to.

The Re-Ed programs have had gratifying success. They have now been accepted as regular parts of the North Carolina and Tennessee state systems of Mental Hygiene. Tennesses is using the model as its basic approach in treating emotionally-disturbed children.

Still, the Re-Ed program is only one model. The general picture is a good deal less gratifying. Why have we not made better use of what we know? Obviously, we have not been bold or radical enough; we have not asked the hard questions.

For instance, why don't we have better coordination between the agencies that are supposed to serve people—especially those people who need it most? Why do we so arbitrarily parcel out human problems among diverse agencies, departments, and professions? The new mental-health revolution is not an isolated phenomenon— it is part of the whole urban revolution, a revolution that poses the question of how we can make urban life more tolerable, satisfying, and effective. And most of us are now urbanites. At present the great proliferation of schools, the great proliferation of public and private welfare agencies, the mental-health system, and the legal-correctional system all nibble at the edges of these problems. We must integrate efforts.

Consider, for example, what happens to an alcoholic. Who handles his case? Whether it is the police, courts and jails, mental-health institutions, or some special welfare agency depends pretty much on circumstances—most of them accidental.

Or what of the unruly, disturbed, truant child who commits an act of vandalism? Will he be handled by the schools and their psychological services or by the police and the courts? (Whether he is rich or poor, black or white, will help decide.)

The absurdity and injustice of all this are obvious. As a result, there is ferment in every field that must deal with the hard-core problems of malfunctioning in a modern, urban society. The basic wrong-headedness of present public-welfare policies is just short of a national scandal, and the search for alternatives has brought on a national debate. The field of justice and corrections is going through its own revolution, modeled largely on the new mental-health revolution—the emphasis has shifted from a punitive-custodial orientation in the prisons to therapy and a greater use of community treatment, especially for juveniles. In the Negro ghettos, at long last—even if we still move with tragic slowness—we have begun to do something about the appalling problems instead of trying to sweep them under a rug. In sum, there are signs of an impending rational attack on urban problems. But the needed coordination is still a hope, not a reality.

In mental-health programming itself, a key impediment to effectiveness has been its separation from such services as schools, courts, and welfare. Agencies often work at cross-purposes, or in ignorance of one another's programs. This is partly because we are still defining mental disturbance as an illness, establishing hospitals and clinics as the appropriate places of treatment, and insisting on semi-medical qualifications for its treatment specialists.

Current recommendations that a person in trouble be admitted to the total mental-health system, and not just to one component of it, fall short of coming to grips with the problem—though the aim is laudable. In treating distressed people, we must not artificially isolate a "mental-health sector." Mental-health professionals should take the lead in ensuring that mental-health activities are no longer isolated from the schools, from urban planning, from the poverty program, and from police recruitment and training.

Let there be no misunderstanding: I do not claim all human welfare is covered by "mental health." But professionals can no longer find smug comfort in some supposedly well-defined area of "mental-health problems." There is no such well-defined area. "Mental health"—a better description is "human effectiveness versus ineffectiveness"—is one aspect of concrete problems that are also likely to be educational, medical, moral, and maybe religious. No single family of professions or institutions can grasp and manage all the mental-health concerns to which we are committed—from serious neurological disorders through the whole fabric of human experience. Mental health is everyone's business. None of us have sufficient competence to deal with all of it. No mental-health center can be comprehensive enough.

Mental-health professionals must therefore ask how their scarce skills can be used best in conjunction with the skills of others. The staff of a community mental-health center must set up joint programs with the other systems—school, industry, welfare, and the rest. As staff members do this, they will need to develop new skills—ways of helping based on action rather than talk, as well as indirect forms of help and consultation.

Consultation is essential. People interact with their social environment; to change aspects of that environment can make great differences in the mental health of whole groups. The people and institutions that in large part influence or determine that environment—government agencies, churches, schools, business, industry—are amateurs when it comes to the psychological effects of their policies and decisions, and they are preoccupied with other matters. This does not mean that the mental-health professionals know best how the community should operate—such a claim is presumptuous and foolish. Rather, they contribute a special perspective that can help the agencies and institutions perform their functions better. Through consultation, at all levels, mental-health people can improve the quality of community and family life for all citizens.

New Approaches to Therapy

What existing programs embody the new approaches? I have already mentioned Nick Hobbs and his Project Re-Ed. I must also hasten to add, in all fairness, that though I have been arguing for a community mental-health program that breaks free of the old medical model, some of the most imaginative programs—and those least medical in the traditional sense—have been launched by physicians.

I have been enormously impressed by the program led by two psychiatrists, Sheppard Kellam and Sheldon Schiff. They have been working primarily with children in the Chicago Negro community of Woodlawn. In developing this community mental-health program, they had the great advantage of building upon an already-active community organization with identified leadership, whom they could work with closely. Consultations, therefore, could go into motion quickly—without the usual faltering.

Woodlawn wanted the program to focus on the problems of first-grade children in their encounter with school. School represents the initial occasion when all children are touched by organized society. The approach taken by Kellam, Schiff, and their associates made the teachers themselves collaborators and principals in the enterprise, drawing heavily on their skills and experience. The program included screening for existing psychological problems, and consultation with teachers and classroom groups of children. The psychiatrists also kept a running assessment of the impact of their program. The scarce skills of the mental-health professionals were used strategically—they even trained the teachers, in effect, to be valuable assistant diagnosticians and treatment specialists.

A couple of other examples might be introduced. Frank Riessman's application of the technique of *role-playing* is especially helpful with the nonverbal poor. (See *Trans-action*, Jan. 1964.) In role-playing, the participants act out parts in selected, simulated situations. Working with slum-dwellers in the Mobilization for Youth program, Riessman found this approach more congenial to them than just talking. The poor prefer doing to talking, presenting their real problems rather than their fantasies. He found that this approach also reduced the gap between practitioner and client—a real barrier when middle-class professionals try to work with the poor, especially in the usual bureaucratic settings. It also tends to develop the articulateness of people who usually lack verbal skill and self-confidence.

Another example of imaginative innovation: In Cambridge, Mass., Charles Slack and R. R. Schwitzgebel, working with delinquents, in effect tried using tape recorders as therapists. They hired the youths to talk at length into the recorders about their lives and problems, carefully using rewards and bonuses to bring them into increasingly responsible relationships, and to give them, and the professionals, insight. Although Slack and Schwitzgebel describe this approach in terms of B. F. Skinner's reinforcement theories, I think that its scrupulous honesty and complete reciprocity were the most important reasons for its success. Help and knowledge were sought from the young people as well as given (at first, in fact, *more* sought than given).

All these new approaches have broken the mold of the doctor-patient relationship, and achieved some success; we can expect many more.

But success is not inevitable. In fact, in a fundamental sense the work has hardly begun, and many snares lie ahead. It was President John F. Kennedy who sponsored this revolution, and the "bold new approaches" he called for are still, for the most part, gleams in the eyes of pioneers, or pilot ventures not yet part of standard practice. Moreover, we are finding to our dismay that we must fight a two-front war: While we try to push ahead, we must also fight vigorously merely to preserve yesterday's gains from short-sighted budget-mindedness. The situation in California provides a good example. In self-defense, mental health has now entered politics, and if we are serious about "bold new approaches," we will have to stay in politics, and fight.

The greatest danger perhaps is that the third mental-health revolution will be (in Harold Lasswell's phrase) "resisted by incorporation"—that is, confined to existing models while lip-service is given to "new" ideas. Already the plans for "comprehensive community mental-health centers," stimulated and supported by federal legislation, are following discouragingly tame and conventional paths. Most are hospital-centered—on the old medical model, under medical control. Do they help orchestrate and coordinate existing services? Generally, no. Usually they appear as just one more package among all the other proliferating, ill-coordinated packages.

What seems to be happening is that the revolution is being frozen in its first phase. This early ossification around the mental-health center idea reflects the thinking of leaders in the National Institute of Mental Health—and it is deplorable. Effective "community mental health" cannot be fitted inside existing professional biases, habits, and territorial rights.

We must have explicit and built-in evaluations of new programs, with continuous feedback of adequate information about results. These we must use, with great flexibility and innovation, to meet *community*—not professional—needs.

We must set forth in new directions. We must be radical. It will be a national shame and scandal if the "third national mental-health revolution" finally peters out into little more than the substitution of shiny, sterile, glass-and-aluminum institutions in the city for the old dismal red brick ones out in the sticks.

Neighborhood Psychiatry: New Community Approach

STEVEN S. SHARFSTEIN

Psychiatrists have been working in a variety of neighborhood settings for several years. With the development of Office of Economic Opportunity Neighborhood Health Centers came the opportunity for psychiatrists to focus on the provision of mental health services to a neighborhood and to integrate these services with comprehensive health and social services. Section 222 (a, 4, A, 1) of the Economic Opportunity Act as amended includes mental health in its definition of comprehensive services, and the *Guidelines for the Comprehensive Neighborhood Health Services* includes mental health services. A recent survey of 26 neighborhood health centers (OEO and HEW funded) in Boston shows that 19 have mental health services (Action for Boston Community Development, 1971).

The literature in "neighborhood psychiatry" is sparse and reflects the lack of a shared experience among these community workers (Scherl & English, 1969; Peck & Kaplan, 1969; Lowenhopf & Zwerling, 1971; Sharfstein & Khajavi, in press).

Psychiatric services based in a neighborhood health center can be delivered in a number of different ways. This paper reports on an evolving 2-year experience in the Model Cities Program in Boston, with one "family life center" as the base of operations for a program of direct patient care and preventive services for a defined neighborhood. It emphasizes the integration of mental health with other services provided at the center and in agencies that serve the neighborhood.

Brookside Park Family Life Center

The Brookside Park Family Life Center (FLC) serves an inner city population of around 15,000, mostly white, Catholic, and Spanish working class, and attempts to provide "one door" service to community residents so that any health, mental health, or social problems can be dealt with in a personal, unfragmented, and effective manner. Comprehensive outpatient services are provided in pediatrics, internal medicine, obstetrics-gynecology, and dentistry. Social services are provided by intake workers who are community residents. These paraprofessional workers often function as patient advocates.

The mental health unit was the first operating service at the Family Life Center and has become an integral part of its function. Direct and consultation services are performed through multidisciplinary teams comprised of service providers at all professional and paraprofessional levels from each service unit.

The mental health unit includes a half-time psychiatrist-director, two full-time psychiatric nurses, one half-time chief resident, one half-time child psychiatrist, and a number of additional part-time staff from the back-up mental hospital. It is the philosophy of the mental health staff to act as a separate department as little as possible and to permeate all aspects of center service delivery through interaction within the teams. Further, the unit uses the center as a home base to consult with a wide variety of community agencies that either are located in or serve the neighborhood. It is also used by the back-up hospital as a major focus for the teaching of community psychiatry to residents in training.

The mental health program is described below, subdividing its role in (1) general health, (2) social service and community advocacy, (3) community agencies, and (4) teaching hospital.

Neighborhood Psychiatry and the General Health Setting

Community based adult, pediatric, and obstetric-gynecological services provide the unique opportunity for mental health workers to have an impact on the treatment planning for large numbers of people. Early detection of mental illness can often take place as patients initially refer themselves for physical complaints. The two intradisciplinary health teams discuss difficult cases and multiprogram families. Each team has one psychiatric nurse as a member and consultant to the team. Much of the teaching of the center's health professionals on the psychological side of a multifaceted situation takes place by the nurses in the teams, and direct referrals for evaluation and treatment by mental health professionals come from the teams with the nurse as the front-line "triage" worker.

Direct outpatient psychiatric treatment is available to neighborhood residents upon request of the neighborhood advisory board to the Family Life Center. They felt that consultation and referral was not enough and insisted on early accessible care with no waiting list. Long-term, office-based, insight-oriented psychotherapy is available only to a minority of patients, as this form of treatment is not only inappropriate for the vast majority of problems, but also would rapidly deplete the team's resources. Emphasis is placed on home visits, crisis intervention, short-term therapy, family therapy, and group therapy. Many evaluations and recommendations are directed to the other health team professionals for implementation with no further work done by the mental health worker. Psychiatric residents perform evaluations of multiproblem families as a service to the center and as part of their training in community psychiatry.

Patients who have been discharged from the mental hospital can be most effectively followed up in a neighborhood setting like the Brookside Park Family Life Center. In addition to the closeness of psychiatric services to the family, other needs of the family can be met in a uniform way. By helping a disorganized family (further disrupted by the return of a member after hospitalization) to organize itself and to adjust, both the individual and the family are better served. Paraprofessionals can be most effectively utilized in this way.

Case 1 A 48–year-old Irish mother of six has been hospitalized almost continuously for the last 12 out of 14 consecutive years following a postpartum psychosis after the birth of her sixth child. She had received multiple ECT treatments, and was considered a "backward" case.

Two years ago she was discharged from the hospital, on a high dosage of phenothiazines, and returned to her family for what was expected to be a brief visit before another long hospitalization. Follow-up was begun at the Family Life Center.

The patient was seen weekly by the psychiatrist to adjust her medications, and a home visit was made. A paraprofessional worker, a woman the same age as the patient, began visiting twice a week; going shopping with the patient and helping her organize the home. A meeting was called of all the community agencies involved including welfare, visiting nurses association, and a probation officer. Crises were handled rapidly by the Family Life Center and rehospitalization was prevented several times.

The patient has remained out of hospital for 2 years as a contributing member of her family. Her phenothiazine dose has been lowered and her level of function is better than before her first breakdown, as judged by her husband.

Direct service delivery, however, is only one important part of the mental health effort in the Brookside Park Family Life Center. The interpersonal skills of all health team members are hopefully enlarged by the ongoing consultations and the teaching done by the psychiatric nurses. One-to-one consultation takes place between the family physicians and the appropriate psychiatrists to implement multiproblem care. Further, several of the nurse-practitioners have taken on psychiatric patients in short-term therapy in order to enhance their learning and to look at alternate ways of handling crisis situations. These nurses receive supervision from the mental health team. Various formats for this have been tried, one in which the psychiatrist sits in with the medical service provider as he sees patients (Zabarenko, Merenstein, & Zabarenko, 1971).

Case 2 A 25–year-old unmarried mother of three came to the Family Life Center wanting an abortion. She spoke with the obstetric nurse practitioner, telling her about her most recent disappointing love affair and suicidal thoughts in relation to this pregnancy and relating a past history of impulsive behavior, including several suicidal gestures.

The nurse consulted the mental health unit and the patient was seen by a psychiatrist and the nurse together. A plan was worked out for short-term therapy by the nurse under the psychiatrist's supervision. The nurse arranged the abortion, and was available to the patient in crisis situations. She was able to set some limits on self-destructive behavior and helped the patient begin a school program. The nurse handled the emotional aspects of the case well, and felt that she had profited by this learning experience.

Neighborhood Psychiatry and Social Services

The "information and evaluation" worker is the primary intake worker and advocate for clients who register at the Brookside Park Family Life Center. As community residents and paraprofessionals they bridge a gap in the translation of the needs of their clients in relation to professional service providers at the center and other service agencies such as housing and welfare. Much of the hopelessness and powerlessness of poor people is rooted in reality. This worker, by getting things accomplished within the reality of these people's lives, functions as a kind of mental health worker. The mental health teams, especially the psychiatrists and nurses, maintain a close working relationship with the information and evaluation specialist in sorting out the psychological problems from the social problems, helping the worker understand his client, and in setting limits with himself and his clients. These workers are also crucial expeditors of service, especially when there is a language barrier.

Case 3 A 26–year-old, Spanish-speaking, unemployed man came with his family to the center because he refused food and was mute. A recent arrival from Puerto Rico, he had broken up with his girlfriend and when he did speak, he spoke only of her. The Spanish worker brought him to the back-up hospital, on recommendation of the center psychiatrist, and helped negotiate day hospitalization for this young man. The worker not only served as a translator of language, but also helped the professionals understand the cultural issues involved and the stresses of migration from Puerto Rico. As the case became clearer, it seemed that the patient believed a curse had been placed on him by his girl friend's mother, and the folk medical practices were discussed.

This patient accomplished short-term therapy with the help of the information and evaluation worker, and after several months was considerably improved.

Neighborhood Psychiatry and Community Agencies

An early function of the mental health unit was to establish links between the Family Life Center and many community organizations. This role has been twofold—that of "network builder" for working relations among community agencies and that of crisis intervention once working relations have been established. By working directly in a neighborhood center and setting up mental health consultations in various other community service agencies, both the agencies and the psychiatrists have gained a clearer picture of the needs and resources within the community and their potential assistance to each other. Consultation services have been or are taking place in the Boston Legal Assistance Project (legal aid, storefront), local welfare office, local neighborhood employment center, several teen drop-in centers, several nursing homes, the local Head Start and Day Care programs, and the public junior high school.

The mental health unit has effectively intervened in several crisis situations in neighborhood programs. Being "right there" is essential in securing acceptance from neighborhood residents and agency workers.

Case 4   A teen drop-in center located in a church was closed abruptly after a series of incidents leading to the vandalizing of the center and assault on several of the counselors. The kids, mostly 14 to 16 years old, were all black. The adults, including the priest-director, were all white. Until 2 years ago, this church was in an all-white neighborhood.

The director of the center asked for outside help in understanding what had happened and in getting the drop-in center open again. The Family Life Center sent in a white psychiatrist and a black psychologist to consult with them on this crisis for a short period.

During the eight meetings, the counselors ventilated their anger at the kids and their guilt in not having set firmer limits in bad behavior earlier in the year. They realized that if this were a group of white kids, they might not have had the same trouble. They also felt that more involvement from the black community was essential, and a parent's group was formed. Several black counselors were recruited. The center reopened after several weeks without incident.

Neighborhood Psychiatry and the Back-up Mental Hospital

Back-up inpatient and day care facilities are provided by a community mental health center. In addition, six residents from one of four treatment services work part time in the neighborhood project as an integral part of their training throughout their residency. This part of the program has been described in detail elsewhere (Sharfstein, Scherl, & Gault, 1972). Other staff from the hospital are becoming interested in community and neighborhood psychiatry and other inpatient services now have their own neighborhood projects. The impact of this program on a large teaching hospital known for its training and research in individual, dynamic psychiatry has been considerable, and the residency training curriculum has been modified.

The integration of many part-time inexperienced professionals in a neighborhood setting is not without its problems, however. There is difficulty in coordinating this part-time staff, and much time is spent in providing a teaching program. Because this group is often the most vocal of the many constituencies of the neighborhood mental health team, care is taken to assure that the priorities of service to the center, the agencies, and the neighborhood are met.

Discussion

Adolph Meyer, writing in the early twentieth century, foresaw the entire concept of "neighborhood psychiatry." He proposed a mental health program in a single geographic area that would consist of an integrated program of prevention, treatment, and aftercare involving all care-giving agencies such as welfare, schools, and clergy. He suggested that the psychiatrist work together with the teachers, police, welfare workers, and family physicians in a given neighborhood (Meyer, 1952).

Psychiatric services as part of a comprehensive, community based health care delivery system provide a unique alternative to either office based or community mental health center based care. It aims at comprehensiveness and unity with other services so that its impact is magnified many fold. This program offers the potential for effective prevention on many levels. Working closely with community agencies, especially agencies that deal with populations at risk of developing mental disorders, such as children (Head Start, Day Care) or welfare recipients, the neighborhood psychiatrist attempts to reduce both the incidence and prevalence of mental disorder (primary and secondary prevention). Further, the easy accessibility of the neighborhood health and multiservice center as well as its comprehensive focus give a natural setting for maximum rehabilitation for those discharged from the back-up hospital (tertiary prevention). At present we are conducting a study to demonstrate the effectiveness of follow-up care of chronic mental disorder in a neighborhood setting.

Mental health has been left out of current "health maintenance organization" objectives. However, the model of neighborhood psychiatry described here fits in well with the overall strategy of "keeping people well." It is an effort to "promote alternatives . . . reform the health care delivery system and provide incentives for health maintenance rather than crisis-oriented medical care," (Meyers, 1971). A psychiatric team provides a new dimension to neighborhood health care delivery and a new potential for psychiatry to meld within the mainstream of medicine.

References

Action for Boston Community Development. *A directory of Boston neighborhood health centers.* Boston: Action for Boston Community Development, Inc., 1971.

Lowenhopf, E., & Zwerling, I. Psychiatric services in a neighborhood health center. *American Journal of Psychiatry*, 1971, *127*, 92–96.

Meyer, A. The problem of the state in the care of the insane. In *The collected papers of Adolph Meyer*, Vol. IV. E. Winters (Ed.), Baltimore: Johns Hopkins Press, 1952.

Meyers, B.A. Health maintenance organizations: Objectives and issues. (USGPO No. 919-2S8) Washington, D.C.: United States Government Printing Office, 1971.

Peck, H., & Kaplan, S. A mental health program for the urban multiservice center. In M. Shore and F. Mannino (Eds.), *Mental health and the community: Problems, programs, and strategies.* New York: Behavioral Publications, 1969.

Scherl, D., & English, J. Community mental health and comprehensive health service programs for the poor. *American Journal of Psychiatry,* 1969, *12S,* 80–88.

Sharfstein, S.S., & Khajavi, F. Mental health care in the neighborhood: The Model City Family Life Center. *Mental Hygiene,* in press.

Sharfstein, S.S., Scherl, D.J., & Gault, W.B. Incorporating community psychiatry in first-year residency training. *Hospital and Community Psychiatry,* 1972, *23,* 38–40.

Zabarenko, R., Merenstein, J., & Zabarenko, L. Teaching psychological medicine in the family practice office. *Journal of the American Medical Association,* 1971, *218,* 392–397.

The "Helper" Therapy Principle

FRANK RIESSMAN

An age-old therapeutic approach is the use of people with a problem to help other people who have the same problem in more severe form (e.g., Alcoholics Anonymous). But in the use of this approach—and there is a marked current increase in this tendency—it may be that emphasis is being placed on the wrong person in centering attention on the individual receiving help. More attention might well be given the individual who needs the help less, that is, the person who is providing the assistance, because frequently it is he who improves!

While it may be uncertain that people *receiving* help are always benefitted, it seems more likely that the people *giving* help are profiting from their role. This appears to be the case in a wide variety of self-help "therapies," including Synanon (for drug addicts), Recovery Incorporated (for psychologically disturbed people), and Alcoholics Anonymous. Mowrer notes that there are over 265 groups of this kind listed in a directory, *Their Brother's Keepers*.[1] The American Conference of Therapeutic Self-Help Clubs publishes an official magazine, *Action*, describing some of the functions of these groups.

While there is still a need for firm research evidence that these programs are effective, various reports (many of them admittedly impressionistic) point to improvement in the givers of help rather than the recipients. Careful research evaluating these programs is needed, because there are numerous contaminating factors that may be contributing to their success, such as the leadership of the therapist, selection of subjects, and the newness or novelty of the program.

Although much of the evidence for the helper principle is observational and uncontrolled, there is one experimental investigation that provides at least indirect verification or support of the principle. In a study by King and Janis in which role-playing was used, it was found that subjects who had to improvise a speech supporting a specific point of view tended to change their opinions in the direction of this view more than subjects who merely read the speech for an equivalent amount of time.[2] They describe this effect in terms of "self-persuasion through persuading others."

Volkman and Cressey formulate this principle as one of their five social-psychological principles for the rehabilitation of criminals:

> The most effective mechanism for exerting group pressure on members will be found in groups so organized that criminals are induced to join with non-criminals for the purpose of changing other criminals. A group in which criminal "A" joins with some non-criminals to change criminal "B" is probably most effective in changing criminal "A", not "B". . .[3]

Perhaps, then, social work's strategy ought to be to devise ways of creating more helpers! Or, to be more exact, to find ways to transform *recipients* of help into *dispensers* of help, thus reversing their roles, and to structure the situation so that recipients of help will be placed in roles requiring the giving of assistance.

In most of the programs mentioned thus far the helpers and the helped have had essentially the same problem or symptom. The approach is carried one step further in Recovery Incorporated, in which emotionally disturbed people help each other even though their symptoms may differ.

A somewhat more indirect expression of the principle is found in the sociotherapeutic approach reported by Wittenberg some years ago.[4] Wittenberg found that participation in a neighborhood block committee formed to help other people in the neighborhood led to marked personality development and growth in a woman who had been receiving public assistance and who also had considerable personality difficulty.

Work of Nonprofessionals

Another variant of this principle is found in the work of indigenous nonprofessionals employed as homemakers, community organizers, youth workers, recreation aides, and the like. Some of these people have had serious problems in the recent past. Some are former delinquents. It has been observed, however, that in the course of their work, their own problems diminished greatly.[5] One of the important premises of the HARYOU program is that "indigenous personnel will solve their own problems while attempting to help others."[6]

The helper therapy principle has at least two important implications for the nonprofessional of lower socioeconomic background: (1) Since many of the nonprofessionals to be recruited are former delinquents, addicts, AFDC mothers, and the like, it seems quite likely that placing them in a helping role can be rehabilitative for them. (2) As the nonprofessionals benefit from their new helping roles, they may actually become more effective workers and thus provide more help to others at a new level.

Thus, what is presented here may be a positive upward spiral in contrast to the better-known downward trend. That is, the initial helping role may be furnishing minimal help to the recipient, but may be highly beneficial to the helper, who in turn becomes more efficient, better motivated, and reaches a new stage in helping skill.

Therapy for the Poor

The helper principle probably has universal therapeutic application, but may be especially useful in low-income treatment projects for these two reasons:

1. It may circumvent the special interclass role distance difficulties that arise from the middle-class-oriented therapy (and therapist) being at odds with the low-income clients' expectations and style; the alienation that many low-income clients feel toward professional treatment agents and the concomitant rapport difficulties may be greatly reduced by utilizing the low-income person himself as the helper-therapist.

For the same reason much wider employment of neighborhood-based nonprofessionals in hospitals and social agencies as aides or social service technicians is recommended. Like the helper-therapist, they are likely to have considerably less role distance from the low-income client than does the professional.

2. It may be a principle that is especially attuned to the co-operative trends in lower socioeconomic groups and cultures. In this sense it may be beneficial to both the helper (the model) and the helped.

Students as Helpers

In Flint, Michigan, a group of fourth-grade pupils with reading problems was assigned to the tutelage of sixth-grade pupils who were also experiencing reading difficulties. It is interesting to note that while the fourth graders made significant progress, the sixth graders also learned from the experience.[7] Mobilization For Youth has used homework helpers with a fair amount of success, in that the recipients of the help showed some measurable academic improvement.[8] It may be that even more significant changes are taking place in the high school youngsters who are being used as tutors. Not only is it possible that their school performance is improving, but as a result of their new role these youngsters may begin to perceive the possibility of embarking on a teaching career.

Schneider reports on a small study in which youngsters with varying levels of reading ability were asked to read an "easy" book as practice for reading to younger children. She observes:

> For the child who could read well, this was a good experience. For the child who could not read well it was an even better experience. He was reading material on a level within his competence and he could read it with pleasure. Ordinary books on his level of interest were too difficult for him to read easily and so he did not read books for pleasure. Reading for him was hard, hard work; often it left him feeling stupid and helpless. This time it was different . . . he would be a giver; he would share his gift with little children just as a parent or teacher does.[9]

In a sense these children were role-playing the helper role in this experience, as they were reading aloud to adults in anticipation of later reading to small children.

The classroom situation illustrates an interesting offshoot of the helper principle. Some children, when removed from a class in which they are below average and placed in a new group in which they are in the upper half of the class, manifest many new qualities and are in turn responded to more positively by the teacher. This can occur independently of whether or not they play a helper role. But some of the same underlying mechanisms are operative as in the direct helper situations: the pupil in the new group is responded to more, he stands out more, more is expected of him, and generally he responds in turn and demands more of himself. Even though he may not be in the helper role as such, similar forces are at work in both cases, stimulating more active responses. (Unfortunately, this principle may be counteracted if the teacher treats the entire group as a "lower" or poorer group and this image is absorbed in an un-differentiated manner by all the members of the class.)

A connected issue worthy of mention is that in the new situations in the schools, where (hopefully) integration will be taking place, youngsters coming from segregated backgrounds will need help in catching up, in terms of reading skills and the like. It is generally argued that the white middle-class children who do not need this extra assistance will suffer. Their parents want these youngsters to be in a class with advanced pupils and not to be "held back" by youngsters who are behind.

However, in terms of the helper principle, it may very well be that the more advanced youngsters can benefit in new ways from playing a teaching role. Not all fast, bright youngsters like to be in a class with similar children. We have been led to believe that if one is fast and bright he will want to be with others who are fast and bright and this will act as a stimulus to his growth. It does for some people, but for others it most certainly does not. Some people find they do better in a group in which there is a great range of ability, in which they can stand out more, and finally—and this is the point of the helper principle—in situations in which they can help other youngsters in the classroom. In other words, some children develop intellectually not by being challenged by someone ahead of them, but by helping somebody behind them, by being put into the tutor-helper role.

As any teacher can report, there is nothing like learning through teaching. By having to explain something to someone else one's attention is focused more sharply. This premise seems to have tremendous potentiality that social workers have left unused.

Leadership Development

Carried one step further, the helper principle allows for the development of leadership in community organizations and the like. It has been found, for example, in tenant groups, that an individual might be relatively inactive at meetings in his own building, but display quite different characteristics when helping to organize another building. In the new situation, forced to play the helper role, leadership begins to emerge. The character of the new group, in which the individual is in a more advanced position vis-á-vis the remainder of the group, contributes toward the emergence of new leadership behavior. This is simply another way of saying that leadership develops through the act of leading. The art of leadership training may lie in providing just the right roles to stimulate the emergence of more and more leadership. While some individuals fall more naturally into the helper or leader role (in certain groups), this role can be distributed more widely by careful planning with regard to the sociometry and composition of the group. When the group is fluid, the introduction of new members often encourages older members who were formerly in the follower role to assume a more active helping role. Following King and Janis' lead, role-playing can be utilized to have a person who formerly was the recipient of help in the group now play a helper role, thus aiding him to persuade himself through persuading others.[10] Many similar group dynamic approaches can be used in order to utilize most fully the potentialities of the helper principle. Seating arrangements can be altered, individuals can be placed in key positions—for example, chairing small committees—and temporary classroom groupings can be formed in which pupils previously submerged by more advanced classmates are now allowed to become helpers or models for less advanced youngsters. The essential idea in all of this is to structure and restructure the groups so that different group members play the helper role at different times.

Helper Therapy Mechanisms

It may be of value to speculate briefly regarding the various possible mechanisms whereby the helper benefits from his helping role. Brager notes the improved self-image that probably results from the fact that a person is doing something worthwhile in helping someone in need.[11]

The King-Janis study suggests that becoming committed to a position through advocating it ("self-persuasion through persuading others") may be an important dimension associated with the helper role. Pearl notes that many helpers (such as the homework helpers) are "given a stake or concern in a system" and this contributes to their becoming "committed to the task in a way that brings about especially meaningful development of their own abilities."[12]

There is undoubtedly a great variety of other mechanisms that will be clarified by further research. Probably also the mechanisms vary depending on the setting and task of the helper. Thus helpers, functioning in a therapeutic context, whether as professional therapeutic agents or as nonprofessional "peer therapists," may benefit from the importance and status associated with this role. They also receive support from the implicit thesis "I must be well if I help others." People who themselves have problems (e.g., alcoholics, drug addicts, unwed mothers) should derive benefit from this formulation. Moreover, their new helper roles as such may function as a major (distracting) source of involvement, thus diverting them from their problem and general self-concern. There is no question also that individual differences are important so that some people receive much greater satisfaction from "giving," "helping," "leading," "controlling," "co-operating," "persuading," and "mothering."

Helpers operating in a teaching context, again both as professionals and nonprofessionals, may profit more from the cognitive mechanisms associated with learning through teaching. They need to learn the material better in order to teach it and more generalized academic sets may emerge from the teacher role. Finally, the status and prestige dimensions attached to the teacher role may accrue unforeseen benefits to them.

The helper in the leader role may benefit from some of the same factors related to the teacher and therapist roles as well as the "self-persuasion through persuading others" mechanism and their "stake in the system." In essence, then, it would seem that the gains are related to the actual demands of the specific helper role (whether it is teacher, leader, or therapist), plus the new feelings associated with the meaning and prestige of the role and the way the helper is treated because of the new role.

Cautions and Conditions

In a sense, the helper principle seems counter to the widely accepted psychological dictum that warns against therapist projection. The well-known danger, called to our attention by all of psychoanalytic theory and practice, indicates that a therapist with a specific problem may, unless he has understanding and control of this problem, project it to the person he is treating. Of course, in many of the cases cited this situation does not arise because both the treater and the treated suffer from the same malady. But in other cases when rehabilitated nonprofessional workers are hired to work with people who either have no specific problem or do not have the problems of the helper, the possibility of projection as well as psychological contagion has to be considered.

Two controlling devices are suggested to guard against the potential risk: (1) the helper should not be involved in any intensive treatment function unless he has considerable awareness of his problem and the projection issue, and (2) professional supervision is absolutely necessary; perhaps one of the difficulties of the amateur therapeutic self-help programs is the antiprofessionalism that frequently characterizes them.

There is another potential danger residing in the helper therapy principle, especially if it is to be applied on a large scale. Much of the intrinsic value of the technique may depend on it operating in a relatively subconscious fashion. Once people know they are being placed in certain helping roles in order to be helped themselves, some of the power of the principle deriving from feelings of self-importance and the like may be reduced. That this is not entirely true is evident from role-playing situations in which the subjects know the object of the game but still are affected. Nevertheless, the question of large-scale manipulation of the principle, with the increased likelihood of mechanical and arbitrary application, does hold some danger that only careful observation and research can accurately evaluate.

Implications

The helper principle may have wide application in hospital groups (both in- and outpatient), prisons, correctional institutions, and so forth. Scheidlinger suggests that the principle may have powerful implications for social work's understanding of the therapeutic process in all group therapy. Not only are individual group members aided through helping other members in the group, but the group as a whole may be greatly strengthened in manifold ways as it continually offers assistance to individual group members.[13]

Levine suggests that in a variety of types of habit change, such as efforts to curtail cigarette smoking, the helper principle may have considerable validity. Smokers who are cast in the role of persuading other smokers to stop smoking have themselves been found to benefit from their commitment to the new antismoking prescription.[14]

The helper principle does not really require that only the helper profit or even that he benefit more than the person receiving help. Thus it is seen in the Flint, Michigan, study that the fourth graders receiving help benefited at least as much as the givers of help.[15] The helper principle only calls attention to the aid the helper receives from being in the helper role.

The helper principle has been utilized with varying degrees of awareness in many group situations. What we are calling for is more explicit use of this principle in an organized manner. Conscious planning directed toward the structuring of groups for the widest possible distribution of the helper role may be a decisive therapeutic intervention, a significant leadership training principle, and an important teaching device. It is probably no accident that it is often said that one of the best ways to learn is to teach. Perhaps also psychiatrists, social workers, and others in the helping professions are helping themselves more than is generally recognized!

Notes

1. O. Hobart Mowrer, *The New Group Therapy* (Princeton, N.J.: D. Van Nostrand Co., 1964), p. iv.

2. B.T. King and I.L. Janis, "Comparison of the Effectiveness of Improvised Versus Non-Improvised Role Playing in Producing Opinion Changes," *Human Relations*, Vol. 1 (1956), pp. 177–186.

3. Rita Volkman and Donald R. Cressey, "Differential Association and the Rehabilitation of Drug Addicts," *American Journal of Sociology*, Vol. 69, No. 2 (February 1963), p. 139.

4. Rudolph M. Wittenberg, "Personality Adjustment Through Social Action," *American Journal of Orthopsychiatry*, Vol. 18, No. 2 (March 1958), pp. 207–221.

5. *See* Gertrude Goldberg, "The Use of Untrained Neighborhood Workers in a Homemaker Program," an unpublished report of Mobilization For Youth, New York, N.Y., 1963; and *Experiment in Culture Expansion* (Sacramento, Calif.: State of California Department of Corrections, 1963).

6. *Youth in the Ghetto* (New York: Harlem Youth Opportunities Unlimited, 1964), p. 609.

7. Frank B.W. Hawkinshire, "Training Needs for Offenders Working in Community Treatment Programs," *Experiment in Culture Expansion* (Sacramento, Calif.: State of California Department of Corrections, 1963), pp. 27–36.

8. "Progress Report" (New York: Mobilization For Youth, July 1964).

9. Gussie Albert Schneider, "Reading of the Children, By the Children, For the Children." Unpublished manuscript, 1964. (Mimeographed.)

10. *Op. cit.*

11. George Brager, "The Indigenous Worker: A New Approach to the Social Work Technician," pp. 33–40, *Social Work*, April, 1965.

12. Arthur Pearl, "Youth in Lower Class Settings," p. 6. Paper presented at the fifth Symposium on Social Psychology, Norman, Okla., 1964.

13. Conversation with Saul Scheidlinger, Community Service Society, New York, N.Y., January 18, 1964.

14. Conversation with Sol Levine, Harvard University School of Public Health, Cambridge, Mass., January 12, 1964.

15. Hawkinshire, *op. cit.*

Delivery of Health Care

RUTH MURRAY and JUDITH ZENTNER

Understanding Health Care Services

In every culture, care of the sick is undertaken by specified persons with a certain status or background who carry out a set of culturally determined practices. The care is given within a system. A theory to help you understand how health care is given as well as the person for whom you are caring, his family, and his community is General Systems Theory. This theory advocates that probably nothing is determined by a single cause or explained by a single factor. Taking a holistic view of man, General Systems Theory instead suggests that interrelationships exist among all elements of a society, institution, situation, family, or organism.[51]

Characteristics of a System *A system is an entity consisting of definable interdependent parts that are in equilibrium. Two or more people interacting together constitute a social system,* —for example, nurse-patient-family or nurse-doctor. Systems have specific characteristics. Change in one part causes change in other parts. A constant *exchange of energy and information* must exist with the surrounding specified *environment* if the system is to be open, useful, and creative. If this information or energy exchange, called *feedback,* does not occur, the system becomes closed and ineffective.

A system is organized, or structured, formally or informally, through *principles, policies,* or *norms,* which in turn maintain balance and control, change, flow of information, and behavior of people. Roles exist for the members and may shift, blur, or remain stable. All systems exist for a *purpose* and to achieve certain *goals* [3,4,45,51]. A person belongs to a system as long as it meets his needs. For example, the public school is formally organized to teach students certain skills and behavior that will help them become self-supporting citizens.

Man as a Social System   Every person is an open social system, made up physically of a hierarchy of components such as cells, organs, and organ systems; emotionally of levels of needs and feelings; and socially of a relative rank in a hierarchy of prestige, such as boss, peasant, adult, or child. While internal stimuli are at work, such as those governed by the nervous and endocrine systems, outer stimuli also affect man—for example, the feelings of others, or the external environment. The boundaries or environment—such as one's skin, the limits set by others, one's status, home, and community—influence the person's needs and goal achievement. To remain healthy, the person must have feedback: the condition of his skin tells him about temperature; an emotional reaction signifies a job well done or a failure; a pain signifies malfunction or injury.

Man is an open system, receiving stimuli from the outer world and in turn influencing that world through its behavior.

Other social systems composed of man are the family, the church, political institutions, and health care agencies.

The American Health Care System   Many patients and most health workers are currently challenging traditional American health care practices and demanding change. Present practices are inadequate for the needs of people in a pluralistic society. The present health care system is closed, controlled by medical physicians, and does not distribute services equitably. There is little interchange among doctors, other health care professionals, and health institutions or agencies, on one hand, and the person, family, and community on the other. Health workers other than doctors of medicine cannot function in an independent, open manner, and thus have to work around the system to provide the kinds of services the public deserves and expects. Presently medical doctors control entry into and the pathway through the health care system.

The present health care system is the result of certain unrelated, independent, and divergently developing health care programs, services, and facilities that have managed to survive and expand. In general, the system grew without a plan. And since the system is organized and coordinated to stabilize and maintain existing facilities, services, and related enterprises, it does not support change.

People seeking preventive services or medical care and the practitioners of medical care may be seen as two components of the social system, often with divergent and conflicting interests. The people component consists of those who may be called patients or clients. *Patients are ill and are primarily concerned with their symptoms and how they feel*, rather than with organic diseases per se. They seek a return to normal functioning rather than physiological health as defined by the doctor. *Clients are not necessarily ill and seek health care workers for services which either maintain or regain health.* Being a client implies active participation in the treatment plan. The patient as a component of the health care system is too often seen as a passive observer rather than as an active participant in his treatment or inward life. As an increasingly enlightened consumer of care, the client will change this outlook unless the system retaliates by becoming even more mechanized and repressive. The medical component, the doctor, is often interested in illness or disease rather than the illness experience or the full social consequences of physical symptoms. The nurse is the liaison person, attempting to understand each aspect when working with the patient.

What about the workers in the health care system? They usually are separated by status levels, each eating and socializing with his own occupational levels. The equivalent of a caste system exists. Communication generally moves downward, deference upward. The worker may or may not feel a part of a specific unit. He is likely to stay employed if he feels a similarity between his attitudes and the philosophy of the agency and if there are pleasant working relationships and conditions. If the worker feels himself to be an outsider, if his competency or skill is higher than the norm, or if the situation is changing too rapidly, he won't remain employed. Job turnover is also influenced less directly by marital status, age, presence of children, and job history.

A registered nurse, even though unemployed, is often looked to or called upon to intervene with friends or relatives. With no specified status, however, it is difficult to break into the caste system and communicate with the health care hierarchy. Consider the following experience of such a nurse.

A Case Study   Mrs. S., a 78-year-old woman without relatives, lives alone on $170 a month Social Security benefits, and recently became a concern to a nurse friend. Mrs. S., while maintaining limited mental ability, became depressed and increasingly forgetful. She often forgot day and time, lost her way several times in the city, forgot that she had turned on the gas stove, ate rotten food, took her medicine too often or not at all, and was twice the victim of vandals.

The nurse friend wished to help Mrs. S. find a living arrangement where she would receive adequate personal and medical care. She called various nursing homes whose representatives said Mrs. S. would need a medical doctor's statement for admittance. The nurse explained the circumstances to Mrs. S.'s doctor, who told her that the only way he could admit Mrs. S. to a nursing home was through Medicare benefits via hospitalization. He said he would give her a complete physical examination and have a psychiatrist and social worker evaluate her condition.

Mrs. S. entered a hospital reputed to be one of the top ten in the United States. After 26 days of hospitalization, a $2500 hospital bill, a $250 physician's bill, a $50 X-ray bill, and $120 in consultation fees, Mrs. S. was *discharged to her home.*

What had happened? Not much. The physician said Mrs. S. initially resisted the nursing home idea, so he didn't pursue the matter. The nurse spoke repeatedly to the doctor of her friend's dire need. Finally he agreed to get a social worker to examine the case. But before the social worker appeared (if she was ever notified) the hospital's Patient Review Committee (composed of physicians who review patients' records and who are empowered to decide which patients will go home or have Medicare benefits terminated) informed Mrs. S.'s physician that her benefits were being canceled.

Mrs. S.'s physician then said he would—and did—send a nurse and social worker from a local religious health organization, who were to assess her home situation and help her make the proper move.

The nurse friend and a neighbor continued to see Mrs. S., who was now more depressed and confused than ever. The nurse friend tried to help her organize her medicines, check her supplies, find her lost items, and pay her bills. The neighbor fed her and did her laundry. Several weeks elapsed with no further plans made. Finally, the nurse friend called the religious health organization to determine the status of the case. The organization nurse had not been given complete background information by the physician, and was only planning to see Mrs. S. on a bimonthly or monthly basis to give an injection.

The nurse friend then called Mrs. S.'s minister and the director of a neighborhood ministry for the aged. Both were aware of some of her problems but had no comprehension of the overall situation.

The health care system had not worked! Unless all persons concerned, even peripherally, can work together, Mrs. S. will eventually destroy herself or be destroyed.

Types of Health Care Subsystems

Today's health challenge is no longer based on survival, but on the quality of being. What is the method of organization that will best enhance the pursuit of and opportunity for optimal health and increased longevity? Understanding the types of present health care agencies and health workers can help determine the changes that are needed.

In America, health care is big business, exceeded only by agriculture and construction in terms of expenditures for services rendered and increase in proportion of the gross national product.[36] As a business, it is organized in a variety of ways, depending on the goals of the particular organization and whether or not planning is through governmental or voluntary efforts. *Governmental or official agencies are tax-supported and are operated by federal, state, or local governments. Private, voluntary agencies function under a board of directors and are supported by donations, fees, membership dues, endowments, payments from insurance plans, and contracts.*[16]

Voluntary Agencies Voluntary agencies historically emerged first and have flourished in the United States because of a democratic society coupled with aggressive, interested persons. At the turn of the nineteenth century only the American Red Cross and a few tuberculosis societies existed, other than some private hospitals. However, increased knowledge from scientific and medical discoveries coupled with economic growth from industrialization stimulated the growth of voluntary agencies. Because government-sponsored programs were sparse, people volunteered their newly found financial resources and time[16].

Early organizations (unrelated to hospitals) were formed because of concern about specific health problems, including tuberculosis, veneral disease, mental health, child care, and maternal mortality. Interest in health problems continued, and during the 1920s and 1930s voluntary organizations were initiated to control cancer, diabetes, and heart disease; to prevent blindness; and to provide for maternal and child health and crippled children.

Present Contributions of voluntary agencies are considerable. Some agencies are concerned with prevention, eradication, or control of certain diseases. They conduct educational programs to improve the utilization of health services. Such organizations include the National Tuberculosis Association, American Cancer Society, American Diabetes Association, and the American Heart Association. These organizations are also concerned about the care people receive within various health facilities. Some contribute to nursing care indirectly; for example, volunteers from the American Cancer Society make dressings and donate them for appropriate use.

Promotion of local health programs is another function of voluntary agencies, particularly foundations. The Ford, W.K. Kellogg, and Rockefeller Foundations, for example, subsidize health programs, especially in rural areas. They also support research and public and professional education.[16]

Professional associations are voluntary. Their activities vary but generally include provision for exchange of information and ideas among health professionals through local, state, or national meetings and conventions; promotion of improved standards for the organization's constituencies; and encouragement of research. Some of these include the American Nurses' Association, American Public Health Association, and American Medical Association.

You should become familiar with your professional organization, the American Nurses' Association. It is primarily concerned with fostering high standards of nursing practice and works continually to improve the quality of nursing care. It also promotes educational advancement of nurses, advises on legal aspects of practice, and has a strong lobby in the nation's capital.

Other voluntary organizations contribute primarily to improved health services. These are the private and nonprofit organizations: hospitals, visiting-nurses' associations, health insurance organizations such as Blue Cross and Blue Shield, privately sponsored clinics, and those health professionals who are in private practice.

Voluntary groups are also involved in setting standards and evaluating existing programs. For example, the Joint Commission on Accreditation of Hospitals makes recommendations concerning care given by hospitals and nursing homes. It is authorized to close those that do not meet established standards. These voluntary groups may need to make frequent revisions in their standards or changes in their programs to keep up with the fast changes in health care in the United States. Ideally there should be no duplication of services between two or more voluntary agencies or between a voluntary and an official agency. But overlap obviously exists in the present system, a fact which has given rise to fragmentation and agency-hopping for patients and clients.

Organization of many voluntary agencies operates on the national, state, and local levels. Usually, these agencies (with the exception of the professional associations) are governed by boards of directors comprised of people from all walks of life—business, industry, politics, the arts, and the professions—who are civic-minded and work without pay in this capacity.

At the national level, general policies and programs are developed and reviewed, positive public image and the agency's cause is stressed, and money is raised. State functions include long-range planning, fund raising, and giving stimulation and guidance to local affiliates about program planning and administration. The local level works with immediate needs, develops and implements community programs, and determines priorities.

Voluntary agencies have financial problems. They have been criticized for conducting numerous campaign drives and questioned about their spending of publicly raised funds. Furthermore, people hesitate to donate to voluntary agencies because they are already paying taxes for government health and welfare programs. Constructive collaboration at the national, state, and local levels among all voluntary agencies is needed. Their primary goal should be to enhance the appropriateness, quality, and efficiency of programs and services within the country.

Official Agencies Official agencies began after numerous epidemics in the 1800s when people realized that government should be responsible for safeguarding the health of the public. The population of the cities was rapidly increasing, adding sanitation and health to the ever-growing list of problems.

Hookworm infestation was a mounting problem in North Carolina. The voluntary Rockefeller Foundation recognized that its efforts in this area to control a single disease without other health services was in vain. So, in 1911, a health department was established in Guilford County, North Carolina. Shortly thereafter, another department began operations, and the growth of official agencies has continued ever since.[8]

Present Agency Contributions are determined by federal and state laws and are operated by federal, state, or local governments.

At the federal level, concern is for national and international health and the health of special population groups. Provisions are made for international meetings and exchange of research findings and of students with other countries. The federal government is responsible for protection against hazards affecting large populations, such as flood relief programs, which cannot be provided by the states. Federal support is given to state and local governments to maintain health services and civil defense programs. Another responsibility is the collection and reporting of national vital and health statistics. Special populations that the federal government is responsible for include armed forces personnel and veterans, the aged, the economically deprived, and the physically and mentally handicapped, among others.[16]

Official state agencies are usually concerned with policy, planning, legislation, consultation to local agencies, indirect services, financial support, organizational relationships, research, and evaluation.

Local agencies provide direct services to the public, including medical care, preventive services, nursing services, and environmental control. Medical and preventive services include treatment of venereal disease and tuberculosis, maternity and well child care, interest in school health problems and services for crippled children. Nurses usually make home visits and provide nursing care in clinics and schools. Environmental health services include sanitation control and inspection, housing and urban planning services, air pollution control, and food and drug control programs.[16]

Social service, laboratory services, and health education are supportive services in state and local health departments.

Organization of official agencies begins with the United States Public Health Service, one of eight agencies within the Department of Health, Education, and Welfare. The Office of the Surgeon General is its main governing body.

Both state and local health departments have a health officer, a board of health, and various numbers of divisions or bureaus to conduct programs and services, with advisory committees and consultants as necessary.

The official agencies are also witnessing the public demand for increased and better health care. Citizens are tired of lengthy bureaucratic proceedings and political power plays for funding. Citizens must increasingly speak up for needed services and vote on the issues. More combining of official and voluntary agencies, or at least more communication among them, might lessen duplication and fragmentation of services.

Additionally, the United States is a part of the World Health Organization (WHO), created by the United Nations in 1948 with the conviction that international health, peace, and security are simultaneous goals.[54] More than 120 countries belong to WHO and contribute to its budget. As an international health system, WHO engages in many activities: health education, research, and publication; statistical services; standardization of drugs, vaccines, and other biologicals; development of international quarantine measures; and care of people during endemics and epidemics.[16,56]

The Hospital as a Subsystem Whether official or voluntary, each hospital (or health care facility) is a subsystem which defines the various functions and skills necessary to maintain the institution and establishes its own kind of social organization through a system of roles and statuses. The hospital is a bureaucratic organization with a hierarchy from the board of trustees on down to the maintenance or housekeeping employee. Increasingly more administrative persons are joining the hierarchy to manage and maintain the growing number of parts within a facility. The general hospital, with the many levels of nonprofessional and professional personnel each having its own values and ideologies, may have ineffective channels of communication and patient care.

The hospital seems to have conflicting goals within itself. To stay financially solvent, it must strive for maximum efficiency. But to provide expert patient care, education, and research, it must have time and money. It needs expert professional judgement from those highly trained in medical skill, but also needs obedience from lesser-trained personnel who are also, indirectly or directly, responsible for life and death. Citizens require that the hospital meet their health needs, yet they cannot afford the spiraling cost of these services.

Obviously, for effective organization and provision for the best patient care, communication and some agreement among *all* working members is essential. Establishing goals, priorities, and methods of achievement is an ongoing process with need of constant revaluation. Hospitals could benefit from industry's plan of considering and rewarding workers' suggestions, whether from doctor or housekeeper.

Not only does the hospital have its own culture exhibited through policies, attitudes, and relationships among workers. Patients, too, if allowed to get acquainted with one another, may develop a subculture of their own which may or may not have much in common with the overall hospital culture. This subculture is seen particularly in psychiatric, rehabilitation, chronic care, and geriatric divisions.

Four Divisions in the Health Care System   In addition to voluntary and official health agencies within the health care system, four divisions of medical health care have been delineated in the United States: two subdivisions of private health care; the charity system (although many Americans may not like to admit the existence of such care); and health professionals (other than medical doctors) who provide special services.[46]

Within the Private Division, One Subdivision Is the Pediatrician-Internist Services, utilized by the upper and upper middle classes. Primary care for the family with children is assumed mainly by two physicians, the internist and the pediatrician. Inpatient care is obtained in private or semiprivate rooms in voluntary hospitals.

The Other Subdivision in the Private Division Is Care by the General Practitioner, used by the lower middle class and skilled laborers. Primary care is received from a single physician, and specialist services may be provided by the general practitioner himself or by qualified specialists. Inpatient care is usually obtained in semiprivate rooms in voluntary hospitals. Such care may be the only choice in rural areas and small towns, and the difficulty in obtaining such health care at all is compounded by the reduced numbers of general practitioners in the United States. Physicians have increasingly felt either that becoming a specialist is more prestigious or that trends in the health care system demand specialization. Presently, however, some renewed emphasis is being given to the training of family physicians.

The Charity Division serves the unskilled or unemployed, their dependents, and the elderly poor. Primary care in this division is provided in hospital out-patient departments by interns and residents or by internists and pediatricians, who also usually provide the specialist services. Inpatient care is usually obtained in the wards of city, county, or voluntary hospitals.

The Fourth Division Includes Several Services for obtaining health care. These are health professionals, like the medical doctors (M.D.), who follow a prescribed course of education and supervised experience, and must adhere to continuously updated standards prescribed by their professional organizations. Persons using these services may also use the other health services just prescribed and may be a member of any social class.

A dentist (D.D.S.) cares for teeth and surrounding tissue, prevents and eliminates decay, replaces missing teeth with artificial ones, and prevents malocclusion. A dentist may specialize in *orthodontics, the correction and prevention of irregularities of the teeth and poor occlusion,* or in *oral surgery, surgical procedures involving structures of the mouth or the teeth.*

A chiropractor (D.C.) employs a method of mechanical therapeutics based on the nervous system as the main determiner of health. He gives specific adjustments to restore normal nerve function and does not use drugs or surgery. He refers the patient to an internist or surgeon when indicated.

An optometrist (O.D.) examines eyes, measures errors of vision, and prescribes glasses to correct defects. He does not treat eye disease or perform eye surgery but refers patients needing such services to an ophthalmologist, a medical doctor who specializes in treating structures, functions, and diseases of the eye. An optician prepares and dispenses eyeglasses.

A podiatrist (D.P.M.) cares for the feet, preventing and treating foot disorders, such as corns and ingrown nails. He prescribes medicine and performs surgery for such disorders. He refers those cases indicated to an orthopedist, a surgeon who specializes in treating deformities, diseases, and injuries of bones, joints, and muscles.

An osteopath (D.O.) employs various methods of diagnosis and treatment, including skeletal manipulation, medicine, and surgery. His practice is similar to that of a medical doctor. Originally his philosophy specifically emphasized the interrelationship of the musculo-skeletal system to all other body systems.

The four divisions, even with some provision for charity patients, points to the obvious but unfortunate fact that more money buys better care. The charity subdivision is underfinanced and does not begin to provide adequate health services. That charity patients receive better health care than others is a myth. Morbidity and mortality statistics show a strong correlation between level of income, on the one hand, and health and longevity on the other.[16]

Quackery within the Health Care System   Self-styled health workers and "quacks" are also offering services. The self-styled health worker may emphasize certain herbs for healing or a special "hand-me-down" formula. He does not relay on professionally set standards. A quack, one who makes pretentious claims about his ability to treat others with little or no foundation, may be found representing any health profession. He raises false hopes and causes loss of money and time—often money and time that could be better used for proven treatment.

Perhaps just as much to blame as the quacks are those people who incessantly want a shortcut—a sure cure. They almost beg someone in authority to give them the answer.

You can help people avoid quacks by helping them set realistic health goals and by helping them recognize the following typical behaviors of the false practitioner:

1. Claims use of a special or secret formula, diet, or machine.
2. Promises an easy or quick cure.
3. Offers only testimonials as proof of his healing power.
4. Claims one product or service is good for a variety of illnesses.
5. States he is ridiculed or persecuted by health professionals.
6. Promotes his product through faithhealers, door-to-door health advisors, or sensational ads.
7. Refuses to accept proven methods of research.
8. Claims his treatment is better than any prescribed by a physician.

Reexamine your knowledge about and attitude toward the givers of health care in the four divisions. Remember that people think in terms of having symptoms and eradicating them. If the latter takes place to their satisfaction, they will place their trust in the health care worker who was responsible for their improvement, regardless of his credentials. After assessment, you can support those who find improvement and refer those who are dissatisfed into another direction, if that dissatisfaction is based on realistic expectations.

Application of Systems Theory for Nursing Appreciating the complexity and interrelationships of the people, social institutions, and organizations giving health care will enable you to understand your role in giving health care. As a nurse, you will have a twofold purpose: to adjust at times to the system as it exists, and at other times to work with people to produce necessary changes. Increasingly the public expects you to do the latter to meet their needs.

Systems theory takes the major responsibility for change from you as an individual person and recognizes the importance of the total situation in creating and maintaining problems that hinder change and are beyond the power of the individual to correct. Each aspect of life is so interrelated and people are so interdependent that one person, for example, the nurse, is unlikely to make much change in a situation unless she works with others and considers many factors.

Fundamental changes come from within the individual or system. They cannot be imposed from without, although an outsider can be an influence. The push for maintaining the status quo and the push for change exist simultaneously. If you strive for better conditions in a health agency, you may find that they can only be achieved by pressures for policy and administrative change on a high level. Through your educational preparation and experiences as a nurse you will be in a position to promote changes in the health care system.

As a member of various health, education, welfare, and regulatory agencies in the community, you may function in the health care system in the following ways:

1. As an advocate for the person or family needing health services.
2. As a concerned, active community member.
3. As an expert in health affairs.
4. As a consumer of health services.

If you understand and are comfortable in the health care system, you can work more effectively for furtherance of health. Community surveys, assessments, and demographic and epidemiologic studies are tools that will help you use the nursing process in the social system of the community and specific health agency.

Intervention on the systems level includes talking with the nursing supervisor, clinical specialist, or dietitian about cold food at mealtimes, or getting a wheelchair for a patient so he can get out of the confining four walls of his room. You may be instrumental in creating a patient council that has at least some effect on improving the environment of a unit. Outside the institution you can participate in starting organizations for older or disabled persons that help to meet their individual needs as well as have an impact on the political life of their community.

While you will not always strive for big institutional upheavals, also avoid accepting the present situation as an unalterable fact. Often when you have worked at the same place for some time, you adapt to distressing situations so that you do not even notice them, even though they cause considerable discomfort or suffering for the patient. Periodically survey your work environment as if you were a stranger to it. You might keep a diary of your reactions to the work setting when you are first employed and then refer to it periodically to determine changes you wish to initiate. In that way you can better work as your patients' advocate.

You may not always be able to make constructive changes in the system. Some changes take longer than others, but you need to keep trying. Often an ideal must be proposed several times before it gains acceptance by others.

Manpower in the Health Care System

There appears to be a shortage of medical physicians, nurses, and other professional and nonprofessional health personnel in the United States today. However, measuring the full extent of the problem is difficult since manpower is unevenly distributed and inefficiently utilized, owing to lack of full cooperation among all health disciplines.

Medical Physicians   The number of physicians has increased in the last decade. Yet the increased number of physicians does not adequately meet the needs of the population because physicians tend to specialize, to concentrate on research, to remain in urban centers to practice, or to become full-time hospital staff with less time for office visits.

Physicians have increased their use of auxiliary personnel, the newest being physicians' assistants. The idea for such a person arose in response to the continuing problem of providing adequate medical services in nonurban areas of the United States. Some former military medical corpsmen have been trained as physicians' assistants. Their allegiance is to the physician they serve, and they may work in a clinic or hospital or assist the physician in his office practice or research. Some health professionals fear that physicians' assistants will unsurp their jobs. Further concern is that they will not have adequate training and ability. Both professional and lay people will need further orientation about the functions of physicians' assistants, and certain safeguards need to be established to ensure their proper supervision and competency.

Nurses and Other Professionals   *Nurses.* The number of nurses has also increased over the past ten years, but this increase has not kept pace with the increasing demand for health services either. There is an uneven distribution of nurses among the population, as well as limited opportunities for the professional nurse to fully use individual abilities, education, and skills. There are adequate numbers of technical and licensed practical nurses, while an inadequate number of nurses are prepared with baccalaureate, master's, and doctoral degrees.

Every nurse should examine his or her level of preparation for and role within the system for delivering health care to delineate more clearly the characteristics and qualifications needed for each level of prepared nurse. Transition from one level of preparation to another is increasingly available to nursing practitioners to allow preparation for clinical specialization, research, and family care positions. With the movement toward improved health care for all, nursing needs dynamic leaders to help change the delivery system and to create and shape the character of nursing within the system. Nurses have moved away from complete dominance by the medical doctors. Yet they have not established themselves as a permanent force in the fourth system—as professionals from whom persons seek primary diagnosis and care. This trend is gaining impetus, however.

Other Professionals who perform important services in the health care system are the psychologist, chaplain, social worker, occupational therapist, physiotherapist, medical and X-ray technologist, dietitian, medical record librarian, and pharmacist, among others. Each member of the health team makes an important contribution to the well-being of the patient or family unit.

Modes of Financing Medical Care

An increase in the numbers of subscriptions to various hospital and health plans has contributed to the increasing demand for medical care and the use of health facilities. However, the rise in the cost of living, including the cost of medical care and use of hospital facilities, has exceeded the ability of many people to pay, especially those in the middle-income range.[47]

Some of the cost escalation has been expected. Inadequately paid hospital employees deserve better pay. Increased technology has provided more complex and costly equipment, along with the need for trained personnel to operate it. Finally, there are more aged persons in the population, and the prevalence of illness increases with age.[46]

Often the person, no matter how ill, cannot be admitted to the hospital unless he has health insurance or can make a down payment of several hundred dollars. Workmen's compensation and private or government health insurance help defray medical costs.

Health insurance companies influence the health care system. In the past, most companies paid only for hospital care, thus encouraging people to enter hospitals for procedures or care which could have been accomplished on an outpatient basis. Thus the hospital subsystem expanded considerably. Today, more insurance policies cover outpatient costs, but other pressures are applied. Insurance companies have special agents who investigate health benefit claims. Benefits are sometimes withheld until a special review board determines that treatment was necessary.

Privately Sponsored Health Insurance *Health insurance is a method for financing personal health service,* but some plans are not adequate in the scope of services covered. One must read the fine print carefully when examining an insurance policy. The American public purchases health insurance from approximately 1800 organizations.

Blue Cross and Blue Shield are perhaps most frequently thought of when referring to insurance plans. Blue Cross pays for most of the cost of hospitalization; Blue Shield pays for physician's care.

Major Medical Plans are a recent addition to health insurance provisions. They may be supplemental to basic health insurance or may be the only coverage a person has. Such plans pay for hospitalization, physician's services, drugs, nursing care, and other related items. Most of these plans have reciprocal arrangements in that the insurance company will pay either the people and institutions giving care or the insured.

Indemnity Plans are offered at reduced rates which are determined by the cost of actual loss experience in past years to the group at risk. Premium rates are thus related to actual use of insurance. This plan might discourage over-utilization of insurance but also might keep the person from seeking early diagnosis and preventive health care to avoid using his insurance and increasing his rates. Predetermined benefits are paid to the insured in cash and he must pay for the remaining costs, another reason to delay care.[44]

Independent Health Plans are another type of private insurance. These plans combine prepayment for medical care with *group practice, where a number of specialists work together in association, sometimes providing care to patients and families at a fixed annual rate.* Insured persons utilize the medical staff who are in the group practice and the specific facilities provided by the medical group and insurance company. Costs are spread among members over a period of time, and the total cost of medical care—prevention, cure, and rehabilitation—are included in the benefits. Disadvantages are that such plans are not available to people in all areas, reciprocal arrangements have not been completely worked out, and the insured must use the physicians and facilities affiliated with the plan.[44] Advantages are that independent companies watch closely the type of medical care rendered to their insured; the trend is thus toward decreased hospitalization, since preventive health measures are stressed.[16] The medical profession has not been too receptive to such plans, but recently some of the leading medical schools—Harvard, Yale, and Johns Hopkins—have started group practice prepayment plans.[46]

Government-Sponsored Health Insurance   Medicare and Medicaid are federally sponsored insurance plans, the latter financed by federal and state matching funds. In 1965, Congress passed Title XVIII—Medicare— as an amendment to the Social Security Act for persons 65 and older. Medicaid (Title XIX) is a medical care program for all those declared eligible for public assistance by individual states, including the blind, those receiving Old-Age Assistance benefits, families with dependent children (ADC), and the permanently and totally disabled. If your patient is on public assistance, check whether or not he has a Medicaid card. If he does not, consult a social worker. Medicare and Medicaid are further discussed by Murray and Zentner in relation to the person in later maturity.[38]

Workmen's Compensation   State workmen's compensation plans make legal provision for treating and rehabilitating workers injured on the job. The injury must be caused by the nature of the job itself, not by obvious negligence on the part of the employer or the worker. This requirement makes both employer and employee assume some responsibility for safety. For example, a mine cave-in would result in compensation for injuries to the victims. Laws related to workmen's compensation are continually being examined to determine that the worker and employer are being fair to one another and that the worker is receiving deserved benefits. As an occupational health nurse, you would be responsible for reporting job-related injuries and assuring that workers received proper compensation. In addition, you would work with management and labor to promote safe working conditions.

Projected Health Plans The needs revealed by studies of Medicare and Medicaid payments along with other factors indicate that the delivery of health care must be improved. Medicaid has not begun to meet the needs of the medically indigent, and Medicare costs keep mounting for the federal government. Yet almost 46 percent of the population are either under 18 or over 65 years old and therefore need assistance with medical care costs because they are frequent users of health services.[12]

Alternative health care plans that have been suggested include a national health service and health maintenance organizations (prepaid group practice).

Health Maintenance Organizations (HMOs), operative in some areas in the Unites States, are discussed in the section on current trends influencing the delivery of health care.

National Health Insurance is the payment method in several European countries and Great Britian. Various national plans have been proposed by politicians and organizations in the United States since the 1920s, but none has been adopted. Each suggested plan has certain distinct features, but some similarities do exist. Taxation, based on income and with a maximum ceiling, would pay for part of the insurance, while the consumer would directly pay the balance of medical care costs. Care for mental illness, dental care, long-term hospital care, and preventive services are generally excluded by these plans.

National health insurance still does not solve the problems of fragmentation of care, of proportionately greater payment by people with lower incomes, and of the need for preventive and comprehensive health services.

Factors Influencing the Delivery of Health Care

Social Changes If, as estimated, 245 million people will be living in the United States by 1980, health care opportunity must increase. The birth rate has declined in the past decade, while the death rate has remained constant; yet the excess of births over deaths is still substantial.[55] Because people are living longer and thus are more likely to develop chronic disease problems, more and more people will need the services of better prepared doctors, nurses, allied health personnel, and service agencies. Technological advances in medical care have caused care to be increasingly fragmented and given more in hospital centers rather than at home or in the local community. However, these same advances, along with medical research, have permitted efficient and effective care and recoveries not possible in the past, in turn contributing to longer life spans and a growing population.

Consumer Involvement Because of a growing belief that health and the services needed to maintain it are everyone's basic right, Americans now have higher health care expectations, which are being incorporated into their value system.

> The public has come to expect the right: to wellness; to receive adequate and qualified health care; to participate in decisions regarding their care; to be helped to understand their health and illness as well as the treatments undertaken in their behalf; to be cared for with concern whey they are ill; to be accepted in a state of dependence when they are unable to care for themselves; to be kept as comfortable as modern science permits; to decline and die in reasonable dignity; to feel that someone cares and that they are not alone in their illness or dying.[29]

Generally, the public is more health-conscious and knowledgeable about the nature of health, health care, and illness because such information is more readily available in schools, in popular literature, and on television. Along with increasing knowledge and sophistication is a tendency for the person to become more critical about his care (or lack of it) and to want to actively participate in planning his care. The practice of being "spoken for" is no longer accepted. To the shame of health professionals, legislative efforts were required to initiate consumer input into the health care system—through programs like neighborhood health centers, Model Cities, and comprehensive health planning that have consumer representatives on policy-making and planning boards.[26]

One nursing organization, the National League for Nursing, includes consumers in its membership and on its advisory councils and works to improve health care delivery as well as the education of nurses.

Professional Response   Professional groups, including nurses, have responded and must continue to respond to the public's health care needs, rights, and expectations. Nursing has become aware of a broader spectrum of patient problems; trends in nursing education favor increased competence in perceiving care problems and better care planning. Nursing has determined that one of its roles is the coordination of health services because so many personnel, professional and nonprofessional, are utilized in providing patient care. Moreover, systematically identifying, analyzing, and planning the patient's nursing care needs along with the patient and family require the expertise of a professionally competent nurse.

Legislative Interest   Over the past decade Congress has exhibited a growing interest in health affairs. Legislators have been concerned about closing the gap between the knowledge people are acquiring and the care they are receiving. The Eighty-ninth Congress (1965–1967) was especially notable in this regard in that it passed 24 health or health-related bills.[18]

Congress has attempted to encourage regional and comprehensive approaches to health care, with continued emphasis on planning and consumer involvement. Because some persons feel that the federal government should take a more active part in health care, pressure is continuously exerted for some type of national health insurance plan.

Nurses, individually and through membership in the nursing organizations, have lobbied and must continue to lobby for legislation that will assist the public in getting maximum health care.

Comprehensive Health Planning   As the concern about health problems and the delivery of health care increased during the 1960's, comprehensive health planning, enacted through federal legislation, had its origin. Federal grants, distributed to various designated state agencies, were the source of funding for the project. Certain stipulations were attached to the federal grants: (1) that a single state agency take responsibility for the grant, and (2) that a state planning council be established that included representatives from local and state governmental units and other agencies concerned about health and the consumer.[12]

Nurses should be included as members of national, state, and local planning boards and advisory councils and active as citizens in promoting health standards.

If you discover a patient or family problem, regardless of your position or care setting, you can take positive action. Perhaps no organizational source of help exists, or a present source may be unable to meet the needs of the persons in question. What would you do? Your combination of creative ability and practical working knowledge can develop a program to meet the specific need. The following are proper steps to take should you find yourself in a position to make changes in organizational sources of help, and as a nurse in the primary care role you may indeed be in such a position.

Be very specific in identifying the problem. An epidemiological study may be needed. Note the number of people who are affected. If only a few isolated people are affected, redirect your plans to meet their needs within the existing care system. Once the problem is identified and found significant, write out the proposed solutions. Involve your supervisor throughout; perhaps that person can help you find unknown resources. Think about attaching the proposed program to one that already exists. If attachment is possible, costs can be cut drastically. Whatever your course—attachment or creation of a new program—inform your agency about your plans and ask for its support.

You are now ready to begin convincing others in the community that a new program is needed. Begin with the power structure of the community—the people known for "getting things done." Select people from various occupations and professions; get a cross section of the community. Visit each personally and ask for his advice, suggestions, and support. Get permission to mention the names of those who react positively when discussing the proposed program with others.

Plan the first group meeting. Invite those people with whom you spoke plus a variety of others from the community. Continue to look for support from valuable individuals or organizations. Don't forget the consumer! At the meeting, present your proposal verbally as well as distribute a written outline. A temporary chairman and interim steering committee need to be elected. The purpose of the committee is to review the proposed program in its entirety, determine cost details and ways to funding, investigate whether it is necessary to develop a new agency or if an existing one can be utilized, and finally, prepare a written report of the findings.

At the second group meeting the findings of the steering com mittee are presented. A permanent board of directors should be elected. All involved people not on the board should be on the advisory council. The board is responsible for making policies, adopting bylaws, and writing a formal, detailed program proposal, including job descriptions of needed staff and facilities. The board must be prepared to state how the program will be financed if and when federal or state funds are discontinued. It should also solicit letters of commitment from organizations and agencies that will give free services. Program proposals may need to be written several times to meet particular funding requirements. Many meetings may be necessary to achieve your goal.[56]

Convincing people that a new program is needed may take determination and fortitude. While keeping your goal in mind, you will constantly integrate new ideas that may change your direction somewhat. Worthwhile programs are created through this difficult process, but time and effort are needed.

Fragmentation of Health Care Services Despite the growing interest and efforts of interested people, the health care system is still fragmented. People receive bits of treatment from various people and places. A given person may utilize a family doctor and several specialists, attend different hospitals for different purposes, maintain a number of insurers (or have no insurance), and rely on many health or health-related agencies. Not only is this pattern expensive, it also encourages duplication of services. No one assumes sole responsibility for the health of the person. Many times different health workers involved in giving care have no idea what the others are doing. When no single worker has a total picture of a person, the latter cannot receive comprehensive individualized care.

Current and Future Trends in Delivery of Health Care

Primary Health Care   Primary health care is a relatively new concept designed to provide comprehensive health services to a family. These include physical and psychological preventive, maintenance, and restorative services; general dental services; and sources for help related to social, economic, legal, and environmental problems. Care is individualized in order to prevent crises as best as possible. The family has a long-term relationship with a small group of professionals who work closely with the family members and involve them in their own care. Ideally, primary health care settings are conveniently located, near or within the community being served, compatible with the life styles of the people served, and have some provision for 24-hour availability for emergencies.[6]

The overall purposes of primary health care are to make care more accessible and equitable and to improve the quality of care delivered. The plan updates the family doctor concept with modern-day support services, in the form of specialists and technology, available on a continuing basis to a specific group of people.

Health Maintenance Organizations   A health maintenance organization (HMO) is a system for delivering primary health care with emphasis on adequate distribution and quality. If such a concept continues to be properly developed, it could drastically reduce the fragmentation, gaps, and duplication of the present system.[35]

An HMO is designed to provide comprehensive health care for the whole person in its own ambulatory and inpatient care facilities. Financing is achieved by a fixed contract fee paid by subscribers each month, regardless of the number of times they use the services (or if they never use them). The plan encourages effective, personal treatment, and subscribers are likely to use the facility for preventive measures and to seek early treatment. The addition of hospital beds and the employment of too many specialists are discouraged, since health personnel and facilities are acquired according to the number enrolled in the HMO program, rather than according to the long-range projection of health care needs in the community. The goal is to give the best and most health care for the money available.

Designers of HMOs leave open the question of specific organizational form. They hope to encourage all kinds of organizational forms—public and private, profit and nonprofit. The consumer will be able to choose the type and level of health care he wishes. Competition will exist; those unhappy will leave if there is another available choice. Thus the HMO will be encouraged to establish and maintain a good reputation.

Problems have been cited with HMOs, and solutions have not been formulated. Cost competition could lead to a reduction in necessary care and hence a loss in quality of care. Physicians could determine their own fees, which would influence the corporate fee that the consumer pays monthly. Coexistence of two forms of practice within one organization could occur, one in the fee-for-service sector and another for those under the corporate fee.[9]

HMOs are a threat to the individual practitioner. Under an HMO, the primary person responsible for an individual or family may not always be a physician, but may be a nurse or other health professional, depending on the needs of the person.

Nurses continue to constitute the largest group of health professionals and thus play a major role in all aspects of health care. In fact, nurses are currently functioning as the primary health care person in HMOs. They are defining problems, assessing needs, implementing and coordinating health care, educating patients and coworkers, and evaluating results. In general, nurses assume major responsibility for providing or securing all required primary health services. They are not substitute physicians or physicians' assistants. The nurses' functions are variously independent of, interdependent with, and dependent on those of other health team members.[6]

Independent functions are performed legally, with the nurse being accountable for professional actions. Examples include health care coordination and implementation for a person with a stable chronic illness; complete history and physical assessment for well babies and adults; family planning counseling, health education, and patient counseling; and laboratory- and other diagnostic-test selection in illness situations. Interdependent functions, performed simultaneously with other members of the health team, include deciding whether to place patients in nursing homes or to maintain home care; planning for patient care with physicians; and dietary planning with nutritionists. Dependent functions are performed under the immediate supervision and guidance of physicians or other professionals. These functions include medical diagnosis; history and physical examination on an acutely ill or unstable chronically ill patient; psychotherapy and family counseling for patients with emotional or behavioral disorders; and performance of minor surgical procedures, such as uncomplicated suturing.[6]

If nursing is to assume a major role in primary health care, more nurses must be graduated from baccalaureate programs that provide education and opportunity for clinical practice of the skills necessary to become a primary-care practitioner. More emphasis must be placed on such practitioners in planning for future health care delivery. Nurses can and should carry more responsibility than they have in the past, assuming they receive the necessary preparation. The nurse-practitioner is no longer a title for the future.[21]

Directions for the Future   Exciting concepts and proposals are being discussed and enacted. Speculating about the outcome is difficult, but many hope for the development of an open system.

An open health care system would offer the client a choice of services from several health disciplines, not only physician services. He might not need to see a doctor at all if a nurse, social worker, physiotherapist, or nutritionist could effectively handle his problem. The person would get prompt care, possibly at less cost, without fragmentation and redundancy of services. The various health professionals would be fully contributing their skills and would be responsible to the client and accountable for their services, whether provided independently or in collaboration with other disciplines. The system would remain responsive to change. There would be an exchange of ideas among all health disciplines as well as consumer input. Consumer demand will hasten realization of this open system, although third-party insurance payments will have to be revised to accomodate the change.

Innovative health care models are few to date, but some suggestions for changes in the present health care system are:

1. Separating the well from the sick, using a multihealth screening plan to meet specific needs of clients.
2. Using interdisciplinary teams, including generalists, specialists, and the judicious use of paraprofessional workers.

3. Considering the cultural, social, psychological, and physiological aspects of the person.
4. Avoiding care that is hospital-based and physician-controlled, and instead delivering care in the community and focusing on the individual, wellness-behavior, and on ways to maintain or restore a healthy state.
5. Using health screening, health education, counseling, and referral more deliberately.
6. Encouraging health personnel to assume personal responsibility for their decisions and actions.
7. Encouraging social and natural scientists, humanists, health professionals, and consumers to become active participants in planning and evaluating care, distributing authority, and control.
8. Increasing emphasis on group approaches and on demographic planning in order to maximize individual potential and health-care services.
9. Avoiding hasty planning that creates situations demanding easy, quick, final answers and leads to abandoning problems too soon when immediate results are not forthcoming. Epidemiological data and scientific problem solving will help prevent the tendency to rely on such fast, unrealistic answers.[5, 15, 27]

Some nurses are presently helping to create an open system of care by working as independent practitioners, performing many of the functions described as nursing roles in relation to HMOs but establishing their own offices or facilities for nursing practice. [For further information, see references 7, 24, 25, 30, 37, 41, 53.]

Changes must occur in order to build an open health care system, and health professionals, among others, must change to meet needs of the client. Educational preparation will have to include greater interdisciplinary study, increased understanding of and responsibility for primary care, and increased skill in caring for people of all ages and backgrounds. The rest of this text and its companion text[38] deal with the educational foundation needed to practice in such an open system.

124   *THE HUMAN SERVICES*

Notes

1. Armiger, Sister Bernadette, "Nursing Shortage—Or Unemployment?" *Nursing Outlook*, 21: No. 5 (1973), 312–16.
2. Bates, Barbara, "Nursing in a Health Maintenance Organization: Report on the Harvard Community Health Plan," *American Journal of Public Health*, 62: No. 7 (1972), 991–94.
3. Bell, Earl, *Social Foundations of Human Behavior*, New York: Harper & Row, 1961.
4. Berrien, F. Kenneth, *General and Social Systems*. New Brunswick, N.J.: Rutgers University Press, 1968.
5. Brill, Naomi, *Working With People: The Helping Process*. Philadelphia: J.B. Lippincott Company, 1973.
6. Brunetto, Eleanor, and Peter Birk, "The Primary Care Nurse: The Generalist in a Structured Health Care Team," *American Journal of Public Health*, 62: No. 6 (1972), 785–94.
7. Burgess, Ann, and J.Burns, "Why Patients Seek Care," *American Journal of Nursing*, 73: No. 2 (1973), 314–16.
8. Coulter, Pearl, *The Nurse in the Public Health Program*. New York: G.P. Putnams' Sons, 1954.
9. Donabedian, Avedis, "An Examination of Some Directions in Health Care Policy," *American Journal of Public Health*, 63: No. 3 (1973), 243–46.
10. "Extending The Scope of Nursing Practice," *Nursing Outlook*, 20: No. 1 (1972), 46–47
11. Fagin, Claire, and Beatrice Goodwin, "Baccalaureate Preparation for Primary Care," *Nursing Outlook*, 20: No. 4 (1972), 240–44.
12. Freeman, Ruth B., *Community Health Nursing Practice*. Philadelphia: W.B. Saunders Company, 1970, pp. 1–30, 74–108.
13. French, Ruth, *The Dynamics of Health Care*. St. Louis: McGraw-Hill Book Company, 1968.
14. Froh, R., and R. Galanter, "The Poor, Health, and the Law," *American Journal of Public Health*, 62: No. 3 (1972), 427–30.
15. Garfield, S.R., "The Delivery of Medical Care," *Scientific American*, 222: No. 4 (1970), 15–23.
16. Goerke, Lenor, and Ernest Stebbins, *Mustard's Introduction to Public Health* (5th ed.). New York: The Macmillan Company, 1968, pp. 43–80, 131–67, 436–60.
17. Greenidge, Jocelyn, Ann Zimmern, and Mary Kohnke, "Independent Group Nursing Practice: Community Nurse Practitioners—A Partnership," *Nursing Outlook*, 21: No. 4 (1973), 228–31.
18. Hanlon, John, *Principles of Public Health Administration*. St. Louis: C.V. Mosby Company, 1969.
19. Hazzard, Mary, "A Systems Approach to Nursing," *Nursing Clinics of North America*, 6: No. 3 (1971), 385–455.
20. Hulka, Barbara, and John Cassel, "The AAFP-UNC Study of the Organization, Utilization, and Assessment of Primary Medical Care," *American Journal of Public Health*, 63: No. 6 (1973), 494–501.
21. Ingles, Thelma, "Where Do Nurses Fit in the Delivery of Health Care?" *Archives of Internal Medicine*, 127: No. 1 (1971), 73–75.
22. Keller, Nancy, "The Nurse's Role: Is It Expanding or Shrinking?" *Nursing Outlook*, 21: No. 4 (1973), 236–40.
23. King, Imogene, *Towards a Theory For Nursing*. New York: John Wiley & Sons, Inc., 1971.

24. Kinlein, M. Lucille, "Independent Nurse Practitioner," *Nursing Outlook*, 20: No. 1 (1972), 22–24.

25. Kosik, S., "Patient Advocacy, or Fighting the System," *American Journal of Nursing*, 72: No. 4 (1972), 694–98.

26. Kramer, Marlene, "The Consumer's Influence on Health Care," *Nursing Outlook*, 20: No. 9 (1972), 574–78.

27. Leininger, Madeline, "An Open Health Care System Model," *Nursing Outlook*, 21: No. 3 (1973), 171–75.

28. Litman, Theodor, "Public Perceptions of the Physician's Assistant: A Survey of the Attitudes and Opinions of Rural Iowa and Minnesota Residents," *American Journal of Public Health*, 62: No. 3 (1972), 343–46.

29. Little, Delores, and Doris Carnevali, *Nursing Care Planning*. Philadelphia: J.B. Lippincott Company, 1969.

30. Logsdon, Audrey, "Why Primary Nursing?" *Nursing Clinics of North America*, 8: No. 2 (1973), 283–86.

31. Lynaugh, Joan, and B. Bates, "The Two Languages of Nursing and Medicine," *American Journal of Nursing*, 73: No. 1 (1973), 66–69.

32. Manor, Gloria, "The Berkeley Free Clinic," *Nursing Outlook*, 21: No. 1 (1973), 40–43.

33. Manthey, Marie, "Primary Care is Alive and Well in the Hospital," *American Journal of Nursing*, 73: No. 1 (1973), 83–87.

34. Marram, Gwen, "Patients' Evaluation of Their Care: Importance to the Nurse," *Nursing Outlook*, 21: No. 5 (1973), 322–24.

35. McClure, Walter, "National Health Insurance and HMOS," *Nursing Outlook*, 21: No. 1 (1973), 44–48.

36. McNerney, W.J., "Personal Health Comprehensive Care Services: A Management Challenge to the Health Professions," *American Journal of Public Health*, 57: No. 10 (1967), 1717–27.

37. Murray, B. Louise, "A Case for Independent Group Nursing Practice," *Nursing Outlook*, 20: No. 1 (1972), 60–63.

38. Murray, Ruth, and Judith Zentner, *Nursing Assessment and Health Promotion through the Life Span*, Englewood Cliffs, N.J.: Prentice-Hall, Inc., 1975.

39. Nehring, Virginia, and Barbara Geach, "Patients' Evaluation of Their Care: Why They Don't Complain," *Nursing Outlook*, 21: No. 5 (1973), 317–21.

40. Paige, David, Edwardo Leonardo, Eve Roberts, and George Graham, "Enhancing the Effectiveness of Allied Health Workers," *American Journal of Public Health*, 62: No. 3 (1972), 370–73.

41. Rafferty, Rita, and Jean Carner, "Independent Group Nursing Practice: Nursing Consultants, Inc.—A Corporation," *Nursing Outlook*, 21: No. 4 (1973), 232–35.

42. Record, Jane, and Harold Cohen, "The Introduction of Midwifery in a Prepaid Group Practice," *American Journal of Public Health*, 62: No. 3 (1972), 354–60.

43. *Report of the National Advisory Commission on Health Manpower*, Vol. 1. Washington, D.C.: U.S. Government Printing Office, November 1967.

44. Report of the National Commission on Community Health Services, *Health is a Community Affair*. Cambridge, Mass.: Harvard University Press, 1967.

45. Sutterly, Doris, and Gloria Donnelly, *Perspectives in Human Development*. Philadelphia: J.B. Lippincott Company, 1973, pp. 3–24.

46. Terris, Milton, "Crisis and Change in America's Health System," *American Journal of Public Health*, 63: No. 4 (1973), 312–17.

47. "The Plight of the U.S. Patient," *Time*, February 21, 1965, pp. 53–58.

48. Tinkham, Catherine, and Eleanor Voorhies, *Community Health, Nursing, Evolution and Process*. New York: Appleton-Century-Crofts, Educational Division,

Meredith Corporation, 1972.

49. United States Department of Commerce, Bureau of the Census, *Pocket Data Book, USA, 1967*. Washington, D.C.: U.S. Government Printing Office, 1967.

50. United States Department of Health, Education, and Welfare, *Health, Education, and Welfare Trends, 1965*. Washington, D.C.: U.S. Government Printing Offices, 1967.

51. von Bertalanffy, Ludwig, *General System Theory*. New York: George Braziller, 1968.

52. Wagner, Dorris L., "Issues in the Provision of Health Care for All," *American Journal of Public Health*, 63: No. 6 (1973), 481–85.

53. Walker, A., "PRIMEX: The Family Nurse Practitioner," *Nursing Outlook*, 20: No. 1 (1972), 28–31.

54. Walsh, Margaret, "On Nursing's Role in Health Care Delivery," *Nursing Outlook*, 20: No. 9 (1972), 592–93.

55. Wilner, Daniel, Rosabelle Walkley, and Lenor Goerke, *Introduction to Public Health* (6th ed.). New York: The Macmillan Company, 1973.

56. World Health Organization, *The First Year of the WHO*. Geneva: The World Health Organization, 1958.

57. Yankauer, Alfred, Sally Tripp, Priscilla Andrews, and John P. Connelly, "The Outcomes and Service Impact of a Pediatric Nurse Practitioner Training Program: Nurse Practitioner Training Outcomes," *American Journal of Public Health*, 62: No. 3 (1972), 347–53.

58. Zentner, Reid, personal directives on project establishment, May 1973.

The Invisible Land

MICHAEL HARRINGTON

There is a familiar America. It is celebrated in speeches and advertised on television and in the magazines. It has the highest mass standard of living the world has ever known.

In the 1950s this America worried about itself, yet even its anxieties were products of abundance. The title of a brilliant book was widely misinterpreted, and the familiar America began to call itself 'the affluent society.' There was introspection about Madison Avenue and tail fins; there was discussion of the emotional suffering taking place in the suburbs. In all this, there was an implicit assumption that the basic grinding economic problems had been solved in the United States. In this theory the nation's problems were no longer a matter of basic human needs, of food, shelter, and clothing. Now they were seen as qualitative, a question of learning to live decently amid luxury.

While this discussion was carried on, there existed another America. In it dwelt somewhere between 40,000,000 and 50,000,000 citizens of this land. They were poor. They still are.

To be sure, the other America is not improverished in the same sense as those poor nations where millions cling to hunger as a defense against starvation. This country has escaped such extremes. That does not change the fact that tens of millions of Americans are, at this very moment, maimed in body and spirit, existing at levels beneath those necessary for human decency. If these people are not starving, they are hungry, and sometimes fat with hunger, for that is

127

what cheap foods do. They are without adequate housing and education and medical care.

The Government has documented what this means to the bodies of the poor. But even more basic, this poverty twists and deforms the spirit. The American poor are pessimistic and defeated, and they are victimized by mental suffering to a degree unknown in Suburbia.

This paper is a description of the world in which these people live; it is about the other America. Here are the unskilled workers, the migrant farm workers, the aged, the minorities, and all the others who live in the economic underworld of American life. In all this, there will be statistics, and that offers the opportunity for disagreement among honest and sincere men. I would ask the reader to respond critically to every assertion, but not to allow statistical quibbling to obscure the huge, enormous, and intolerable fact of poverty in America. For, when all is said and done, that fact is unmistakable, whatever its exact dimensions, and the truly human reaction can only be outrage. As W.H. Auden wrote:

> Hunger allows no choice
> To the citizen or the police;
> We must love one another or die.

1

The millions who are poor in the United States tend to become increasingly invisible. Here is a great mass of people, yet it takes an effort of the intellect and will even to see them.

I discovered this personally in a curious way. After I wrote my first article on poverty in America, I had all the statistics down on paper. I had proved to my satisfaction that there were around 50,000,000 poor in this country. Yet, I realized I did not believe my own figures. The poor existed in the Government reports; they were percentages and numbers in long, close columns, but they were not part of my experience. I could prove that the other America existed, but I had never been there.

My response was not accidental. It was typical of what is happening to an entire society, and it reflects profound social changes in this nation. The other America, the America of poverty, is hidden today in a way that it never was before. Its millions are socially invisible to the rest of us. No wonder that so many misinterpreted Galbraith's title and assumed that 'the affluent society' meant that everyone had a decent standard of life. The misinterpretation was true as far as the actual day-to-day lives of two-thirds of the nation were concerned. Thus, one must begin a description of the other America by understanding why we do not see it.

There are perennial reasons that make the other America an invisible land.

Poverty is often off the beaten track. It always has been. The ordinary tourist never left the main highway, and today he rides interstate turnpikes. He does not go into the valleys of Pennsylvania where the towns look like movie sets of Wales in the thirties. He does not see the company houses in rows, the rutted roads (the poor always have bad roads whether they live in the city, in towns, or on farms), and everything is black and dirty. And even if he were to pass through such a place by accident, the tourist would not meet the unemployed men in the bar or the women coming home from a runaway sweatshop.

Then, too, beauty and myths are perennial masks of poverty. The traveler comes to the Appalachians in the lovely season. He sees the hills, the streams, the foliage—but not the poor. Or perhaps he looks at a run-down mountain house and, remembering Rousseau rather than seeing with his eyes, decides that 'those people' are truly fortunate to be living the way they are and that they are lucky to be exempt from the strains and tensions of the middle class. The only problem is that 'those people,' the quaint inhabitants of those hills, are undereducated, underprivileged, lack medical care, and are in the process of being forced from the land into a life in the cities, where they are misfits.

These are normal and obvious causes of the invisibility of the poor. They operated a generation ago; they will be functioning a generation hence. It is more important to understand that the very development of American society is creating a new kind of blindness about poverty. The poor are increasingly slipping out of the very experience and consciousness of the nation.

If the middle class never did like ugliness and poverty, it was at least aware of them. 'Across the tracks' was not a very long way to go. There were forays into the slums at Christmas time; there were charitable organizations that brought contact with the poor. Occasionally, almost everyone passed through the Negro ghetto or the blocks of tenements, if only to get downtown to work or to entertainment.

Now the American city has been transformed. The poor still inhabit the miserable housing in the central area, but they are increasingly isolated from contact with, or sight of, anybody else. Middle-class women coming in from Suburbia on a rare trip may catch the merest glimpse of the other America on the way to an evening at the theater, but their children are segregated in suburban schools. The business or professional man may drive along the fringes of slums in a car or bus, but it is not an important experience to him. The failures, the unskilled, the disabled, the aged, and the minorities are right there, across the tracks, where they have always been. But hardly anyone else is.

In short, the very development of the American city has removed poverty from the living, emotional experience of millions upon millions of middle-class Americans. Living out in the suburbs, it is easy to assume that ours is, indeed, an affluent society.

This new segregation of poverty is compounded by a well-meaning ignorance. A good many concerned and sympathetic Americans are aware that there is much discussion of urban renewal. Suddenly, driving through the city, they notice that a familiar slum has been torn down and that there are towering, modern buildings where once there had been tenements or hovels. There is a warm feeling of satisfaction, of pride in the way things are working out: the poor, it is obvious, are being taken care of.

The irony in this is that the truth is nearly the exact opposite to the impression. The total impact of the various housing programs in postwar America has been to squeeze more and more people into existing slums. More often than not, the modern apartment in a towering building rents at $40 a room or more. For, during the past decade and a half, there has been more subsidization of middle- and upper-income housing than there has been for the poor.

Clothes make the poor invisible too: America has the best-dressed poverty the world has ever known. For a variety of reasons, the benefits of mass production have been spread much more evenly in this area than in many others. It is much easier in the United States to be decently dressed than it is to be decently housed, fed, or doctored. Even people with terribly depressed incomes can look prosperous.

This is an extremely important factor in defining our emotional and existential ignorance of poverty. In Detroit the existence of social classes became much more difficult to discern the day the companies put lockers in the plants. From that moment on, one did not see men in work clothes on the way to the factory, but citizens in slacks and white shirts. This process has been magnified with the poor throughout the country. There are tens of thousands of Americans in the big cities who are wearing shoes, perhaps even a stylishly cut suit or dress, and yet are hungry. It is not a matter of planning, though it almost seems as if the affluent society had given out costumes to the poor so that they would not offend the rest of society with the sight of rags.

Then, many of the poor are the wrong age to be seen. A good number of them (over 8,000,000) are sixty-five years of age or better; an even larger number are under eighteen. The aged members of the other America are often sick, and they cannot move. Another group of them live out their lives in loneliness and frustration: they sit in rented rooms, or else they stay close to a house in a neighborhood that has completely changed from the old days. Indeed, one of the worst aspects of poverty among the aged is that these people are out of sight and out of mind, and alone.

The young are somewhat more visible, yet they too stay close to their neighborhoods. Sometimes they advertise their poverty through a lurid tabloid story about a gang killing. But generally they do not disturb the quiet streets of the middle class.

And finally, the poor are politically invisible. It is one of the cruelest ironies of social life in advanced countries that the dispossessed at the bottom of society are unable to speak for themselves. The people of the other America do not, by far and large, belong to unions, to fraternal organizations, or to political parties. They are without lobbies of their own; they put forward no legislative program. As a group, they are atomized. They have no face; they have no voice.

Thus, there is not even a cynical political motive for caring about the poor, as in the old days. Because the slums are no longer centers of powerful political organizations, the politicians need not really care about their inhabitants. The slums are no longer visible to the middle class, so much of the idealistic urge to fight for those who need help is gone. Only the social agencies have a really direct involvement with the other America, and they are without any great political power.

To the extent that the poor have a spokesman in American life, that role is played by the labor movement. The unions have their own particular idealism, an ideology of concern. More than that, they realize that the existence of a reservoir of cheap, unorganized labor is a menace to wages and working conditions throughout the entire economy. Thus, many union legislative proposals—to extend the coverage of minimum wage and social security, to organize migrant farm laborers—articulate the needs of the poor.

That the poor are invisible is one of the most important things about them. They are not simply neglected and forgotten as in the old rhetoric of reform; what is much worse, they are not seen.

One might take a remark from George Eliot's *Felix Holt* as a basic statement of what this paper is about:

> . . . there is no private life which has not been determined by a wider public life, from the time when the primeval milkmaid had to wander with the wanderings of her clan, because the cow she milked was one of a herd which had made the pasture bare. Even in the conservatory existence where the fair Camellia is sighed for by the noble young Pineapple, neither of them needing to care about the frost or rain outside, there is a nether apparatus of hotwater pipes liable to cool down on a strike of the gardeners or a scarcity of coal.
>
> And the lives we are about to look back upon do not belong to those conservatory species; they are rooted in the common earth, having to endure all the ordinary chances of past and present weather.

Forty to 50,000,000 people are becoming increasingly invisible. That is a shocking fact. But there is a second basic irony of poverty that is equally important: if one is to make the mistake of being born poor, he should choose a time when the majority of the people are miserable too.

J.K. Galbraith develops this idea in *The Affluent Society*, and in doing so defines the 'newness' of the kind of poverty in contemporary America. The old poverty, Galbraith notes, was general. It was the condition of life of an entire society, or at least of that huge majority who were without special skills or the luck of birth. When the entire economy advanced, a good many of these people gained higher standards of living. Unlike the poor today, the majority poor of a generation ago were an immediate (if cynical) concern of political leaders. The old slums of the immigrants had the votes; they provided the basis for labor organizations; their very

numbers could be a powerful force in political conflict. At the same
time the new technology required higher skills, more education, and
stimulated an upward movement for millions.

Perhaps the most dramatic case of the power of the majority poor
took place in the 1930s. The Congress of Industrial Organizations
literally organized millions in a matter of years. A labor movement
that had been declining and confined to a thin stratum of the highly
skilled suddenly embraced masses of men and women in basic industry. At the same time this acted as a pressure upon the Government, and the New Deal codified some of the social gains in laws like
the Wagner Act. The result was not a basic transformation of the
American system, but it did transform the lives of an entire section
of the population.

In the thirties one of the reasons for these advances was that
misery was general. There was no need then to write books about
unemployment and poverty. That was the decisive social experience
of the entire society, and the apple sellers even invaded Wall Street.
There was political sympathy from middle-class reformers; there
were an elan and spirit that grew out of a deep crisis.

Some of those who advanced in the thirties did so because they
had unique and individual personal talents. But for the great mass,
it was a question of being at the right point in the economy at the
right time in history, and utilizing that position for common
struggle. Some of those who failed did so because they did not have
the will to take advantage of new opportunities. But for the most
part the poor who were left behind had been at the wrong place in
the economy at the wrong moment in history.

These were the people in the unorganizable jobs, in the South, in
the minority groups, in the fly-by-night factories that were low on
capital and high on labor. When some of them did break into the
economic mainstream—when, for instance, the CIO opened up the
way for some Negroes to find good industrial jobs—they proved to
be as resourceful as anyone else. As a group, the other Americans
who stayed behind were not originally composed primarily of individual failures. Rather, they were victims of an impersonal process
that selected some for progress and discriminated against others.

Out of the thirties came the welfare state. Its creation had been
stimulated by mass impoverishment and misery, yet it helped the
poor least of all. Laws like unemployment compensation, the
Wagner Act, the various farm programs, all these were designed for

the middle third in the cities, for the organized workers, and for the upper third in the country, for the big market farmers. If a man works in an extremely low-paying job, he may not even be covered by social security or other welfare programs. If he receives unemployment compensation, the payment is scaled down according to his low earnings.

One of the major laws that was designed to cover everyone, rich and poor, was social security. But even here the other Americans suffered discrimination. Over the years social security payments have not even provided a subsistence level of life. The middle third have been able to supplement the Federal pension through private plans negotiated by unions, through joining medical insurance schemes like Blue Cross, and so on. The poor have not been able to do so. They lead a bitter life, and then have to pay for that fact in old age.

Indeed, the paradox that the welfare state benefits those least who need help most is but a single instance of a persistent irony in the other America. Even when the money finally trickles down, even when a school is built in a poor neighborhood, for instance, the poor are still deprived. Their entire environment, their life, their values, do not prepare them to take advantage of the new opportunity. The parents are anxious for the children to go to work; the pupils are pent up, waiting for the moment when their education has complied with the law.

Today's poor, in short, missed the political and social gains of the thirties. They are, as Galbraith rightly points out, the first minority poor in history, the first poor not to be seen, the first poor whom the politicians could leave alone.

The first step toward the new poverty was taken when millions of people proved immune to progress. When that happened, the failure was not individual and personal, but a social product. But once the historic accident takes place, it begins to become a personal fate.

The new poor of the other America saw the rest of society move ahead. They went on living in depressed areas, and often they tended to become depressed human beings. In some of the West Virginia towns, for instance, an entire community will become shabby and defeated. The young and the adventurous go to the city, leaving behind those who cannot move and those who lack the will to do so. The entire area becomes permeated with failure, and that is one more reason the big corporations shy away.

Indeed, one of the most important things about the new poverty is that it cannot be defined in simple, statistical terms. Throughout this book a crucial term is used: aspiration. If a group has internal vitality, a will—if it has aspiration—it may live in dilapidated housing, it may eat an inadequate diet, and it may suffer poverty, but it is not impoverished. So it was in those ethnic slums of the immigrants that played such a dramatic role in the unfolding of the American dream. The people found themselves in slums, but they were not slum dwellers.

But the new poverty is constructed so as to destroy aspiration; it is a system designed to be impervious to hope. The other America does not contain the adventurous seeking a new life and land. It is populated by the failures, by those driven from the land and bewildered by the city, by old people suddenly confronted with the torments of loneliness and poverty, and by minorities facing a wall of prejudice.

In the past, when poverty was general in the unskilled and semiskilled work force, the poor were all mixed together. The bright and the dull, those who were going to escape into the great society and those who were to stay behind, all of them lived on the same street. When the middle third rose, this community was destroyed. And the entire invisible land of the other Americans became a ghetto, a modern poor farm for the rejects of society and of the economy.

It is a blow to reform and the political hopes of the poor that the middle class no longer understands that poverty exists. But, perhaps more important, the poor are losing their links with the great world. If statistics and sociology can measure a feeling as delicate as loneliness, the other America is becoming increasingly populated by those who do not belong to anybody or anything. They are no longer participants in an ethnic culture from the old country; they are less and less religious; they do not belong to unions or clubs. They are not seen, and because of that they themselves cannot see. Their horizon has become more and more restricted; they see one another, and that means they see little reason to hope.

Galbraith was one of the first writers to begin to describe the newness of contemporary poverty, and that is to his credit. Yet because even he underestimates the problem, it is important to put his definition into perspective.

For Galbraith, there are two main components of the new poverty: case poverty and insular poverty. Case poverty is the plight of those who suffer from some physical or mental disability that is personal and individual excludes them from the general advance. Insular poverty exists in areas like the Appalachians or the West Virginia coal fields, where an entire section of the country becomes economically obsolete.

Physical and mental disabilities are, to be sure, an important part of poverty in America. The poor are sick in body and in spirit. But this is not an isolated fact about them, an individual "case," a stroke of bad luck. Disease, alcoholism, low IQs, these express a whole way of life. They are, in the main, the effects of an environment, not the biographies of unlucky individuals. Because of this, the new poverty is something that cannot be dealt with by first aid. If there is to be a lasting assault on the shame of the other America, it must seek to root out of this society an entire environment, and not just the relief of individuals.

But perhaps the idea of "insular" poverty is even more dangerous. To speak of "islands" of the poor (or, in the more popular term, of "pockets of poverty") is to imply that one is confronted by a serious, but relatively minor, problem. This is hardly a description of a misery that extends to 40,000,000 or 50,000,000 people in the United States. They have remained impoverished in spite of increasing productivity and the creation of a welfare state. That fact alone should suggest the dimensions of a serious and basic situation.

And yet, even given these disagreements with Galbraith, his achievement is considerable. He was one of the first to understand that there are enough poor people in the United States to constitute a subculture of misery, but not enough of them to challenge the conscience and the imagination of the nation.

Finally, one might summarize the newness of contemporary poverty by saying: these are the people who are immune to progress. But then the facts are even more cruel. The other Americans are the victims of the very inventions and machines that have provided a higher living standard for the rest of the society. They are upside-down in the economy, and for them greater productivity often means worse jobs; agricultural advance becomes hunger.

In the optimistic theory, technology is an undisguised blessing. A general increase in productivity, the argument goes, generates a higher standard of living for the whole people. And indeed, this has been true for the middle and upper thirds of American society, the people who made such striking gains in the last two decades. It tends to overstate the automatic character of the process, to omit the role of human struggle. (The CIO was organized by men in conflict, not by economic trends.) Yet it states a certain truth—for those who are lucky enough to participate in it.

But the poor, if they were given to theory, might argue the exact opposite. They might say: Progress is misery.

As the society became more technological, more skilled, those who learn to work the machines, who get the expanding education, move up. Those who miss out at the very start find themselves at a new disadvantage. A generation ago in American life, the majority of the working people did not have high-school educations. But at that time industry was organized on a lower level of skill and competence. And there was a sort of continuum in the shop: the youth who left school at sixteen could begin as a laborer, and gradually pick up skill as he went along.

Today the situation is quite different. The good jobs require much more academic preparation, much more skill from the very outset. Those who lack a high-school education tend to be condemned to the economic underworld—to low-paying service industries, to backward factories, to sweeping and janitorial duties. If the fathers and mothers of the contemporary poor were penalized a generation ago for their lack of schooling, their children will suffer all the more. The very rise in productivity that created more money and better working conditions for the rest of the society can be a menace to the poor.

But then this technological revolution might have an even more disastrous consequence: it could increase the ranks of the poor as well as intensify the disabilities of poverty. At this point it is too early to make any final judgment, yet there are obvious danger signals. There are millions of Americans who live just the other side of poverty. When a recession comes, they are pushed onto the relief rolls. (Welfare payments in New York respond almost immediately to any economic decline.) If automation continues to inflict more and more penalties on the unskilled and the semiskilled, it could have the impact of permanently increasing the population of the other America.

Even more explosive is the possibility that people who participated in the gains of the thirties and the forties will be pulled back down into poverty. Today the mass-production industries where unionization made such a difference are contracting. Jobs are being destroyed. In the process, workers who had achieved a certain level of wages, who had won working conditions in the shop, are suddenly confronted with impoverishment. This is particularly true for anyone over forty years of age and for members of minority groups. Once their job is abolished, their chances of ever getting similar work are very slim.

It is too early to say whether or not this phenomenon is temporary, or whether it represents a massive retrogression that will swell the numbers of the poor. To a large extent, the answer to this question will be determined by the political response of the United States in the sixties. If serious and massive action is not undertaken, it may be necessary for statisticians to add some old-fashioned, pre-welfare-state poverty to the misery of the other America.

Poverty in the 1960s is invisible and it is new, and both these factors make it more tenacious. It is more isolated and politically powerless than ever before. It is laced with ironies, not the least of which is that many of the poor view progress upside-down, as a menace and a threat to their lives. And if the nation does not measure up to the challenge of automation, poverty in the 1960s might be on the increase.

2

There are mighty historical and economic forces that keep the poor down; and there are human beings who help out in this grim business, many of them unwittingly. There are sociological and political reasons why poverty is not seen; and there are misconceptions and prejudices that literally blind the eyes. The latter must be understood if anyone is to make the necessary act of intellect and will so that the poor can be noticed.

Here is the most familiar version of social blindness: 'The poor are that way because they are afraid of work. And anyway they all have big cars. If they were like me (or my father or my grandfather), they could pay their own way. But they prefer to live on the dole and cheat the taxpayers.'

This theory, usually thought of as a virtuous and moral statement, is one of the means of making it impossible for the poor ever to pay their way. There are, one must assume, citizens of the other America who choose impoverishment out of fear of work (though, writing it down, I really do not believe it). But the real explanation of why the poor are where they are is that they made the mistake of being born to the wrong parents, in the wrong section of the country, in the wrong industry, or in the wrong racial or ethnic group. Once that mistake has been made, they could have been paragons of will and morality, but most of them would never even have had a chance to get out of the other America.

There are two important ways of saying this: The poor are caught in a vicious circle; or, The poor live in a culture of poverty.

In a sense, one might define the contemporary poor in the United States as those who, for reasons beyond their control, cannot help themselves. All the most decisive factors making for opportunity and advance are against them. They are born going downward, and most of them stay down. They are victims whose lives are endlessly blown round and round the other America.

Here is one of the most familiar forms of the vicious cycle of poverty. The poor get sick more than anyone else in the society. That is because they live in slums, jammed together under unhygienic conditions; they have inadequate diets, and cannot get decent medical care. When they become sick, they are sick longer than any other group in the society. Because they are sick more often and longer than anyone else, they lose wages and work, and find it difficult to hold a steady job. And because of this, they cannot pay for good housing, for a nutritious diet, for doctors. At any given point in the circle, particularly when there is a major illness, their prospect is to move to an even lower level and to begin the cycle, round and round, toward even more suffering.

This is only one example of the vicious circle. Each group in the other America has its own particular version of the experience, but the pattern, whatever its variations, is basic to the other America.

The individual cannot usually break out of this vicious circle. Neither can the group, for it lacks the social energy and political strength to turn its misery into a cause. Only the larger society, with its help and resources, can really make it possible for these people to help themselves. Yet those who could make the difference too often refuse to act because of their ignorant, smug moralisms. They view the effects of poverty—above all, the warping of the will and spirit that is a consequence of being poor—as choices. Understanding the vicious circle is an important step in breaking down this prejudice.

There is an even richer way of describing this same, general idea: Poverty in the United States is a culture, an institution, a way of life. There is a famous anecdote about Ernest Hemingway and F. Scott Fitzgerald. Fitzgerald is reported to have remarked to Hemingway, "The rich are different." And Hemingway replied, 'Yes, they have money.' Fitzgerald had much the better of the exchange. He understood that being rich was not a simple fact, like a large bank account, but a way of looking at reality, a series of attitudes, a special type of life. If this is true of the rich, it is ten times truer of the poor. Everything about them, from the condition of their teeth to the way in which they love, is suffused and permeated by the fact of their poverty. And this is sometimes a hard idea for a Hemingway-like middle-class America to comprehend.

The family structure of the poor, for instance, is different from that of the rest of the society. There are more homes without a father, there are less marriage, more early pregnancy and, if Kinsey's statistical findings can be used, markedly different attitudes toward sex. As a result of this, to take but one consequence of the fact, hundreds of thousands, and perhaps millions, of children in the other America never know stability and 'normal' affection.

Or perhaps the policeman is an even better example. For the middle class, the police protect property, give directions, and help old ladies. For the urban poor, the police are those who arrest you. In almost any slum there is a vast conspiracy against the forces of law and order. If someone approaches asking for a person, no one there will have heard of him, even if he lives next door. The outsider is 'cop,' bill collector, investigator (and, in the Negro ghetto, most dramatically, he is 'the Man').

While writing this paper, I was arrested for participation in a civil-rights demonstration. A brief experience of a night in a cell made an abstraction personal and immediate: the city jail is one of the basic institutions of the other America. Almost everyone whom I encountered in the 'tank' was poor: skid-row whites, Negroes, Puerto Ricans. Their poverty was an incitement to arrest in the first place. (A policeman will be much more careful with a well-dressed, obviously educated man who might have political connections than he will with someone who is poor.) They did not have money for bail or for lawyers. And, perhaps most important, they waited their arraignment with stolidity, in a mood of passive acceptance. They expected the worst, and they probably got it.

There is, in short, a language of the poor, a psychology of the poor, a world view of the poor. To be impoverished is to be an internal alien, to grow up in a culture that is radically different from the one that dominates the society. The poor can be described statistically; they can be analyzed as a group. But they need a novelist as well as a sociologist if we are to see them. They need an American Dickens to record the smell and texture and quality of their lives. The cycles and trends, the massive forces, must be seen as affecting persons who talk and think differently.

I am not the novelist, yet I have attempted to describe the faces behind the statistics, to tell a little of the "thickness" of personal life in the other America. I work on a assumption that cannot be proved by Government figures or even documented by impressions of the other America. It is an ethical proposition, and it can be simply stated: In a nation with a technology that could provide every citizen with a decent life, it is an outrage and a scandal that there should be such social misery. Only if one begins with this assumption is it possible to pierce through the invisibility of 40,000,000 to 50,000,000 human beings and to see the other America. We must perceive passionately, if this blindness is to be lifted from us. A fact can be rationalized and explained away; an indignity cannot.

What shall we tell the American poor, once we have seen them? Shall we say to them that they are better off than the Indian poor, the Italian poor, the Russian poor? That is one answer, but it is heartless. I should put it another way. I want to tell every well-fed and optimistic American that it is intolerable that so many millions should be maimed in body and in spirit when it is not necessary that they should be. My standard of comparison is not how much worse things used to be. It is how much better they could be if only we were stirred.

The Positive Functions of Poverty[1]

HERBERT J. GANS

I

Over 20 years ago, Merton (1949, p. 71), analyzing the persistence of the urban political machine, wrote that because "we should ordinarily . . . expect persistent social patterns and social structures to perform positive functions which are at the time not adequately fulfilled by other existing patterns and structures . . . perhaps this publicly maligned organization is, under present conditions, satisfying basic latent function." He pointed out how the machine provided central authority to get things done when a decentralized local government could not act, humanized the services of the impersonal bureaucracy for fearful citizens, offered concrete help (rather than law or justice) to the poor, and otherwise performed services needed or demanded by many people but considered unconventional or even illegal by formal public agencies.

This paper is not concerned with the political machine, however, but with poverty, a social phenomenon which is as maligned as and far more persistent than the machine. Consequently, there may be some merit in applying functional analysis to poverty, to ask whether it too has positive functions that explain its persistence. Since functional analysis has itself taken on a maligned status among some American sociologists, a secondary purpose of this paper is to ask whether it is still a useful approach.[2]

143

II

Merton (1949, p. 50) defined functions as "those observed consequences which make for the adaptation or adjustment of a given system; and dysfunctions, those observed consequences which lessen the adaptation or adjustment of the system." This definition does not specify the nature or scope of the system, but elsewhere in his classic paper "Manifest and Latent Functions," Merton indicated that social system was not a synonym for society, and that systems vary in size, requiring a functional analysis "to consider a *range* of units for which the item [or social phenomenon—H.G.] has designated consequences: individuals in diverse statuses, subgroups, the larger social system and cultural systems" (1949, p. 51).

In discussing the functions of poverty, I shall identify functions for *groups* and *aggregates;* specifically, interest groups, socioeconomic classes, and other population aggregates, for example, those with shared values or similar statuses. This definitional approach is based on the assumption that almost every social system—and of course every society—is composed of groups of aggregates with different interests and values, so that, as Merton put it (1949, p. 51), "items may be functional for some individuals and subgroups and dysfunctional for others." Indeed, frequently one group's functions are another group's dysfunctions.[3] For example, the political machine analyzed by Merton was functional for the working class and business interests of the city but dysfunctional for many middle class and reform interests. Consequently, functions are defined as those observed consequences which are positive *as judged by the values of the group under analysis;* dysfunctions, as those which are negative by these values.[4] Because functions benefit the group in question and dysfunctions hurt it, I shall also describe functions and dysfunctions in the language of economic planning and systems analysis as benefits and costs.[5]

Identifying functions and dysfunctions for groups and aggregates rather than systems reduces the possibility that what is functional for one group in a multigroup system will be seen as being functional for the whole system, making it more difficult, for example, to suggest that a given phenomenon is functional for a corporation or political regime when it may in fact only be functional for their officers or leaders. Also, this approach precludes reaching a priori conclusions about two other important empirical questions raised by

Merton (1949, pp. 32–36), whether any phenomenon is ever functional or dysfunctional for an entire society, and, if functional, whether it is therefore indispensable to that society.

In a modern heterogeneous society, few phenomena are functional or dysfunctional for the society as a whole, and most result in benefits to some groups and costs to others. Given the level of differentiation in modern society, I am even skeptical whether one can empirically identify a social system called society. Society exists, of course, but it is closer to being a very large aggregate, and when sociologists talk about society as a system, they often really mean the nation, a system which, among other things, sets up boundaries and other distinguishing characteristics between societal aggregates.

I would also argue that no social phenomenon is indispensable; it may be too powerful or too highly valued to be eliminated, but in most instances, one can suggest what Merton calls "functional alternatives" or equivalents for a social phenomena, that is, other social patterns or policies which achieve the same functions but avoid the dysfunctions.

III

The conventional view of American poverty is so dedicated to identifying the dysfunctions of poverty, both for the poor and the nation, that at first glance it seems inconceivable to suggest that poverty could be functional for anyone. Of course, the slum lord and the loan shark are widely known to profit from the existence of poverty; but they are popularly viewed as evil men, and their activities are, at least in part, dysfunctional for the poor. However, what is less often recognized, at least in the conventional wisdom, is that poverty also makes possible the existence or expansion of "respectable" professions and occupations, for example, penology, criminology, social work, and public health. More recently, the poor have provided jobs for professional and paraprofessional "poverty warriors," as well as journalists and social scientists, this author included, who have supplied the information demanded when public curiosity about the poor developed in the 1960s.

Clearly, then, poverty and the poor may well serve a number of functions for many nonpoor groups in American society, and I shall describe 15 sets of such functions—economic, social, cultural, and political—that seem to me most significant.

First, the existence of poverty makes sure that "dirty work" is done. Every economy has such work: physically dirty or dangerous, temporary, dead-end and underpaid, undignified, and menial jobs. These jobs can be filled by paying higher wages than for "clean" work, or by requiring people who have no other choice to do the dirty work and at low wages. In America, poverty functions to provide a low-wage labor pool that is willing—or, rather, unable to be unwilling—to perform dirty work at low cost. Indeed, this function is so important that in some Southern states, welfare payments have been cut off during the summer months when the poor are needed to work in the fields. Moreover, the debate about welfare—and about proposed substitutes such as the negative income tax and the Family Assistance Plan—has emphasized the impact of income grants on work incentive, with opponents often arguing that such grants would reduce the incentive of—actually, the pressure on—the poor to carry out the needed dirty work if the wages therefore are no larger than the income grant. Furthermore, many economic activities which involve dirty work depend heavily on the poor; restaurants, hospitals, parts of the garment industry, and industrial agriculture, among others, could not persist in their present form without their dependence on the substandard wages which they pay to their employees.

Second, the poor subsidize, directly and indirectly, many activities that benefit the affluent.[6] For one thing, they have long supported both the consumption and investment activities of the private economy by virtue of the low wages which they receive. This was openly recognized at the beginning of the Industrial Revolution, when a French writer quoted by T.H. Marshall (1979, p. 7) pointed out that "to assure and maintain the prosperities of our industries, it is necessary that the workers should never acquire wealth." Examples of this kind of subsidization abound even today; for example, domestics subsidize the upper middle and upper classes, making life easier for their employers and freeing affluent women for a variety of professional, cultural, civic, or social activities. In addition, as Barry Schwartz pointed out (personal communication), the low income of the poor enables the rich to divert a higher proportion of their income to savings and investment, and thus to fuel economic growth. This, in turn, can produce higher incomes for everybody, including the poor, although it does not necessarily improve the position of the poor in the socioeconomic hierarchy, since the benefits of economic growth are also distributed unequally.

At the same time, the poor subsidize the governmental economy. Because local property and sales taxes and the ungraduated income taxes levied by many states are regressive, the poor pay a higher percentage of their income in taxes than the rest of the population, thus subsidizing the many state and local governmental programs that serve more affluent taxpayers.[7] In addition, the poor support medical innovation as patients in teaching and research hospitals, and as guinea pigs in medical experiments, subsidizing the more affluent patients who alone can afford these innovations once they are incorporated into medical practice.

Third, poverty creates jobs for a number of occupations and professions which serve the poor, or shield the rest of the population from them. As already noted, penology would be miniscule without the poor, as would the police, since the poor provide the majority of their "clients." Other activities which flourish because of the existence of poverty are the numbers game, the sale of heroin and cheap wines and liquors, pentecostal ministers, faith healers, prostitutes, pawn shops, and the peacetime army, which recruits its enlisted men mainly from among the poor.

Fourth, the poor buy goods which others do not want and thus prolong their economic usefulness, such as day-old bread, fruit and vegetables which would otherwise have to be thrown out, second-hand clothes, and deteriorating automobiles and buildings. They also provide incomes for doctors, lawyers, teachers, and others who are too old, poorly trained, or incompetent to attract more affluent clients.

In addition, the poor perform a number of social and cultural functions:

Fifth, the poor can be identified and punished as alleged or real deviants in order to uphold the legitimacy of dominant norms (Macarov 1970, pp. 31–33). The defenders of the desirability of hard work, thrift, honesty, and monogamy need people who can be accused of being lazy, spendthrift, dishonest, and promiscuous to justify these norms; and as Erikson (1964) and others following Durkheim have pointed out, the norms themselves are best legitimated by discovering violations.

Whether the poor actually violate these norms more than affluent people is still open to question. The working poor work harder and longer than high-status jobholders, and poor housewives must do more housework to keep their slum apartments clean than their middle-class peers in standard housing. The proportion of cheaters among welfare recipients is quite low and considerably lower than among income taxpayers.[8] Violent crime is higher among the poor, but the affluent commit a variety of white-collar crimes, and several studies of self-reported delinquency have concluded that middle-class youngsters are sometimes as delinquent as the poor. However, the poor are more likely to be caught when participating in deviant acts and, once caught, to be punished more often than middle-class transgressors. Moreover, they lack the political and cultural power to correct the stereotypes that affluent people hold of them, and thus continue to be thought of as lazy, spendthrift, etc., whatever the empirical evidence, by those who need living proof that deviance does not pay.[9] The actually or allegedly deviant poor have traditionally been described as undeserving and, in more recent terminology, culturally deprived or pathological.

Sixth, another group of poor, described as deserving because they are disabled or suffering from bad luck, provide the rest of the population with different emotional satisfactions; they evoke compassion, pity, and charity, thus allowing those who help them to feel that they are altruistic, moral, and practicing the Judeo-Christian ethic. The deserving poor also enable others to feel fortunate for being spared the deprivations that come with poverty.[10]

Seventh, as a converse of the fifth function described previously, the poor offer affluent people vicarious participation in the uninhibited sexual, alcoholic, and narcotic behavior in which many poor people are alleged to indulge, and which, being freed from the constraints of affluence and respectability, they are often thought to enjoy more than the middle classes. One of the popular beliefs about welfare recipients is that many are on a permanent sex-filled vacation. Although it may be true that the poor are more given to uninhibited behavior, studies by Rainwater (1970) and other observers of the lower class indicate that such behavior is as often motivated by despair as by lack of inhibition, and that it results less in pleasure than in a compulsive escape from grim reality. However, whether the poor actually have more sex and enjoy it more than affluent people is irrelevant; as long as the latter believe it to be so, they can share it vicariously and perhaps enviously when instances are reported in fictional, journalistic, or sociological and anthropological formats.

Eighth, poverty helps to guarantee the status of those who are not poor. In a stratified society, where social mobility is an especially important goal and class boundaries are fuzzy, people need to know quite urgently where they stand. As a result, the poor function as a reliable and relatively permanent measuring rod for status comparison, particularly for the working class, which must find and maintain status distinctions between itself and the poor, much as the aristocracy must find ways of distinguishing itself from the *nouveau riche*.

Ninth, the poor also assist in the upward mobility of the nonpoor, for, as Goode has pointed out (1967, p. 5), "the privileged . . . try systematically to prevent the talent of the less privileged from being recognized or developed." By being denied educational opportunities or being stereotyped as stupid or unteachable, the poor thus enable others to obtain the better jobs. Also, an unknown number of people have moved themselves or their children up in the socioeconomic hierarchy through the incomes earned from the provision of goods and services in the slums: by becoming policemen and teachers, owning "Mom and Pop" stores, or working in the various rackets that flourish in the slums.

In fact, members of almost every immigrant group have financed their upward mobility by providing retail goods and services, housing, entertainment, gambling, narcotics, etc., to later arrivals in America (or in the city), most recently to blacks, Mexicans, and Puerto Ricans. Other Americans, of both European and native origin, have financed their entry into the upper middle and upper classes by owning or managing the illegal institutions that serve the poor, as well as the legal but not respectable ones, such as slum housing.

Tenth, just as the poor contribute to the economic viability of a number of businesses and professions (see function 3 above), they also add to the social viability of noneconomic groups. For one thing, they help to keep the aristocracy busy, thus justifying its continued existence. "Society" uses the poor as clients of settlement houses and charity benefits; indeed, it must have the poor to practice its public-mindedness so as to demonstrate its superiority over the *nouveaux riches* who devote themselves to conspicuous consumption. The poor play a similar function for philanthropic enterprises at other levels of the socioeconomic hierarchy, including the mass of middle-class civic organizations and women's clubs engaged in volunteer work and fundraising in almost every

American community. Doing good among the poor has traditionally helped the church to find a method of expressing religious sentiments in action; in recent years, militant church activity among and for the poor has enabled the church to hold on to its more liberal and radical members who might otherwise have dropped out of organized religion altogether.

Eleventh, the poor perform several cultural functions. They have played an unsung role in the creation of "civilization," having supplied the construction labor for many of the monuments which are often identified as the noblest expressions and examples of civilization, for example, the Egyptian pyramids, Greek temples, and medieval churches.[11] Moreover, they have helped to create a goodly share of the surplus capital that funds the artists and intellectuals who make culture, and particularly "high" culture, possible in the first place.

Twelfth, the "low" culture created for or by the poor is often adopted by the more affluent. The rich collect artifacts from extinct folk cultures (although not only from poor ones), and almost all Americans listen to jazz, blues, spirituals, and country music which originated among the Southern poor—as well as rock, which was derived from similar sources. The protest of the poor sometimes becomes literature; in 1970, for example, poetry written by ghetto children became popular in sophisticated literary circles. The poor also serve as culture heroes and literary subjects, particularly, of course, for the Left, but the hobo, cowboy, hipster, and the mythical prostitute with a heart of gold have performed this function for a variety of groups.

Finally, the poor carry out a number of important political functions:

Thirteenth, the poor serve as symbolic constituencies and opponents for several political groups. For example, parts of the revolutionary Left could not exist without the poor, particularly now that the working class can no longer be perceived as the vanguard of the revolution. Conversely, political groups of conservative bent need the "welfare chiselers" and others who "live off the taxpayer's hard-earned money" in order to justify their demands for reductions in welfare payments and tax relief. Moreover, the role of the poor in upholding dominant norms (see function 5 above) also has a significant political function. An economy based on the ideology of laissez faire requires a deprived population which is allegedly unwilling to work; not only does the alleged moral inferiority of the poor reduce the moral pressure on the present political economy to eliminate poverty, but redistributive alternatives can be made to look quite unattractive if those who will benefit from them most can be described as lazy, spendthrift, dishonest, and promiscuous. Thus, conservatives and classical liberals would find it difficult to justify many of their political beliefs without the poor; but then so would modern liberals and socialists who seek to eliminate poverty.

Fourteenth, the poor, being powerless, can be made to absorb the economic and political costs of change and growth in American society. During the 19th century, they did the backbreaking work that built the cities; today, they are pushed out of their neighborhoods to make room for "progress." Urban renewal projects to hold middle-class taxpayers and stores in the city and expressways to enable suburbanites to commute downtown have typically been located in poor neighborhoods, since no other group will allow itself to be displaced. For much the same reason, urban universities, hospitals, and civic centers also expand into land occupied by the poor. The major costs of the industrialization of agriculture in America have been borne by the poor, who are pushed off the land without recompense, just as in earlier centuries in Europe, they bore the brunt of the transformation of agrarian societies into industrial ones. The poor have also paid a large share of the human cost of the growth of American power overseas, for they have provided many of the foot soldiers for Vietnam and other wars.

Fifteenth, the poor have played an important role in shaping the American political process; because they vote and participate less than other groups, the political system has often been free to ignore them. This has not only made American politics more centrist than would otherwise be the case, but it has also added to the stability of the political process. If the 15% of the population below the federal "poverty line" participated fully in the political process, they would almost certainly demand better jobs and higher incomes, which would require income redistribution and would thus generate further political conflict between the haves and the have-nots. Moreover, when the poor do participate, they often provide the Democrats with a captive constituency, for they can rarely support Republicans, lack parties of their own, and thus have no other place to go politically. This, in turn, has enabled the Democrats to count on the votes of the poor, allowing the party to be more responsive to voters who might otherwise switch to the Republicans, in recent years, for example, the white working class.

IV

I have described fifteen of the more important functions which the poor carry out in American society, enough to support the functionalist thesis that poverty survives in part because it is useful to a number of groups in society. This analysis is not intended to suggest that because it is functional, poverty *should* persist, or that it *must* persist. Whether it should persist is a normative question; whether it must, an analytic and empirical one, but the answer to both depends in part on whether the dysfunctions of poverty outweigh the functions. Obviously, poverty has many dysfunctions, mainly for the poor themselves but also for the more affluent. For example, their social order is upset by the pathology, crime, political protest, and disruption emanating from the poor, and the income of the affluent is affected by the taxes that must be levied to protect their social order. Whether the dysfunctions outweigh the functions is a question that clearly deserves study.

It is, however, possible to suggest alternatives for many of the functions of the poor. Thus, society's dirty work (function 1) could be done without poverty, some by automating it, the rest by paying the workers who do it decent wages, which would help considerably to cleanse that kind of work. Nor is it necessary for the poor to subsidize the activities they support through their low-wage jobs (function 2), for, like dirty work, many of these activities are essential enough to persist even if wages were raised. In both instances, however, costs would be driven up, resulting in higher prices to the customers and clients of dirty work and subsidized activity, with obvious dysfunctional consequences for more affluent people.

Alternative roles for the professionals who flourish because of the poor (function 3) are easy to suggest. Social workers could counsel the affluent, as most prefer to do anyway, and the police could devote themselves to traffic and organized crime. Fewer penologists would be employable, however, and pentecostal religion would probably not survive without the poor. Nor would parts of the second- and third-hand market (function 4), although even affluent people sometimes buy used goods. Other roles would have to be found for badly trained or incompetent professionals now relegated to serving the poor, and someone else would have to pay their salaries.

Alternatives for the deviance-connected social functions (functions 5–7) can be found more easily and cheaply than for the economic functions. Other groups are already available to serve as deviants to uphold traditional morality, for example, entertainers, hippies, and most recently, adolescents in general. These same groups are also available as alleged or real orgiasts to provide vicarious participation in sexual fantasies. The blind and disabled function as objects of pity and charity, and the poor may therefore not even be needed for functions 5–7.

The status and mobility functions of the poor (functions 8 and 9) are far more difficult to substitute, however. In a hierarchical society, some people must be defined as inferior to everyone else with respect to a variety of attributes, and the poor perform this function more adequately than others. They could, however, perform it without being as poverty-stricken as they are, and one can conceive of a stratification system in which the people below the federal "poverty line" would receive 75% of the median income rather than 40% or less as is now the case—even though they would still be last in the pecking order.[12] Needless to say, such a reduction of economic inequality would also require income redistribution. Given the opposition to income redistribution among more affluent people, however, it seems unlikely that the status functions of poverty can be replaced, and they—together with the economic functions of the poor, which are equally expensive to replace—may turn out to be the major obstacles to the elimination of poverty.

The role of the poor in the upward mobility of other groups could be maintained without their being so low in income. However, if their incomes were raised above subsistence levels, they would begin to generate capital so that their own entrepreneurs could supply them with goods and services, thus competing with and perhaps rejecting "outside" suppliers. Indeed, this is already happening in a number of ghettoes, where blacks are replacing white storeowners.

Similarly, if the poor were more affluent, they would make less willing clients for upper- and middle-class philanthropic and religious groups (function 10), although as long as they are economically and otherwise unequal, this function need not disappear altogether. Moreover, some would still use the settlement houses and other philanthropic institutions to pursue individual upward mobility, as they do now.

The cultural functions (11 and 12) may not need to be replaced. In America, the labor unions have rarely allowed the poor to help build cultural monuments anyway, and there is sufficient surplus capital from other sources to subsidize the unprofitable components of high culture. Similarly, other deviant groups are available to innovate in popular culture and supply new culture heroes, for example, the hippies and members of other counter-cultures.

Some of the political functions of the poor would, however, be as difficult to replace as their economic and status functions. Although the poor could probably continue to serve as symbolic constituencies and opponents (function 13) if their incomes were raised while they remained unequal in other respects, increases in income are generally accompanied by increases in power as well. Consequently, once they were no longer so poor, people would be likely to resist paying the costs of growth and change (function 14); and it is difficult to find alternative groups who can be displaced for urban renewal and technological "progress." Of course, it is possible to design city-rebuilding and highway projects which properly reimburse the displaced people, but such projects would then become considerably more expensive, thus raising the price for those now benefiting from urban renewal and expressways. Alternatively, many might never be built, thus reducing the comfort and convenience of those beneficiaries. Similarly, if the poor were subjected to less economic pressure, they would probably be less willing to serve in the army, except at considerably higher pay, in which case war would become yet more costly and thus less popular politically. Alternatively, more servicemen would have to be recruited from the middle and upper classes, but in that case war would also become less popular.

The political stabilizing and "centering" role of the poor (function 15) probably cannot be substituted for at all, since no other group is willing to be disenfranchised or likely enough to remain apathetic so as to reduce the fragility of the political system. Moreover, if the poor were given higher incomes, they would probably become more active politically, thus adding their demands for more to those of other groups already putting pressure on the political allocators of resources. The poor might continue to remain loyal to the Democratic party, but like other moderate-income voters, they could also be attracted to the Republicans or to third parties. While improving the economic status of the presently poor would not necessarily drive the political system far to the left, it would enlarge the constituencies now demanding higher wages and more public funds. It is of course possible to add new powerless groups who do not vote or otherwise participate to the political mix and can thus serve as "ballast" in the polity, for example, by encouraging the import of new poor immigrants from Europe and elsewhere, except that the labor unions are probably strong enough to veto such a policy.

In sum, then, several of the most important functions of the poor cannot be replaced with alternatives, while some could be replaced, but almost always only at higher costs to other people, particularly more affluent ones. Consequently, *a functional analysis must conclude that poverty persists not only because it satisfies a number of functions but also because many of the functional alternatives to poverty would be quite dysfunctional for the more affluent members of society.*[13]

V

I noted earlier that functional analysis had itself become a maligned phenomenon and that a secondary purpose of this paper was to demonstrate its continued usefulness. One reason for its presently low status is political; insofar as an analysis of functions, particularly latent functions, seems to justify what ought to be condemned, it appears to lend itself to the support of conservative ideological positions, although it can also have radical implications when it subverts the conventional wisdom. Still, as Merton has pointed out (1949, p. 43; 1961, pp. 736–37), functional analysis per se is ideologically neutral, and "like other forms of sociological analysis, it can be infused with any of a wide range of sociological values" (1949, p. 40). This infusion depends, of course, on the purposes—and even the functions—of the functional analysis, for as Wirth (1936, p. xvii) suggested long ago, "every assertion of a 'fact' about the social world touches the interests of some individual or group," and even if functional analyses are conceived and conducted in a neutral manner, they are rarely interpreted in an ideological vacuum.

In one sense, my analysis is, however, neutral; if one makes no judgment as to whether poverty ought to be eliminated—and if one can subsequently avoid being accused of acquiescing in poverty— then the analysis suggests only that poverty exists because it is useful to many groups in society.[14] If one favors the elimination of poverty, however, then the analysis can have a variety of political implications, *depending in part on how completely it is carried out.*

If functional analysis only identifies the functions of social phenomena without mentioning their dysfunctions, then it may, intentionally or otherwise, agree with or support holders of conservative values. Thus, to say that the poor perform many functions for the rich might be interpreted or used to justify poverty, just as Davis and Moore's argument (1945) that social stratification is functional because it provides society with highly trained professionals could be taken to justify inequality.

Actually, the Davis and Moore analysis was conservative because it was incomplete; it did not identify the dysfunctions of inequality and failed to suggest functional alternatives, as Tumin (1953) and Schwartz (1955) have pointed out.[15] Once a functional analysis is made more complete by the addition of functional alternatives, however, it can take on a liberal and reform cast, because the alternatives often provide ameliorative policies that do not require any drastic change in the existing social order.

Even so, to make functional analysis complete requires yet another step, an examination of the functional alternatives themselves. My analysis suggests that the alternatives for poverty are themselves dysfunctional for the affluent population, and it ultimately comes to a conclusion which is not very different from that of radical sociologists. To wit: *that social phenomena which are functional for affluent groups and dysfunctional for poor ones persist; that when the elimination of such phenomena through functional alternatives generates dysfunctions for the affluent, they will continue to persist; and that phenomena like poverty can be eliminated only when they either become sufficiently dysfunctional for the affluent or when the poor can obtain enough power to change the system of social stratification.*[16]

Notes

1. Earlier versions of this paper were presented at a Vassar College conference on the war on poverty in 1964, at the 7th World Congress of Sociology in 1971, and in *Social Policy 2* (July-August 1971): 20–24. The present paper will appear in a forthcoming book on poverty and stratification, edited by S.M. Lipset and S.M. Miller, for the American Academy of Arts and Sciences. I am indebted to Peter Marris, Robert K. Merton, and S.M. Miller for helpful comments on earlier drafts of this paper.

2. The paper also has the latent function, as S.M. Miller has suggested, of contributing to the long debate over the functional analysis of social stratification presented by Davis and Moore (1945).

3. Probably one of the few instances in which a phenomenon has the same function for two groups with different interests is when the survival of the system in which both participate is at stake. Thus, a wage increase can be functional for labor and dysfunctional for management (and consumers), but if the wage increase endangers the firm's survival, it is dysfunctional for labor as well. This assumes, however, that the firm's survival is valued by the workers, which may not always be the case, for example, when jobs are available elsewhere.

4. Merton (1949, p. 50) originally described functions and dysfunctions in terms of encouraging or hindering adaptation or adjustment to a system, although subsequently he has written that "dysfunction refers to the particular inadequacies of a particular part of the system for a designated requirement" (1961, p. 732). Since adaptation and adjustment to a system can have conservative ideological implications, Merton's later formulation and my own definitional approach make it easier to use functional analysis as an ideologically neutral or at least ideologically variable method, insofar as the researcher can decide for himself whether he supports the values of the group under analysis.

5. It should be noted, however, that there are no absolute benefits and costs just as there are no absolute functions and dysfunctions; not only are one group's benefits often another group's costs, but every group defines benefits by its own manifest and latent values, and a social scientist or planner who has determined that certain phenomena provide beneficial consequences for a group may find that the group thinks otherwise. For example, during the 1960s, advocates of racial integration discovered that a significant portion of the black community no longer considered it a benefit but saw it rather as a policy to assimilate blacks into white society and to decimate the political power of the black community.

6. Of course, the poor do not actually subsidize the affluent. Rather, by being forced to work for low wages, they enable the affluent to use the money saved in this fashion for other purposes. The concept of subsidy used here thus assumes belief in a "just wage."

7. Pechman (1969) and Herriott and Miller (1971) found that the poor pay a higher proportion of their income in taxes than any other part of the population: 50% among people earning $2,000 or less according to the latter study.

8. Most official investigations of welfare cheating have concluded that less than 5% of recipients are on the rolls illegally, while it has been estimated that about a third of the population cheats in filing income tax returns.

9. Although this paper deals with the functions of poverty for other groups, poverty has often been described as a motivating or character-building device for the poor themselves; and economic conservatives have argued that by generating the incentive to work, poverty encourages the poor to escape poverty. For an argument that work incentive is more enhanced by income than lack of it, see Gans (1971, p. 96).

10. One psychiatrist (Chernus 1967) has even proposed the fantastic hypothesis that the rich and the poor are engaged in a sadomasochistic relationship, the latter being supported financially by the former so that they can gratify their sadistic needs.

11. Although this is not a contemporary function of poverty in America, it should be noted that today these monuments serve to attract and gratify American tourists.

12. In 1971, the median family income in the United States was about $10,000, and the federal poverty line for a family of four was set at just about $4,000. Of course, most of the poor were earning less than 40% of the median, and about a third of them, less than 20% of the median.

13. Or as Stein (1971, p. 171) puts it: "If the non-poor make the rules . . . antipoverty efforts will only be made up to the point where the needs of the non-poor are satisfied, rather than the needs of the poor."

14. Of course, even in this case the analysis need not be purely neutral, but can be put to important policy uses, for example, by indicating more effectively than moral attacks on poverty the exact nature of the obstacles that must be overcome if poverty is to be eliminated. See also Merton (1961, pp. 709–12).

15. Functional analysis can, of course, be conservative in value or have conservative implications for a number of other reasons, principally in its overt or covert comparison of the advantages of functions and disadvantages of dysfunctions, or in its attitudes toward the groups that are benefiting and paying the costs. Thus, a conservatively inclined policy researcher could conclude that the dysfunctions of poverty far outnumber the functions, but still decide that the needs of the poor are simply not as important or worthy as those of other groups, or of the country as a whole.

16. On the possibility of radical functional analysis, see Merton (1959, pp. 40–43) and Gouldner (1970, p. 443). One difference between my analysis and the prevailing radical view is that most of the functions I have described are latent, whereas many radicals treat them as manifest: recognized and intended by an unjust economic system to oppress the poor. Practically speaking, however, this difference may be unimportant, for if unintended and unrecognized functions were recognized, many affluent people might then decide that they ought to be intended as well, so as to forestall a more expensive antipoverty effort that might be dysfunctional for the affluent.

References

Chernus, J. 1967. "Cities: A Study in Sadomasochism." *Medical Opinion and Review* (May), pp. 104–9.

Davis, K., and W.E. Moore. 1945. "Some Principles of Stratification." *American Sociological Review* 10 (April): 242–49.

Erikson, K.T. 1964. "Notes on the Sociology of Deviance." In *The Other Side*, edited by Howard S. Becker. New York: Free Press.

Gans, H.J. 1971. "Three Ways to Solve the Welfare Problem." *New York Times Magazine*, March 7, pp. 26–27, 94–100.

Goode, W.J. 1967. "The Protection of the Inept." *American Sociological Review* 32 (February): 5–19.

Gouldner, A. 1970. *The Coming Crisis of Western Sociology.* New York: Basic.

Herriot, A., and H.P. Miller. 1971. "Who Paid the Taxes in 1968." Paper prepared for the National Industrial Conference Board.

Macarov, D. 1970. *Incentives to Work*. San Francisco: Jossey-Bass.

Marshall, T.H. 1979. "Poverty and Inequality." Paper prepared for the American Academy of Arts and Sciences volume on poverty and stratification.

Merton, R.K. 1949. "Manifest and Latent Functions." In *Social Theory and Social Structure*. Glencoe, Ill.: Free Press.

Merton, R.K. 1961. "Social Problems and Sociological Theory." In *Contemporary Social Problems*, edited by R.K. Merton and R. Nisbet. New York: Harcourt Brace.

Pechman, J.A. 1969. "The Rich, the Poor, and the Taxes They Pay." *Public Interest*, no. 17 (Fall), pp. 21–43.

Rainwater, L. 1970. *Behind Ghetto Walls*. Chicago: Aldine.

Schwartz, R. 1955. "Functional Alternatives to Inequality." *American Sociological Review* 20 (August): 424–30.

Stein, B. 1971. *On Relief*. New York: Basic.

Tumin, M.B. 1953. "Some Principles of Stratification: A Critical Analysis." *American Sociological Review* 18 (August): 387–93.

Wirth, L. 1936. "Preface." In *Ideology and Utopia*, by Karl Mannheim. New York: Harcourt Brace.

Implementing the Objectives of Family Planning Programs

GITTA MEIER

Assistance with family planning [1] has only recently been accorded recognition as a legitimate and valuable component of health and welfare services. It was not until 1968 that a comparatively large amount of public money was allocated for the provision of family planning services.[2] And because of decades of almost complete neglect, the gross deficiencies in contraceptive assistance to the poor and the near poor may be expected to be only partly overcome in the years ahead.[3] Nevertheless, social workers will no longer be prevented by a lack of appropriate resources or by agency prohibitions from making this essential service accessible to their clients. They may even be required to do so, since, almost overnight, affirmative prescription in agency manuals and staff orientation programs have replaced former taboos, restrictive eligibility rules, or total disregard.[4] Workers are now free to use established approaches based on nonthreatening exploration of the client's feelings in regard to birth control and to offer frequent or routine counseling and referrals for help with child spacing and family limitation.[5]

The problems associated with reaching unreached persons and encouraging the sustained use of contraception by ambivalent, less committed, and less competent clients will doubtless continue. Now, however, such problems may be appropriately viewed within

161

the context of rapid but uneven and awkwardly timed progress and of reduced but persistent flaws in available methods.

Least Accessible Clients

Several important groups are not likely to be reached by organized family planning services in time to prevent unwanted pregnancies. Three identifiable groups include a very large proportion of the least sophisticated and least economically secure persons.

Women in rural areas and small towns   One group is composed of women in rural areas and small towns. This group includes about one third of all very low income women who are estimated to be in need of family planning services.[6] The dynamics of program expansion favor the areas in which there are medical institutions offering obstetric and other care to nonprivate patients and in areas in which family planning services are provided under health department, Office of Economic Opportunity, or Planned Parenthood-World Population auspices. Social workers who function outside the large cities must therefore complement and extend the efforts being made by public health nurses to bring knowledge and understanding of birth control to all families.[7] They may have to work out special arrangements with local physicians to accept patients who are unable to pay for an examination and contraceptive prescriptions. Transportation arrangements may be needed for visits to a physician's office or to the nearest health department clinic. In order to provide such services, social workers will probably have to prod their agencies to take full advantage of the funds available under federal and state law for innovative program development.

Newcomers to the ghettos   The women in families that migrate between the white, black, and Spanish-speaking inner-city ghettos and the disorganized urban fringe settlements make up another group. Most of these women, or at least members of their families, come into contact with social workers *before* receiving professional contraceptive assistance. It is therefore very important for the social worker to take the initiative in exploring the need for such service along with other relevant services and in removing any obstacles.

The worker's questions about birth control may seem inappropriate when his primary contact is with a son or a younger brother of the person in need of such service. Particularly for clients who are newcomers to a community, however, such assistance is well worth the worker's effort, even in implementing immediate agency objectives. Too often the crisis created by a mother's or a sister's unwanted or ill-timed pregnancy wreaks havoc with the other family members' use of agency services and with the adjustment to a new environment. In general the worker will find the additional task neither excessively time consuming nor frustrating. Most of the newcomers do not fall into the hard-to-reach category. Once they have been appropriately introduced to existing family planning services, they do not require sustained casework services to continue using them on their own.[8]

Persons in custodial care and in related programs Another group includes the patients or inmates of institutions for retarded and emotionally disturbed persons and for juvenile and adult delinquents, as well as their spouses, at the time of discharge, temporary leave, parole, or probation. These institutions have only just begun to include contraceptive assistance in their programs, despite the heavy personal and social cost involved in pregnancies and childbearing for their patients. With some modification, the statement may also be made about the noncustodial programs, such as those for moderately retarded adolescents. When contraceptive services are omitted from institutional programs, social workers can document the need for them and take the initiative in using the institutions' resources, as well as those of the larger community, in developing appropriate services.[9] At present such personal initiative is needed to overcome institutional inertia aggravated by shortages of staff and funds.

The Shift to Private Medical Care

As a result of recent legislation many indigent and medically indigent persons now receive obstetric and other care as private patients. Free contraceptive assistance is included among the services to which most of them are legally entitled.[10] Problems in communication between the busy physicians and their poorly educated patients are not uncommon as such patients are brought into the main stream of medical practice and care. With respect to family planning, such difficulties are compounded by the widely differing views physicians have about the circumstances under which they should initiate contraceptive counseling or prescribe contraceptives. Private practice is less readily standardized than that in hospitals and clinics. Moreover, many patients are no longer included in the routine arrangements for home visits by public health nurses to maternity patients discharged from county hospitals. In the past such visits have probably been the most effective professional means of providing family planning information and instruction for the patients in this group.

Social workers in contact with families entitled to medical care under Title XIX of the Social Security Amendments of 1965 should make certain that both physicians and patients are informed about the right to obtain contraceptive service at no cost. In order to prevent rebuffs or neglect, some health and welfare departments have conducted inquiries to determine which general practitioners, internists, and obstetricians will accept such patients for contraceptive assistance and under what circumstances. Knowledge of the physicians' attitudes toward contraceptive service to unmarried patients, especially minors, is particularly important. Although many physicians are prepared to discuss contraception with any patient over eighteen years of age, some will do so only for mothers or only for single women over twenty-one. Such advance information is also important for clients who are not entitled to free services.

Deterrents to Service

The family planning movement — within and outside Planned Parenthood-World Population — has been able in the past to draw on the devotion and enthusiasm of professional and lay people who have seen themselves as pioneers in an important cause. Their cause has now been incorporated into the services of well-established health and welfare agencies that rely on conventional incentives for staff performance. The staff orientation to family planning in such agencies is likely to be perfunctory at best. Moreover, longstanding deterrents to the use of other services often carry over to the newly introduced family planning services. For example, contraceptive assistance has been introduced in the postpartum clinics of some county hospitals and other hospitals that have nonprivate maternity patients. In almost every instance the new service has resulted in improvement of the rate of return for postpartum checkups. Even so, return visits still occur at a level approximating that of private patients only in the institutions that concentrate on ensuring patient satisfaction and confidence in all aspects of their medical care. Another deterrent often encountered is the institution, by administrative fiat, of residential or financial eligibility requirements to family planning assistance. Sometimes these requirements even apply to patients who are charged for the particular service. Clearly such rulings are made without consideration of their consequences for the mobile population served. In addition, the random assignment of staff members who are fundamentally opposed to family planning, or to its provision for unmarried women, still may discourage clients in subtle, not immediately apparent ways.

The clients best known to social workers are also the persons who are most easily deterred by organizational shortcomings. It is therefore important for the worker to relay such information about the client in the referral to the hospital or health department providing family planning service. Recently two social workers tested telephone replies in medical and social agencies to requests for birth control assistance and thereby discovered a serious loophole in their referral system.[11] Similarly, social workers who function within institutions that provide family planning assistance must search out procedures that deter its acceptance.

Unfortunately the long overdue expansion and the legitimation of family planning services have coincided with cutbacks in many other important health and welfare services. Moreover, the federal legislation in support of family planning services is being implemented just when restrictive amendments have been added with respect to the very group to whom such services are being made available. The new emphasis on family planning also comes at a time of sharpened racial suspicion and antagonism. Under the circumstances it is not surprising that the success of the effort to assure equal opportunity for protection against unwanted pregnancies has brought the new programs under attack by the militant black organizations as a means of cutting welfare costs, if not as thinly veiled attempts at genocide. Social workers should be aware of the replacement of earlier, church-led opposition by opposition along racial lines. They need to be aware of the scattered cases of persons "sentenced" to birth control and sterilization for promiscuity, child neglect, or nonsupport. Advocacy of compulsory birth control, sterilization, or abortion for unmarried women who have more than one child has lent another edge to clients' fears, reinforcing their acknowledged or submerged opposition to interference with sexual and procreative matters. Few of these extreme negative reactions have been documented in surveys of contraceptive knowledge and use, but they unquestionably contribute to non-acceptance or rapid abandonment of contraception by a small but important fraction of potential users.[12]

Minimizing Opposition

Beyond careful adherence to a well-publicized policy of the client's right to refuse service, several indirect ways of minimizing antagonism and mistrust seem feasible. Clearly the workers in agencies that are viewed with suspicion or hostility by many of the people they serve are not in an advantageous position to encourage use of birth control. And yet not only welfare recipients and county hospital patients but also many families served by probation and parole departments, juvenile courts, and aftercare programs of mental hospitals and private protective agencies are in need of assistance with family planning, and agency workers are their main contact with community services. It is rarely realistic, however, to refer a client who is being investigated on a battered-child charge to a family planning clinic or to recommend birth control to an AFDC recipient whose request for an increased grant has just been turned down. In such cases it seems advisable for the worker to ask that the public health nurse discuss child spacing and family limitation as health-preserving measures in independent contacts with the families. Alternatively, a neighborhood aide could be called upon to visit the family and others in the area to talk about family planning.

A recommendation to recruit outside help does not carry the implication that the social worker should abdicate his responsibility and fail to use his counseling skill. He certainly should be able to explain in simple terms the greater risks involved for mother and offspring in childbearing by the very young woman and by the woman who is over thirty-five and in frequent, too rapid pregnancies at all ages. The worker should also be prepared to discuss persistent medical or genetic contraindications to child-bearing.[13] With some clients an informed discussion of the parallels between the birth control movement and the civil rights movement can be helpful in dispelling unwarranted misconceptions. When the client's stated objections and fears are inconsistent with his general attitudes, the worker should listen for clues to an explanation rather than consider such feelings irrational and based on deep-seated emotions.

Mrs. G, a mother of seven children, steadfastly refused to agree to tubal ligation after the birth of her eighth, unwanted child. Other contraceptive methods were contraindicated, and another un-wanted pregnancy would have been risky. The physicians strongly suspected that the refusal was based on fears that are prevalent among Negroes concerning the sexual implications of the operation. By exploring problems related to Mrs. G's confinement and af-tercare the social worker learned that her refusal was based on problems related to the additional hospital stay needed for the operation. Mrs. G had been too embarrassed to tell the physicians that she did not want her husband to stay home with the children because it could cost him his tenuous job. Once a homemaker was assured, she accepted sterilization with relief.

When relations between staff members and clients are based on mutual respect and demonstrated concern for the client's welfare, acceptance of family planning assistance is rarely hindered by suspicion and hostility. Hence the establishment of agency policies and procedures in consonance with social work principles is at least as important as is concern for the technical aspects of providing this particular service. Such favorable conditions are not found in every agency, however. The individual workers nevertheless can and often do maintain high standards. An AFDC mother, referring to a worker in an agency that has restrictive assistance policies, com-mented, "Sure it was all right for the welfare worker to talk to me about birth control. She is more like a friend."

It is important that publicity, orientation, and other means of increasing the client's understanding and interest in family planning be geared to reducing suspicion and fear. Notices sent out by welfare departments explaining relaxation of previous prohibitions on family planning should therefore be phrased to encourage clients to request assistance rather than to arouse suspicion and doubts. In addition, family planning procedures should be discussed with local client organizations and welfare rights organizations before they are introduced. Informal discussions with groups of clients, rather than with individual recipients, may serve a similar purpose.

In family planning programs the medically oriented members of the team traditionally tend to be concerned with the technical details of delivering the service. Because for some persons and groups birth control still carries connotations that gravely conflict with its acceptance as a simple medical service, mere attention to satisfactory clinical procedures may not suffice. Consequently, social workers must be prepared to take the initiative in assuring the meaningful participation of patients, aides, and other persons in the community. It is well known that such participation does not eradicate the operational problems of community agencies or the opposition to community programs. Nevertheless, with respect to family planning it is essential to avoid the spread of unfounded suspicions and hostility by establishing co-operation and trust from the outset or by persistent efforts to earn such trust.[14]

Nonacceptance and Ineffective Use of Service

At present family planning services are being given to a cross section of low-income women, most of whom are anxious to space their pregnancies or to limit the size of their families. The majority of these women can be expected to make an effort to follow instructions for regular return visits, refills of prescriptions, self-examination, and checking complaints or doubts with the clinic. Of necessity priority has been given to initial and continuing service to this "motivated" group. Reaching women who have failed to respond to publicity, orientation, and informal or formal referral systems is much more difficult and expensive. The same holds true for follow-up on patients who fail to return after initial acceptance.

The elimination of obvious barriers, the application of relevant research findings, and intelligent experimentation have greatly reduced the incidence of nonacceptance, dropout, and failure in many family planning programs. Nevertheless, even in the most efficient programs there remains a small but troubling percentage of women whose nonacceptance or ineffective use of contraceptives appears to be related, at least in part, to factors extraneous to the quality of the service. And since the most committed and competent contraceptive users tend to shift from clinic to prepaid or private medical care, the percentage is likely to remain constant or even increase in organized family planning clinics.

It is rarely practicable and perhaps not even desirable to adapt mass services to the capacity of the least effective users. What is needed, however, is early identification of the women who are potential "dropouts" or "failures" and provision of effective means of forestalling such outcomes. Such an approach involves looking beyond the standard service "package" required by the average patient. It can be made successfully with the single most important group of women in need of at least temporary protection against pregnancy: those who have just given birth or aborted.

Several factors may be seen as obstacles to successful use of contraceptives. The danger signals, listed below, are easily identified from a quick screening of the case record and from brief personal contacts with the patients. More than one such signal may be present; they are mutually reinforcing.

1. *External obstacles to clinic attendance and continued use:* problems in regard to access to service (expense of transportation or baby-sitting); anticipated changes in eligibility for service (change of residence, increased income); anticipated move to area without services; confusing arrangements for return visits obtaining prescription.

2. *Difficulties in communication:* language; cultural barriers (objection to male doctors, discussion of sex); see item 5.

3. *Contraception-related difficulties:* history of repeated discontinuation and failure, especially if involving oral contraception and intra-uterine contraceptive devices; expressed ambivalence or fear; opposition from husband; rejection of contraception, although last and future pregnancies unwanted.

4. *Lack of orientation to prevention:* little or no prenatal care; little or no preventive care for children; complete fatalism.

5. *Emotional and intellectual obstacles:* evidence of below-normal intelligence; disorganized or very disturbed be-

havior prior to or after confinement; depressed and indifferent response to infant, hospital situation, planning
for return home; see items 2 and 7.

6. *Crisis-created obstacles or related obstacles:* other urgent
and overwhelming problems; apparent isolation from
friends and relatives; illness; reaction to abortion, still-
birth, fetal death; see item 5.

7. *Care-related obstacles:* hostility to hospital, clinic, or staff
members; embarrassment at being dependent on public
care.

8. *Lack of immediate relevance:* separation from or loss of
lover or husband prior to confinement.

9. *Lack of goal orientation:* school dropout, indifference to
school completion and eventual employment after confinement.

Since social workers are often called upon to assist obstetric
patients at the time of their discharge from the hospital, the
following description of the general characteristics of two important kinds of patients may prove helpful in identifying nonac-
cepters and short-term users of contraception.

The psychologically immobilized client The term psychologically immobilized seems to describe most accurately the state
in which purposive action becomes very difficult if not impossible. The condition may not be readily recognized in many
obstetric patients who are very discouraged because of their immediate life situation and prospects for the forseeable future.[15] In
the main such women are responsible and competent and have
genuine aspirations for themselves or their family. They are well
aware of the importance of preventive medical care and anxious to
prevent future pregnancies. They may have strong feelings of guilt
related to the consequences of having another child, their abandonment by husband or lover, or their failure to complete schooling.
They may also suffer from voluntary or involuntary isolation from
their friends or from embarrassment at having to seek care at public
expense. Poor general health or the aftereffects of abortions,
stillbirths, or fetal deaths may produce a similar state of mind. The
professional staff members should be alert to the fairly obvious signs
that such patients require more than routine attention, even during

a brief hospital stay. They exhibit persistently low spirits; indifference to fellow patients, staff members, and after-discharge arrangements; and minimal response to the infant. Their symptoms, however, are not so severe as to indicate postpartum breakdown.

Maternity patients who do not have visitors or who anticipate living alone without close friends and relatives to assist them are also prone to become overwhelmed by their problems once they return home. Contraceptive counseling during and after the hospital stay must become part of the individualized concern for such patients.[16] Transportation assistance and frequent home visits, telephone calls, and reminders of appointments can help overcome protracted indecision and inactivity for the clients for whom even a phone call seems to require too much effort. Because protection against another pregnancy is recognized as an urgent need by most of these patients, social workers and public health nurses may be able to use contraceptive service as a lever in overcoming the clients' lingering inertia in other areas.

A few of the maternity patients who are brought to the attention of social workers may suffer from serious emotional disturbance. Although no generalized approach seems feasible, social workers should see to it that such patients are protected against another pregnancy when they are able to return home. Too often preoccupation with all the other problems arising at the time of discharge interferes with arrangements for birth control.

Below-average intelligence also creates both subtle and concrete barriers to family planning assistance. Residents, interns, and nurses often tend to be brief and impatient with dull, unresponsive patients. The routine contraceptive orientation in ward sessions and at discharge may not be sufficient for such patients. Social workers should therefore take additional time in making sure that patients are not confused about the nature of contraception and about specific instructions, or they should arrange for instruction to be given before discharge and again at home. Often the cooperation of mothers or husbands makes it possible for the patients to follow instructions. Actual prescription or fitting of contraceptives at the time of discharge, as well as long-acting hormonal preparations and intrauterine devices, are of particular importance in minimizing some of the obstacles to successful contraceptive protection for seriously disturbed or retarded patients. Nevertheless, they do not eliminate the need for careful counseling and attention to follow-up.

The indifferent client For a majority of unmarried women and for some married women pregnancy and childbirth are associated with a breakup of their relationship with lover or husband. They do not anticipate a resumption of sexual intercourse in the foreseeable future and feel no urgent need for contraceptive protection. Such patients rarely make eager listeners in orientation sessions, and some may decline contraceptives altogether when they are offered to them. Others may accept contraception as part of their medical care and discontinue its use in short order.

Since so many of the women who say they are "through with sex" resume relations with the same or another partner within a comparatively short period and often become pregnant again,[17] it is very important for the social worker to explore their plans and hopes for the future. Anticipatory, realistic advice about nonprescriptive contraceptive methods and alternative sources of contraceptive assistance should be given to clients who refuse contraceptive service or doubt that they will need prescribed methods. Many mothers of young maternity patients are anxious to have such information so that they can remind their daughters to seek protection when they begin to date steadily again. Social workers probably are more skilled than other members of the hospital staff in handling such counseling without on the one hand seeming to impugn or condone promiscuous behaviour or on the other hand discussing contraceptive methods in a limbo divorced from the circumstances of the patients anticipated sexual involvement. In such counseling after childbirth, or preferably early in pregnancy, the worker should always bear in mind the knowledge that reliable contraceptive protection makes it easier for the persons involved to continue a mutually satisfactory relationship even though lack of income and maturity make marriage a questionable solution at the time. And because a child has been born, it is more often realistic to build on the relationship.

The programs for unmarried young mothers that are combining individualized medical care starting early in pregnancy, social services, group discussion and counseling, and contraceptive assistance, as well as strong emphasis on continuing education and training, appear to have considerable success in the prevention of additional pregnancies.[18] They are also achieving substantial educational and occupational goals. For many reasons, a combination of high-quality professional services, peer-group support, and alternatives to continuing dependency and illegitimacy holds greater promise than exclusive emphasis on contraceptive assistance.[19] Social workers should work toward the development of such programs in the hospital and the community, especially now that federal support is available. Even when comprehensive and coordinated programs are not feasible, workers still can fit the various components together and thereby meet the needs of young mothers.

Conclusions

This article has focused exclusively on what may possibly be considered highly traditional and conventional concerns related to family planning in the United States. It has neglected the innovative programs slowly evolving in pediatric clinics and other settings that provide medical and other services along with contraceptive assistance to young patients who are at high risk of becoming pregnant in the near future.[20] It has disregarded the possible implications of legalizing abortions, of more stringent measures for slowing down population growth, of far-reaching changes in the status of women and the relationship between the sexes, or of the impact of world-wide population pressures. Even given this narrow, perhaps myopic focus, the challenges to social workers and social agencies implied in the incomplete and conservative agenda set forth below are considerable. They are most urgent with respect to the poor and the poorly educated but are not confined to such groups by any means. At a minimum the agenda must include the following tasks:

1. Counseling and providing referrals; being alert for individual persons and subgroups that continue to be bypassed by established family planning services; and working toward the appropriate extension of services to such groups
2. Leading the other members of the family planning team in the development of community acceptance and support of family planning service and in minimizing misunderstandings, suspicion, and hostility

3. Searching for better means of identifying women who may require more than routine orientation and prescription to become successful contraceptive users and adapting standard services to their special needs

4. Seeing that services and counseling provided to clients in other areas also strengthen, as far as possible, the clients' motivation and capacity for effective child spacing and family limitation

5. Encouraging and helping clients to make constructive use of the new choices open to them in regard to effective family planning and promoting the facilities, services, and opportunities provided, so that such choices can indeed be exercised.

Notes

1. In conformity with current popular usage and common administrative jargon, the terms *assistance with family planning* and *family planning services* are used interchangeably in this article with *assistance with child spacing and family limitation* and the somewhat narrower *contraceptive assistance* and *birth control*. Since the major changes have occurred so far in the area of conception control, the other important components of family planning, such as sterility treatment, "interconceptual care" adoption services, and premarital counseling will not be dealt with here. The views expressed in this article are entirely the author's and should not be attributed to the Council on Family Planning.

2. *Family Planning: Nationwide Opportunities for Action* (U.S. Department of Health, Education, and Welfare, Washington, D.C., 1968).

3. *Five Million Women: Who's Who Among Americans in Need of Subsidized Family Planning Services* (Planned Parenthood–World Population, New York, 1967).

4. See *Family Planning . . .*; and Johan W. Eliot and others, "Family Planning Activities of Official Health and Welfare Agencies, United States, 1966," *American Journal of Public Health and the Nation's Health*, 58:700–12 (April, 1968).

5. See *For Caseworkers: Experience in Counseling Birth Control* (Planned Parenthood of Colorado, Denver, Colorado, 1965); Hannah D. Mitchell, "How Do I Talk? — Family Planning," *American Journal of Public Health and the Nation's Health*, 56:738–41, (May, 1966); and Naomi Thomas Gray, "Family Planning and Social Welfare's Responsibility," *Social Casework*, 47:487–93 (October, 1966).

6. *Five Million Women . . .*

7. Hazel Ann Hutcheson and Nicholas H. Wright, "Georgia's Family Planning Program," *American Journal of Nursing*, 68:332–35 (February, 1968).

8. See Stewart B. Gross, Wilma Johnson, Laura Anderson, and James C. Malcolm, "The Alameda County Health Department Family Planning Program," *American Journal of Public Health and the Nation's Health*, 56:34–39 (Supplement to January, 1966), report of a demonstration project specifically directed to newcomers.

9. Population Crisis Committee, National Institute of Mental Health, *Family Planning and Mental Health*, summary of discussions held at National Institutes of

Health, January 13, 1966 (Population Crisis Committee, Washington, D.C., 1966); Ames Fischer, "Community Psychiatry and the Population Explosion," *California Medicine*, 106:189–95 (March 1967); and Harriet Hills Stinson, "Family Planning Workers Ought To Be in Jail," *The Family Planner*, 2 (January, 1969).

10. See Frederick S. Jaffe, "Family Planning and the Medical Assistance Program," *Medical Care*, 6:69–77 (January-February, 1968) for a report of the implications of restrictive state plans for medical care as they affect access to family planning services.

11. Jane Castor and Pamela Sue Hudson, "Social Workers and Fertility Regulation: Involvement or Non-Involvement?" *New Perspectives: The Berkeley Journal of Social Welfare*, 2:35–44 (Spring, 1968).

12. Mary Smith, "Birth Control and the Negro Woman," *Ebony*, 23:29ff. (March, 1968). Among other revealing examples of suspicion and misinformation, this article tells about the belief that there are two kinds of contraceptive pills — one for white women and one for Negro women. The latter is believed to produce sterility.

13. See Frederick S. Jaffe and Steven Polgar, *Medical Indications for Fertility Control* (Planned Parenthood–World Population, New York, 1963, mimeographed); and William B. Neser and Grace B. Sudderth, "Genetics and Casework," *Social Casework*, 46:22–25 (January, 1965).

14. See Jesse W. Johnson, discussant, "The Client — Reaching and Keeping," in *Public Family Planning Clinics* (G.D. Searle & Son., San Francisco, 1967), 23–24; and Dorothy N. Kirk, "A Family Planning Clinic on Wheels," *Nursing Outlook*, 15:36–38 (December, 1967).

15. Richard E. Gordon and Katherine K. Gordon, "Factors in Postpartum Emotional Adjustment," paper presented at the 44th annual meeting of the American Orthopsychiatric Association, digested in *American Journal of Orthopsychiatry*, 37:359–60 (March, 1967), report of interesting attempts to predict emotional and other difficulties after birth from information and observation obtained in prenatal contacts with a group of middle-class patients seen in private practice. It would seem that a predictive instrument of this sort would be of even greater value for nonprivate patients or for patients from a poor home environment.

- 16. See David M. Kaplan, "Observations on Crisis Theory and Practice" *Social Casework*, 49:151–55 (March, 1968).

17. Mignon Sauber, "The Role of the Unmarried Father," *Welfare in Review*, 4:15–18 (November, 1966); and Hallowell Pope, "Unwed Mothers and Their Sex Partners," *Journal of Marriage and the Family*, 29:555–67 (August, 1967).

18. Mattie K. Wright, "Comprehensive Services for Adolescent Unwed Mothers," *Children*, 13:170–76 (September/October, 1966); and Philip M. Sarrel and Clarence D. Davis, "The Young Unwed Primipara," *American Journal of Obstetrics & Gynecology*, 95:722–25 (July 1, 1966).

19. One of the incidental benefits derived from such a comprehensive approach should be the reduction of the intense and often patently unhealthy interaction between the young mother and her growing child. Too often, without the opening up of alternative opportunities, the persisting strains of precocious maturity, uncertain male support, dependency, and loneliness tend to be poured out on the only available object. Such situations will probably be encountered with increasing frequency. They offer challenges that are more closely related to the classic conflicts of small middle class families than the never ending needs of the rapidly expanding AFDC families.

20. Leon Gordis and others, "Adolescent Pregnancy: A Hospital-Based Program for Primary Prevention," *American Journal of Public Health and the Nation's Health*, 58:849–58 (May, 1968).

Services and Programs in Early Childhood Education

LILIAN OXTOBY and PAULA L. ZAJAN

One of the most important decisions that an individual must make in his life is his choice of vocation. For those who are sure of their interests and skills, it may be a relatively simple task but for others it may take years of soul searching and experimenting until they find their niche.

Aside from the obvious economic factors, choices depend in large part on the feelings and attitudes of people. There are those who enjoy working individually or in situations that demand attention to detail or working with one's hands. Others prefer the type of work that brings them into daily contact with people. Such persons may also be highly motivated to serve others in the helping professions such as nursing, dentistry, education, social work, etc. Frequently, societal factors influence an individual's choice of vocation because of sexual, religious, racial and ethnic discriminations or even geographical location.

The desire to contribute to society, to change and improve the quality of life and derive a sense of satisfaction from one's chosen work, are goals with which adults can identify. Working with young children may have great appeal, but the reasons for selection of this profession are many and varied.

The purpose of this reading is to provide the student who is considering entering the field of early childhood education with a general understanding of the principles and practices of working with young children.

Why Work with Young Children?

If you were to make a survey of adults who work with young children as to why they chose this profession, you would hear a wide variety of answers. Some would say that young children are loving and fun to be with. They would tell you that the work is interesting; the hours short; the pay adequate; the benefits good; and that they derive a feeling of great satisfaction from working with children and their parents. Others would point to the respect and status they attain in their community, while others enjoy their role as surrogate parents.

While all of these reasons may be valid, nevertheless, the education of young children has many more implications. Being in contact with young children requires certain bodies of knowledge, training and a genuine commitment.

Who Works with Young Children?

- Are you a giving individual who genuinely likes other people . . . little people? . . . big people?
- Are you someone with a sense of humor . . . someone who can laugh with others and at oneself?
- Are you someone in good health who has the ability to get through a busy day working with children who are constantly on the move and full of energy and high spirits?
- Are you someone who is aware of one's own limitations and shortcomings and moods? Are you able to recognize your own varying moods such as fatigue, depression and joy? Can you accept behavior that is different from that which you are accustomed to?
- Are you someone who is flexible and open to change? Are you able to act spontaneously when the occasion calls for it or are you locked into a rigid pattern or point of view? Are you able to accept ideas and ways of working other than your own?

- Are you someone who is able to accept criticism? Are you able to take suggestions from supervisors, colleagues and parents?
- Are you some one who is firm but flexible in ideas? Are you someone willing to stand by your principles but willing to explore new ideas and approaches?
- Are you someone who accepts the idea that parents can and should be actively involved in their children's school experiences?
- Are you someone who sees himself/herself as part of a team of adults who are working together. This team might include immediate supervisors, other teachers, main tenance workers, kitchen staff, office workers, staff members as well as those who provide the auxiliary services such as the doctor, nurse, social worker, guidance counselor and psychologist.
- Are you someone who is able to accept the confidences and intimate knowledge of children and their families without disclosing these details to colleagues, friends and people in the community?

What Are the Requirements to Work with Young Children?

In many communities throughout the U.S. it is possible to obtain employment to work with young children, without any specified education or training, all that may be required is a person who is of good health and character.

In other communities, requirements may be very specific with state education certification as the ultimate goal.

One of the advantages of working with young children is that one can enter the profession with a minimum of training and then proceed with additional education and experience to higher levels of responsibilities.

What then are the specific jobs that would be available?

At the entry level, individuals who work with young children are frequently given the title of *Teacher Aide*. All that may be required for such positions is an elementary education and a minimum age of

18 years. Even such minimal requirements may vary from community to community and depend in large part on the need for people to fill such positions. Usually Teachers Aides are encouraged to further their education so they can enhance their performance level. Such additional education and training may be obtained in various ways. If the center is part of a larger agency, on-site or local in-service training may be provided. In many areas two-year or community colleges will provide early childhood education programs that will grant associate degrees.

Once the individual has received some training, or in lieu of training several years of experience, the next step on the career ladder would be that of Teacher Assistant. There are many names given to this level of teaching positions. In some communities they will be called Assistant Teacher or Educational Associates or Child Development Associate. Those Early Childhood Education Programs that have a large staff frequently employ workers at various job levels, the terms used for all these categories of workers are paraprofessional, auxiliary worker, the nonprofessional and the indigenous worker.

The next step on the career ladder would be the Certified Teacher. Although requirements vary from State to State, certification usually implies a Baccalaureate degree with a specialization in Early Childhood Education or Elementary Education. Persons with these are able to work as leaders of a classroom team, or perhaps will consider allied areas.

Many persons who are interested in working with children who are mentally or physically disabled, find that, for them, it is important to have a thorough grounding in the growth and development of the typical child before doing specialized work with the atypical child. Many students become interested in supervision and administration of an Early Childhood setting. In order to attain this level of endeavor one should have an excellent background in child development, human relations; curriculum development as well as several years of working with young children. For the students who become interested in speech and physical therapy there is advanced training available in these areas. For the students who are interested in working with the families of young children, there are positions as Parent Counselors and Social Workers. For those who become interested in the psychological aspects, there is the possibility of graduate work in Child Psychology.

If an individual possesses all the characteristics mentioned above why then is it necessary to have additional schooling and why do some states maintain such stringent requirements?

Many people have the misguided notion that working with young children requires little in the way of knowledge, skills and techniques. They believe that early childhood programs should provide healthy and safe custodial care and emphasize good social experiences. While these characteristics are basic to every good early childhood program, research and study in the field of Early Childhood Education has shown that early learning experiences can enhance and in many instances compensate for the limitations that young children may encounter in growing up in today's world.

For the past forty years physical and social scientists have been actively involved in research dealing with young children. They have examined the physical, emotional, social and intellectual growth and development of the young child. They have studied the cultural and environmental effects of living in a highly complex society and how these factors have influenced growth and learning patterns. As these various disciplines contributed more and more to what was already known of child growth and development, the ways in which we worked with children was influenced and changed.

Since World War II many changes have occurred which have greatly affected the number and type of early childhood programs as well as the philosophies that underlined them. Such influences as the post war baby boom and the information explosion which resulted from the launching of the Soviet Union's first manmade satellite had a direct relationship on how a larger segment of the population came to view the education of the young child. In the first instance, early childhood programs continued to flourish and proliferate. What had been a wartime measure to provide child care for working mothers now became an accepted and needed institution practice for mothers who continued to work. In the second, the competition and motivation to produce a more scientifically and technologically trained populace encouraged scientists and scholars such as Robert Karplus and Patrick Suppes to turn their attention toward the elementary schools and such ways to teach the basic principles of their disciplines to young children.

(1) Jerome Bruner, a social scientist from Harvard University, became interested in the general content of what children could learn. His hypothesis "that any subject can be taught effectively in

some intellectually honest form to any child at any stage of development" (2) sparked interest and change in the curriculum of many early childhood programs. Psychologists such as J. Mc Vicker Hunt questioned the theories of fixed intelligence and predetermined development. (3) And Benjamin Bloom on the strength of his research stated that intelligence is a developmental concept, just as height, weight or strength. (4) Another greatly renowned psychologist, Jean Piaget, contributed a vast amount of factual information related to children's cognitive development. Teachers and those who work with young children must be aware and knowledgeable of the changes and trends as new ideas and information are brought to light. Just as the doctor or dentist continues to study, read journals and attend conferences, so does the concerned and truly professional early childhood teacher.

While many students are familiar with the more usual kinds of early childhood programs such as the kindergarten or day care center, there now exists a wide variety of early learning opportunities for children.

The names of such programs may vary from community to community but generally speaking similarities are to be found in the various categories of programs. Differences exist with regard to funding, purpose of program, ages of the children who attend, and the length of time the children attend the programs. (see Table 1).

Some of the more familiar types of programs are described below. Although programs may vary from locality to locality there are still several distinct categories that commonly exist. It is important that the student become familiar with these types of programs for they represent opportunities for field experience and ultimate employment.

Types of Early Childhood Settings

Laboratory School   These schools were among the first of the nursery schools established in the United States during the early 1920s. They were primarily utilized for research relating to child development, teacher-training preparation and experimenting with new styles and methods of teaching.

TABLE 1. GENERAL DESCRIPTIONS OF CHILD CARE PROGRAMS,
AND TYPES OF FUNDING AVAILABLE

Funding:	Federal. State. Local: Tax levy or capital budget funds voluntary monies such as those donated by private agencies, e.g. the United Fund, Community Chest, Y's, settlement houses, etc. religiously oriented organizations such as churches and synagogues. Strictly private and profit making organizations.
Purpose of Program:	Custodial care. Social experiences. Cognitively oriented. Child development approach.
Ages of Children:	Infant. Toddler. Preschool. School-age.
Length of Time the Children May Attend:	24 hour shelter. 24 hour care. All day care (8:00 am – 6:00 pm). Part time care (morning and/or after- noons) from 2 or 3 days per week to 5 days per week. Informal play group.

Cooperative School   The Cooperative Schools are usually organized as non-profit by a group of parents in order to offset the cost of operating a school. The parents often times act as teacher, assistant teacher, kitchen staff and maintenance personnel. Some cooperatives employ a Director and Teachers but mandate that parents serve in some type of voluntary capacity at the school. Other cooperatives only hire either a Director or Teacher in order to comply with licensing requirements. The parents in this type of setting must serve as volunteer teachers, teacher aides, assistant teachers as well as office staff, kitchen and maintenance personnel.

Day Care "Day Care is a loose label for child care services outside the family. It can apply to evening as well as daytime services. It can apply to care in a home or in a center. It can mean minimal custodial care, or it can mean comprehensive, developmental care." (League of Women Voters.)

Family Care   The various kinds of Day Care include Family Day Care where a child is cared for in someone else's home while the parent must be away during the day.

Group Day Care   Where children are cared for in a group setting. In some communities the child's total needs are met which include the social, emotional, physical and intellectual development for the child's growth and development. In other communities, the child's physical needs are only looked after. This type of day care is often referred to as custodial care.

Half-Day Care   This is a service provided in many communities because of the change in family structure. Where at one time older relatives such as grandparents, aunts, cousins would care for a youngster, the reliance on this type of care has lessened because families have greater mobility and usually live too far a distance for this kind of care.

Drop-In Day Care   This is somewhat similar to half-day care. The distinction is that children do not attend on a regular basis, but only as need arises.

24-Hour Group Day Care   This provides facilities for families to place their children in a group setting where working hours differ from the usual day of 9:00 A.M. to 5:00 P.M.

Group Infant Care   Facilities for Group Care of Infants and Toddlers are being provided for children throughout the country. The criteria and requirements are similar to those mentioned in the paragraph for group day care.

Private Day Care   This type of group day care setting is usually owned and operated for profit individually or through a franchise arrangement.

Non-Profit Voluntary Programs   Usually these programs are non-profited and sponsored by groups such as churches, synagogues, settlement houses, and philanthropic organizations.

Play Group   Play groups are loosely organized groups where parents usually share their homes, take turns baby sitting, and provide play activities and socialization. Usually no tuition is charged. In some communities, these groups may be the Department of Parks, or some such group.

Head Start   This program was initiated as a component on the "War Against Poverty" during the summer of 1965. A federally funded and locally sponsored program in urban and rural communities which emphasizes a child development program with parent and community involvement. The purpose of the program was to insure the fact that young children who were economically poor would have the opportunity to catch up to children who were in a higher socio-economic bracket. Emphasis was placed on health, nutrition and language development. The program has continued on a year round basis since that time.

Public School   In most states, the public school system does provide Early Childhood Education experiences for children in the community. Five year olds may attend kindergarten for either half or full day sessions. In some communities, there may be opportunities for 4 year olds in the pre-kindergarten.

Shelters And Institutions   These are 24-hour institutions where children are placed temporarily or permanently when they are unable to be cared for by their families.

Industrial Day Care Centers   These centers are provided for the children of workers who are employed by a specific company. Parents bring the children to work with them, and are free to visit the children at specified times. Many companies provide these services because they alleviate absenteeism and improve the morale of their employees.

The study of early childhood education provides many alternatives for students who are interested in working with young children. The opportunities for advanced study as well as the possibilities of a career with varied options are inherent in this profession. In addition, young men and women who expect to raise their own families will find that knowledge of young children and how they grow and develop will assist them in the important job of being parents.

Bibliography

Braun, Samuel J. and Ester P. Edwards. *History and Theory of Early Childhood Education*. Worthington, Ohio: Charles A. Jones Publishing Co., 1972.

Bruner, Jerome S. *Toward a Theory of Instruction*. New York, N.Y.: W.W. Norton and Company, Inc., 1968.

Cohen, Dorothy H. and Virginia Stern. *Observing and Recording the Behavior of Young Children*. New York, N.Y.: Teachers College Press, 1978.

Hildebrand, Verna. *Introduction to Early Childhood Education*. New York, N.Y.: Macmillan Publishing Company, Inc., 2nd. edition, 1976.

Lindberg, Lucille and Rita Swedlow. *Early Childhood Education: A Guide for Observation and Participation*. Rockleigh, New Jersey: Longwood Division, Allyn and Bacon, Inc., 1976.

Persky, Barry and Leonard Golubchic, (editors). *Early Childhood Education*. Wayne, New Jersey: Avery Publishing Group, Inc., 1977.

Read, Katherine H. *The Nursery School*. Philadelphia, Pennsylvania: W.B. Saunders, 6th. edition, 1976.

Robison, Helen S. *Exploring Teaching in Early Childhood Education*. Rockleigh, New Jersey: Longwood Division, Allyn and Bacon, Inc., 1977.

Spodek, Bernard. *Teaching in the Early Years*. Englewood Cliffs, New Jersey: Prentice-Hall, Inc., 1978.

Todd, Virginia E. and Helen Heffernan. *The Years Before School*. New York, N.Y.: Macmillan Publishing Co. Inc., 3rd. Edition, 1977.

Wadsworth, Barry J. *Piaget for the Classroom Teacher*. New York, N.Y.: Longman, Inc., 1978.

How to Look at Day-Care Programs

PAMELA ROBY

Over recent years child-care and child-development services have been proposed as a means to achieve six primary, partially overlapping, often conflicting purposes or goals. These objectives, which often are seen in two or three different perspectives, are:

1. Child Development
   a. To fulfill children's right to develop to their full potential during their early years by providing them
      — with an opportunity to enjoy stimulating group experiences,
      — with the opportunity to interact with mothers who are relaxed and fulfilled because they may define how much time they spend with their children and how much time they spend pursuing interests other than their children,
      — with opportunities for intellectual stimulation to enhance children's conceptual development and to increase their awareness of their community.
   b. To provide the nation with physically and mentally healthy future citizens by providing children with nutrition, health care, and intellectual stimulation.
2. Social Services
   a. To provide the proper developmental environment

that will meet the special needs of handicapped
children.
  b. To ameliorate the situation of neglected and abused
children.
  c. To help troubled families remain intact by
      — sharing with parents the responsibility of care for
        their children,
      — by helping parents better understand their
        children,
      — by linking parents with available social services.
3. Women's Rights
  a. To provide a necessary, although not sufficient,
      condition for women to have full opportunity to
      participate in America's economic, political, and
      cultural life.
4. Reduction of Inequality
  a. To provide to all young children health care,
      nutritious meals, toys, recreation, and education, paid
      for on a sliding scale with the price of care rising with
      family income.
  b. To provide a catalyst for the economic development of
      total communities through community participation
      and control in the construction, provision of materials,
      maintenance, and administration of child-
      development centers.
5. Income Maintenance
  a. To free mothers receiving welfare for work training
      that will make them self-sufficient, and to enable
      families struggling to remain off welfare to do so
      through the provision of services.
  b. To provide well-paying training and jobs within child
      care for members of the community.
6. Female Participation in the Labor Force
  a. To maximize females' contribution to the labor force
      during the years when they have young children.
  b. To enable women to maintain and further their
      knowledge and skills during their early childrearing
      years, so that in their postchildrearing years their
      contribution to the labor force will not be diminished.

Wherever and whenever child care is discussed, one finds that not only do numerous issues revolve around each of the goals enumerated above, but also the goals themselves are at issue.

Eligibility   Who, for example, are to be the recipients of child-development services? Is child care only for low-income children, working mothers' children, four and five year olds but not toddlers and infants? Or is it to be for everyone who wants it? Today child care is available to only a tiny fraction of our children. What should our short-range and long-range goals be for the inclusion of our preschool children in child-development services?

Advocates of child-development services for children from *all* income groups and social categories argue on behalf of both low-income and middle-income children. James Hymes, a noted early childhood educator, points to the benefits that *all* young children derive from good group experiences with other young children. Constantina Rothschild, director of the Wayne State University Family Research Center, reports that young children and their mothers are far more isolated in America than in other societies today or in past cultures. She recommends that women of all income classes be freed from twenty-four-hour mothering so that they may become more relaxed, fulfilled mothers and human beings.

Others have argued that since our national resources are limited, we should concentrate what funds we have on low-income children and other special groups. Congresswoman Shirley Chisholm has replied to this argument, stating, "Our funds aren't limited. . . . We scrimp on programs for people because we choose to spend our money on tanks, guns, missiles and bombs."

Still others have also argued on behalf of low-income children that if middle-income children, whose parents have greater political resources than low-income families, are not included in child-development services, the programs will soon be thwarted by inadequate funding. Speaking for middle-income mothers, on the other hand, Sheila Cole has noted that "the discussion within the government of day care both as a way of 'breaking the cycle of poverty' and as a way to get women off welfare roles has inevitably raised the question with many women who do not claim to be poor: why not us too?[1] Other middle-income women press for federally supported child care for all so that their children may grow up in a socioeconomically integrated setting. "One thing children *do not* need is to grow up in a sterile, homogeneous environment," Vicki Lathom of the National Organization for Women has declared.

Although many argue that universal child-development programs are more likely than selective programs to better the lot of low-income children, others maintain that without explicit attempts to help the poor, children of the well-to-do are more likely to enroll in and benefit from the programs than are children of the disadvantaged. A means test is the most efficient way to direct limited resources to children most in need. Some who argue for universal programs as an eventual goal support selective programs for the near future. They maintain that with or without limited funds it is impossible to develop suitable facilities and to train the staff for millions of children within a two- or three-year period. However, the creation during World War II, within a twenty-four-month period filled with wartime pressures, of nurseries and child-care centers enrolling over one and a half million American youngsters suggests that the task, although difficult, is not impossible. Today, unlike during World War II, many unemployed construction workers, teachers, women experienced from mothering their own children, and teen-agers eager to find some purpose for their lives stand ready to build and run children's centers. Those who need training will have the opportunity to receive it on the job, where early childhood growth and development can be observed firsthand.

A final group that believes that public provision of child care should be limited to "welfare children" consists of persons who view child care primarily as a means for mothers to work and families to get off welfare rolls. Whether the income maintenance goal should be primary is discussed in greater detail below.

Discussions concerning eligibility are not limited to the question of family income. The age at which children should be admitted to the centers and the hours that the centers should be open (which indirectly affects eligibility) are also heatedly debated issues. John Bowlby's findings about the effects of institutional care and maternal deprivation on infants and young children greatly discouraged the development of children and infant centers in the United States as well as in England and Wales during the 1950s and much of the 1960s. Recently studies have shown that, indeed, two year olds who are placed in residential nurseries where they were separated from their parents from a few weeks to six months—

institutions such as those Bowlby studied—do cry more, get sick more often, regress in speech and toilet training, and become more hostile. *But* those who are placed in institutional settings *part*-day every day and reunited with their parents every evening appeared to behave normally and not to suffer any of the effects that policy makers generalizing from Bowlby's orphanage studies had expected.

Paying For Child Care Who is to pay for child care? Is it to be "free" for all who wish it, that is, supported through taxes? Is it to be "free" only for the poor and other selected groups, or is it to be provided on a sliding scale with the price of care rising with family income? These questions are related to the issue of eligibility discussed above but are discussed separately, for they will remain issues after child-development services are made available to all. If middle-income families are to be eligible for services, are they to pay the full cost of the services, receive them on a subsidized basis, or obtain them free of charge?

Advocates of child care that is free for all argue on behalf of both middle-income and low-income families. Vicki Lathom, a member of the National Organization of Women, has testified to the difficulty middle-income families experience in finding adequate child care that they can afford. The National Women's Political Caucus has noted in addition that "the high cost of day-care services" as well as "the lack of day-care facilities has forced many women onto the welfare roles."

Persons speaking on behalf of low-income groups argue that means tests, which would be required if the cost of child care were to be contingent on family income, affront human dignity and that their stigmatizing effects may discourage many persons who qualify for services from using them. On the other hand, the Black Child Development Institute and others have argued that means-tested child care is better than inadequately funded child care. They urge that sliding fees for economically advantaged children be considered unless the legislature provides funds for quality child-development programs for all.

Governing The creation of nationwide child-development services necessitates the creation of a coordinating apparatus (if not a bureaucratic monster), thus raising the issues of finance and power. Regardless of the setting, one soon finds that the issue of how much can we afford serves to disguise the question of how much do we actually *wish* to spend on young children instead of on highways, defense, and other national priorities. Very often as well it acts as a diversion from the more basic question—who controls day-care facilities once we have them? Who is to decide the nature of the influence they are to have upon the children in them? Parents? The community? Professionals? State or city politicians?

Issues about government span two major concerns: (1) what should be the role of parents and local communities in policy making; and (2) how should the federal government coordinate and disburse funds to federally funded child-care programs.

Minority group representatives, city politicians, feminist organizations, and political coalitions formed for community control of schools all want child-care programs to be locally controlled. But what *is* local control?

Minority representatives and radical groups demand that they set policy for centers in areas where they are a majority. Every large city of the nation has Black, Puerto Rican, or Chicano ghetto communities. Residents of these communities wish to make their own policies concerning child-development services for their children. If the boundaries for "local" control of child care are drawn in line with city, SMSA, or county boundaries rather than along the lines of smaller "communities of interest," including those of ghettos, ghetto residents will again be without a voice in decisions significantly affecting their lives. The nation does not have one set of social values or one life style. It has many. Local control at the community level where persons share somewhat similar values is the only way to avoid one group being oppressed by another. Black and other minority people have learned that institutions nominally serving them but controlled by the white majority *may* serve the needs of whites but do *not* serve their needs.

Issues concerning parent control resemble those of local control. At the 1970 White House Conference on Children and Youth the Task Force on Delivery of Developmental Child-Care Services recommended that parents should control programs whenever feasible and that at least one-half of the places on the governing boards of publicly funded programs should go to parents. Others, believing that parent control is the best mechanism through which to ensure quality programs, recommend that parents or parents and community residents make up the entire board. What are these boards to do? What is "community" and "parent involvement" to mean?

The Delivery Task Force of the White House Conference recommended that "parents of enrolled children must control the program at least by having the power to hire and fire the director and by being consulted on other positions," and that "parents and local communities must also control local distribution of funds and community planning and coordination . . . and play a role in the flexible administration of standards, licensing and monitoring" of programs. Boards were not to be advisory but policy-making bodies.

Opposing advocates of parent and community control are not only spokesmen for professional interests but also persons concerned with racial and class integration, administration, redistribution, political feasibility, and maximum utilization of the state's inputs into child care. Community control, many liberals fear, spells the end of racial and class integration. Integration, they maintain, is a prerequisite for the children of the poor to learn the language, manners, and life style required to enter the mainstream of the American economy. Many minority and ghetto community representatives answer this argument by saying that the economy and social system must adapt to their needs, values, and culture; that it must allow them to be successful on their own terms. For example, Ruth Turner Perot, organizer and former director of the Black Child Development Institute, states:

> What we have to recognize in America is that, one, black vitality and creativity cannot be nurtured in white institutions. Two, we must make it possible for institutions to develop in which blacks can search for their own routes to liberation. And, three, it is only on this basis that effective partnerships can be made with others.

Finally, related to the issue of local control, is the whole question of states' roles in the delivery of child-care services. States are already considerably involved in early childhood programs and their interest is growing. State governments now contribute sizable funds to kindergartens and child care.

On the other hand, the Black Child Development Institute and groups representing minority people strongly oppose state involvement in the administration of federally funded child-development programs. While minority representation at the state level is scanty in most states and directly opposed in other states such as Mississippi, *local* control enables minority groups to set policy in areas where they live. Both those who feel positively and those who feel negatively about the states' role in early childhood programs agree that state politicians have significant strength and that established state early childhood bureaucracies, like any bureaucracy, will be difficult to dissolve, ignore, or prevent from growing.

Staff   Closely related to the question of governing is the question of who will work in the newly created day-care agencies? The issues revolving around the staffing of centers can be summarized, if not solved, fairly easily. What characteristics are child-care workers to have? Are they to meet specific professional standards? If so, what? Are they to reflect the ethnic and racial characteristics of the population? If so, how is this representation to be obtained?

On one side professionals and their respective associations urge that all federally supported child-development centers have "adequately trained professional staffs" and that institutions of higher education develop preparatory programs and "encourage individuals to pursue degrees in early childhood education." These professionals generally believe that relatively untrained paid paraprofessionals or volunteers and a career hierarchy are useful concepts. But they emphasize the need for paraprofessionals to work toward professionalization and for all child-development center staffs to include persons certified with at least a B.A., and preferably an M.A. in early childhood education.

Minority and feminist representatives stand on the other side of the question. They maintain that whatever the merits of credentials, the attainment of a racially and sexually balanced staff is a more important consideration. The Black Child Development Institute urges that priority be given to the hiring of community residents and that at the minimum the racial and ethnic composition of the staff should reflect the specific geographic area served.

The National Organization of Women and other feminist groups seek policy provisions ensuring equitable employment of women and men in the child-care field. This requires more men relating to children in the preschool setting as well as more women participating in administration of the overall program. Men must be a part of preschool staffs, they argue, for children to avoid developing at a young age the sex-role stereotype that child care is a woman's job.

Custodial Care or Comprehensive Child-Development Services What is comprehensive child development? Child-development programs are most often contrasted with custodial child care. Developmental programs address the total needs of the child—physical, social, emotional, and intellectual—and of his family to enable him to realize his fullest potential. They have a small child-staff ratio, parent involvement, well-trained and well-paid personnel, and good facilities. Custodial programs, on the other hand, purport to give children good care but have no special developmental or educational component. In practice children do learn when they are in good custodial care, and many programs that purport to be developmental are nothing more than good babysitting operations with a few minutes of "educational games" thrown in.

In policy discussions concerning child care, the term " child-development programs" has come to stand for higher quality child care and "custodial care" for lower quality care. In addition to parent and community control discussed above, "quality" has been measured primarily in terms of the staff-child ratio, with the rationale that if at the very minimum we seek child care that is equivalent to good home care, we must take into consideration that most homes have fewer than four children per adult.

And, of course, to expect child-development programs to equalize existing social inequities (as Head Start was expected to do) would not only be misleading but harmful to low-income groups. The provision of eight or nine hours of good developmental child care plus good health care and nutrition will *not* give children of the poor a "head start" or even an equal start in life. For equal opportunity to be a reality in this nation, children must begin with equal conditions. But comprehensive child-development programs can grant a significant and sometimes even crucial bit of sunshine to children whose parents are burdened by bad health caused by lack of medical attention; whose own health is not what it should be because as infants they did not have the checkups and shots that are taken for granted for middle-class babies; whose psychological and emotional stability is shattered by fears of rat attacks or by their parents' constant worries about basic finances and the junkie down the street.

Income Maintenance and Community Development The Nixon administration's primary reason for including child care in its

Family Assistance Plan is to reduce welfare rolls by enabling welfare mothers to become self-sufficient.[2] Work is primary; child care is secondary. The wording of the plan as well as administrative discussions regarding it have provoked intense concern among many that the legislation when eventually implemented will force low-income mothers to work and their children to attend child-care centers and will provide child-care facilities of very low quality as a result of inadequate funding and the exclusion of parent and community participation in the governing of the child-care programs.

Although adequate child-care programs are unlikely to be provided under the Nixon income maintenance plan, good child-development programs *can* provide income maintenance and contribute to community development. The creation of child-development services does, after all, require hundreds of thousands of additional professional and paraprofessional child-care workers, cooks, administrators, maintenance workers, and construction workers as well as equipment for the centers. All of these can come from and bring money into low-income communities.

A good child-development program that is *also* a good income maintenance and community development program would, for the sake of the children involved, for the sake of the workers, and for the sake of community development, pay all its staff adequate salaries—something well above the minimum wage. It would, unlike most urban school systems and federal programs today, "buy Black," buy Puerto Rican, buy Chicano, and buy inner city. Not only its lower echelon personnel but also its middle and top level administrators in local, regional, and federal offices would—unlike those in the Office of Economic Opportunity, HEW, and Labor Department programs today—come primarily from low-income communities.

The program *would* provide many of today's poverty-level families with adequate incomes. It *would* serve as a catalyst for the economic and social revitalization of low-income communities. And it might begin to reduce the divisions and crime within this nation.

Although child-development services are unlikely to change national income distribution, they could be used directly to shift other resources from rich to poor. A federally sponsored program could provide *all* children with adequate nutrition, good health care, and stimulating educational experiences, as well as provide jobs for the many unemployed parents who wish to work, and it *could* be financed through a program of progressive taxation. The Comprehensive Child Development Program vetoed by Nixon might have redistributed resources and thereby reduced inequality, even if only ever so slightly. In addition to being highly unethical, the Welfare Reform Plan (H.R. 1), by requiring mothers to register for work in order to obtain monthly income benefits of approximately $200 (the proposed amount for a family of four), is likely to flood the low-wage market (where unemployment is already high) and thereby to further depress wages for both men and women and increase inequality. In the short run this policy would benefit employers and hurt workers. In the long run it is likely to hurt the entire nation by creating greater bitterness and division.

Although increased differentials between the wages of high and low paid groups can be almost guaranteed to result from the implementation of the Nixon administration's Welfare Reform Plan as currently constructed, increased inequality is not a necessary consequence of child care. Although the provision of child care and other social services by itself is unlikely to affect economic inequalities, income inequality *can* be reduced or increased by direct manipulation of the economy through taxation; wage supplements; income transfers (similar to veterans' benefits, welfare payments, and farm subsidies); government creation of good-paying jobs in child care, education, housing, construction, park renovation, and other areas where personnel are badly needed to improve general levels of well-being; and wage or profit freezes (the 1971 wage freeze severely affected the income of persons earning under $20,000 while barely touching those of persons in the over $100,000 income bracket). To reduce inequality through direct manipulation of income will require the political will to do so.

Conclusion The preschool years are nearly one-tenth of the average person's life. They are also the basis for an individual's development throughout the rest of life. Do we value these years and human life? Today we obviously value inequality, military aircraft, highways, and lunar landings more. Thousands of children of working mothers are currently left to care for themselves or are cared for by a sibling who is still a child. When we fully value children and spend our important dollars on them, when the political will to do that is strong—supported by mothers who want relief from the monotony of suburban housekeeping as well as by those mothers who need to work—we can then perhaps look forward to the guaranteed adequate housing, good health care, and decent and secure income we currently and somehow quite comfortably, despite our stated values, deny to the parents of our children and thereby (like it or not) to our children themselves.

Notes

1. Sheila Cole, "The Search for Truth about Day Care," *New York Times Magazine*, December 12, 1971.
2. Economist Gilbert Steiner doubts whether day care will reduce welfare costs. He points out that 43 percent of mothers currently receiving welfare have less than a ninth-grade education. This group will require extensive training leading to high training and day-care bills.

Battered Children

SERAPIO R. ZALBA

In 1962 a group of doctors in Denver wrote a landmark paper reporting on the "alarming number" of children being admitted to hospitals for traumatic injuries for which the parents could not provide plausible explanations.

One news story in a Cleveland paper, for example, reported that a court hearing had been set "to determine the cause of injuries suffered by an eight-month-old baby hospitalized for a month . . . with two broken arms, a broken left leg, a fingernail missing from his left hand and body scars. . . . The child's mother said he fell forward from an upholstered chair and that his arms apparently caught in the sides of the chair, policewomen reported."

Generally these children are in poor health, with unsatisfactory skin hygiene, multiple soft tissue injuries, deep bruises and malnutrition. An indication of the problem's gravity was provided by Dr. C. Henry Kempe, who cited one day in November 1961 when there were four battered children in Colorado General Hospital alone—two died of central nervous system traumas, and one was released to his home in satisfactory condition but subsequently died "suddenly" in an unexplained manner (a not unusual occurrence). A new term was coined to describe such situations: the "battered child syndrome."

Solving or even managing this problem is not easy. Despite evidence that serious physical assault on children is not rare, incidents are not generally brought to the attention of the

199

authorities. And the authorities have relatively few resources to turn to for help in ameliorating the problem.

To begin with, it is often difficult for agents of societal institutions—physicians, nurses, social workers, teachers, police, prosecutors, judges—as well as concerned relatives and neighbors—to decide when the line has been crossed between severe punishment and physical assault or abuse, even though the polar extremes are fairly clear: a mild spanking on the buttocks of a two-year-old child is quite different from the case of abuse that finds its way into a protective agency, where a child may have had scalding water poured on his genitals.

The most extreme cases probably end up in hospitals (when they don't end in the death of the child), especially since the younger children typically seen there are unable to defend themselves by running away from battering or abuse. Yet some studies of nonhospital cases reveal equally serious abuse. Edgar Merrill, an official of the Massachusetts Society for the Prevention of Cruelty to Children (SPCC), gives examples of the kind of cases seen at that agency:

☐ A five-year-old girl went onto her porch though told not to do so; she was kicked into the house, thrown across the room and hit on the face and head with a frying pan.

☐ A nine-month-old boy's eyes were blackened, his fingers, face and neck burned and his skull fractured by his father.

☐ A 13-month-old girl was X-rayed at the hospital; revealed were multiple skull fractures—some old, some new—and marked subdural hematoma.

☐ X rays on a seven-month-old boy showed healed fractures of one arm, the other one currently broken, healed fractures on both legs and multiple skull fractures.

The physical abuse of a child does not generally occur only once. In fact, in most of the cases in a study by Shirley Nurse the abuse had been going on for one to three years. Indeed, one of the medical indicators that physical injuries may have been inflicted rather than accidental is X-ray evidence of prior, often multiple, injuries, such as fractures of the limbs and skull.

In the hospital studies of Elizabeth Elmer and Helen Boardman, the children were very young, over half of them being under one year of age. There was a high mortality rate among them: in 12 of the 56 cases followed up (21 percent) the children died. Of the 46 homicides of infants and preadolescents in Lester Adelson's Cleveland study, 21 were under three years old. In contrast, in the private agency protective service studies reported by Harold Bryant and Edgar Merrill in Massachusetts and James Delsordo in Philadelphia, the children were older, with half of them (in a combined sample of over 260 children) under seven years old, and with no report made of any deaths. The abusers of children were usually their own parents with whom they were currently living—mothers and fathers were identified as the abusers in equal numbers of cases. While there was a great deal of marital and family conflict found in these cases, the non-abusive parent tended to protect the abusive one, supporting his or her denial of having assaulted the child. As a way of hiding the effects of their cruelty, many parents shopped around for medical care—one child under one year of age had been hospitalized three times in three different hospitals. The grim fact is, to quote Adelson: "It is relatively simple to destroy the life of a child in almost absolute secrecy without the necessity of taking any elaborate precautions to ensure the secrecy."

Characteristics of Abusive Parents In the child abuse cases I have seen or read about, the parents came from the complete range of socioeconomic classes. Many were middle class and self-supporting, with well-kept homes. All, however, could be characterized as highly impulsive, socially isolated and in serious difficulties, with their marriage, with money and so forth.

Irving Kaufman has taken a psychoanalytic view that the physical abuse of children implies a distortion of reality: the child as a target is perceived by the parent in a symbolic or delusional way; he stands for the psychotic portion of himself he wishes to destroy, his own abusive parent or the like. But the vast majority of abusive parents do not fall into any easy psychiatric categories, even though some of the most violent and abusive might be called schizophrenic. In Adelson's study, for example, 17 of the 41 murderers of children were patently mentally ill; that is, they had been hospitalized or had shown profound mental disturbance for some time before the eruption of violence.

The Massachusetts SPCC reported that in 50 percent of the 115 families they studied there was premarital conception. Other studies also point out the typicality of youthful marriages, unwanted pregnancies, illegitimacies and "forced" marriages. How much we can make of this is, however, questionable, since many, if not most, American families share one or another of these characteristics. More important, perhaps, is the finding that parents had themselves been abused and neglected as children. The epidemiological implications are, consequently, rather serious. While the 180 children in the Massachusetts study were generally normal physically, all of them were found to have a seriously impaired relationship with the abusive parent. These children tended to overreact to hostility, were depressive, hyperactive, destructive and fearful. The Philadelphia study characterized the children in their cases as bed wetting, truant, fire setters and withdrawn.

How Many Children Are Being Abused?   It is difficult to assess the number of children being physically abused or battered. For one thing, even the number of abuse cases that actually get reported is not known. For another, figures given by individual protective agencies or hospitals may be typical only for their geographic localities. Reported statistics on referrals to protective agencies generally include cases of both neglect and abuse; no definitive statement of how many of each are involved can be made. Eustace Chesser of England's National Society for the Prevention of Cruelty to Children concluded that between 6 and 7 percent of all children in England are at some time during their life "so neglected or ill-treated or become so maladjusted as to require the protection of community agencies." On the basis of a 1964 study in California, it would appear that a minimum of approximately 20,000 children were in need of protective services in that state alone. The American Public Welfare Association reported that in 1958 approximately 100 cases were referred monthly to the public welfare department in Denver, Colorado, for protective services. Elizabeth Barry Philbrook cited the figure of 250,000 children living outside their own homes in 1960. She indicated that one-third of the children had been moved to at least two or three different foster homes and that protective services were needed in those cases, implying that this would serve a preventive as well as restorative function.

David Gil's reports from a nationwide study on child abuse conducted by Brandeis University for the United States Children's Bureau demonstrate once again the difficulty of determining the actual incidence of child abuse. Gil found that approximately 6,000 cases were reported in 1967. But when a sample of people were asked if they personally know of cases of abuse, their reports, if extrapolated to the total population of the United States, would have indicated an incidence of from two to three million cases *annually*. Gil charges us to be careful in interpreting the findings; it was not possible to determine whether the abuse represented only a slap on the face or something more ominous.

Extrapolation on the basis of the data from California and Colorado produces a conservative estimate of between 200,000 and 250,000 children in the United States needing protective services each year, of which 30,000 to 37,500 may have been badly hurt.

How New Is Child Abuse? The basic problem of serious child abuse by parents and parent substitutes is not new. Indeed, as Elizabeth Elmer has pointed out, it is only comparatively recently that there has been any community consensus and sanction for recognizing and protecting the rights of children. In much of recorded history, infanticide, child abandonment, maiming as an aid in begging and the selling of children have been common rather than exceptional. It was common to flog children without provocation in colonial times in America in order to "break them of their willfulness" and make them tractable, ostensibly for the good of their souls. Not until the last half of the nineteenth century was the first Society for the Prevention of Cruelty to Children organized in the United States. And it came about as a result of New York City's infamous Mary Ellen case in 1866 which brought out that the American Society for the Prevention of Cruelty to *Animals* was the only agency willing and able to intervene to protect a child suffering from abuse.

As Norris Class points out, early workers in the field of child welfare proceeded on the assumption that physical abuse and neglect were associated almost exclusively with poverty, slums, ignorance, industrial exploitation and immigration. Physical mistreatment was quite open in these sectors, and it was not difficult to introduce admissible and dramatic evidence into the courts in the prosecution of abusive and neglectful parents. But as the conditions they associated with physical neglect and abuse abated, so did its visibility.

During America's intensive romance with psychoanalysis and dynamic psychiatry in the 1920s and 1930s the child welfare people became concerned more with emotional factors and treatment, and

greater emphasis was given to permissive, voluntarily sought services, with a consequent confusion about the role of authority and
legal sanctions in social services. Acceptable legal evidence of
emotional neglect or abuse was and still is more difficult to define or
produce than is its physical counterpart. Interest in protective
services declined, and the close working relationship between the
protective agency and the court deteriorated. On the positive side,
however, there was an increase in the public's awareness that
prosection of abusive and neglectful parents does not solve the
problems of the victimized children or their families. As the family
system came to be seen first as the diagnostic and eventually the
treatment unit of reference, we began to pay greater attention to the
possibility of treating the parents and attempting to maintain the
structural integrity of the family. In child welfare today we still face
the basic problem: at what point does the harm of leaving a child in
a poor home override the negative consequences of splintering the
family by use of foster homes or other placement facilities outside
the parental home?

An important factor in providing protective services, and an
important value in American society, has been the tradition of
parental rights regarding the rearing of children. The intervention
of the state in parent-child matters is for the most part invoked
reluctantly and carefully. When there is a reasonable question as to
parental adequacy, the tendency has been to rule in favor of the
parent. This may reflect a "folk wisdom" about the child's need for
enduring family ties; however, children are sometimes left in homes
that are neglectful and even dangerous.

The relatively recent interest in more aggressive (that is, reaching-
out) approaches in social work, greater clarification of the role of
authority and accumulated experience and knowledge in work with
those persons psychiatrically categorized as character-disordered
have brought us to the place where we are better able to consider
what we can or should do about the abuse of children.

The Child Abusers Who are the parents that abuse their
children? Are they "normal" people who have overreacted? Or are
they a clearly distinguishable group?

The picture that emerges in studies done in hospitals and
protective agencies is of a number of different types of abusers. One
grouping can be made of abusing parents with personality problems

that could be characterized in the following ways: patent psychosis, pervasive anger, depressive passive-aggressive personality and cold, compulsive disciplinarians.

A second grouping consists of parents who are impulsive but generally adequate, with marital conflicts or identity-role crises. In the first group we would expect to find a representative cross section of American families. Findings from a national study by David Gil, however, indicate there are more cases of child abuse among the socioeconomically disadvantaged, especially in broken homes and in large families. But if there is a significantly greater proportion of abuse cases among the disadvantaged populations, it is likely to consist of cases of the second type. The reporting of such cases, and the interventions of protective services with legal sanctions, does not necessarily reflect its pattern of incidence. Police, schools, hospitals and social agencies are more likely to intervene in the lives of lower income families than they would in the lives of the more affluent. Practitioners have not tended to agree with Gil. They do not think there is a social class difference in the incidence rate. They argue that the abused child in a more affluent family will probably be taken to a private physician who will, where necessary, make arrangements to hospitalize the child. The source of injury may not be reported. If the family is poor, the child would probably be taken to the emergency room of the hospital, where the staff is likely to complete a report of suspected abuse.

It is interesting to speculate on why we tend to turn our faces away from much of the child abuse that occurs around us. Kempe and others have pointed out that physicians, teachers, social workers, nurses and others in positions where they might identify cases of abuse are reluctant to do so. They wish to avoid court appearances. They prefer not to confront or estrange patient-families (or clients). And frequently they are less than certain that they are correct in their suspicions. Thus it becomes easy not to "notice" abusive behavior.

There is still another explanation for what appears to be widespread lack of awareness of incidents of child abuse. Is there any mother or father who has not been "provoked" almost to the breaking point by the crying, wheedling, whining child? How many parents have not had moments of concern and self-recrimination after having, in anger, hit their own child much harder than they had expected they would? How many such incidents make a "child abuser" out of a normal parent? There may be a tracit agreement among us not to meddle in each other's private matters unless it is simply impossible to ignore the behavior involved.

All 50 states have attempted to counteract our "know-nothing" tendencies by passing laws regarding the reporting of suspected child abuse: some states provide protection against claims of slander and other defamatory "injuries" against persons in certain professional categories (doctors, for example).

Another interesting speculation can be made on the societal level: why has our society provided so *little* protection for children?

Despite the historical trend toward increased children's rights and protection—the SPCC, child labor laws, the day care movement, Head Start and the *Gault* decision of the Supreme Court—it seems clear that the perception of children as property or chattels has strong roots in our society. Parental rights are still rated high on the scale of values.

Related to the issue of personal versus social control is the question about the extent to which our society is willing to invest in broad social welfare services. Our national willingness to invest heavily in public education in the past few years seems to have lost its impetus. Mental hygiene and correctional reform have likewise lost momentum. The progressive strides of the period starting with Franklin Roosevelt and ending with the first Johnson term of office have slowed almost to a standstill.

We do not seem willing to provide adequate protective services or institutional care for children in need of them. An example of our low priority for such services is the role and status of the child care worker which is quite different in the United States as compared to Scandinavian countries. In those countries the work has been professionalized through training programs that adequately prepare the worker—a preparation that is reflected in his relative income.

In the United States, in contrast, child care work is low status work. Little is invested in professional preparation or in in-service training. And the pay is typically quite poor. The result is that few child care institutions are able to provide the quality of care and treatment that is needed.

It seems obvious that protective services *in the community*— counseling and supervision of parents and children—are called for. But it is also clear that the level of investment in community protective services is also inadequate.

Why, then, is there not *more* child abuse? Major forces work against it: 1) our society stresses the desirability of youth, the "happiness" of childhood and the reliving—with desirable modifications—of our own childhoods through our children; 2) our standard of living has increased, which attenuates the stress of physical survival—one of the sources of family stress that can lead to child abuse; and 3) for better or worse, there is a higher level of screening and surveillance in our highly organized society, where increasing amounts of information about each of us are collected and recorded at schools, hospitals, banks, license bureaus and so forth.

What, then, is to be done about child abuse? We cannot wait for all men and women to become angels to their children. One sensible, concrete proposal has been made to offer preventive mental and social hygiene services at the most obvious points of stress in the family. One such point is reached when a child is born and introduced into the family. This may be especially true for the first child, when husband and wife must now take on the additional roles of father and mother. Assistance for men and women who seem under unusual strain because of this role change might lead to fewer incidents of child abuse.

More effective remedial efforts will await our willingness to spend greater sums of money on community-based health and welfare services. Protective services are understaffed for the number of cases requiring their help and surveillance. And the alternative child care resources—whether they are institutions or paid individual or group foster homes—require additional resources if they are to be adequate either in terms of the number of children they can handle or in the quality of personnel.

What will we do about this tragic problem, apart from venting our concern for the child, and our rage and disgust toward the abuser? We could try to develop a more sensitive social monitoring network for the early identification of possible abuse cases. But our past efforts in this direction have resulted in only a slight improvement in reporting cases, and these, predictably, came primarily from lower socioeconomic classes and from racial minority groups. We are still, rightly, reluctant to invade the privacy and sanctity of most people's homes. And with the increasing encroachments on our privacy through telephone taps and recording devices, one is reluctant to propose another opportunity for the informers, however "benign" their intentions might be.

There is another part to this terrible dilemma. Neither professionals nor nonprofessionals are likely to report suspected cases of abuse when it is doubtful that such cases will subsequently receive adequate and effective service. Only when they are convinced that involving themselves in these difficult situations will result in positive benefits for the child, and his abuser, will the average citizen be willing to risk reporting cases of suspected child abuse.

Battered Women and Their Assailants

BONNIE E. CARLSON

For centuries there have been battered women—or battered or abused wives—but only recently has their battering gained public attention as a social problem. In the past few years numerous professional and lay publications have begun to provide information about the problem in an attempt to educate the public about its causes and consequences, as well as to stimulate the provision of services for its victims. However, little systematic research has been conducted in this area, and the limited data collected tend not to be oriented toward service delivery. Before services can be provided both to the victims of domestic violence and their assailants, it is essential to understand the dynamics of the problem and what services the affected population needs.

Currently, many myths and misconceptions regarding domestic or conjugal violence exist among both the general public and the helping professionals who are likely to be confronted with domestic violence in their work.

As Schultz noted, the prevailing stereotypes regarding battered women are these:

1. They are basically sadomasochistic. That is, they enjoy being abused and have a need to be abused. Therefore the problem is difficult to eradicate since its roots lie deep in the victim's psyche.

2. They actually instigate the assaults through antagonistic

verbal behavior (for example, nagging, insults, and so on); if they would refrain from such verbal abuse, the battering would cease.

3. They are "very masculine, outspoken, domineering women" (castrating by implication) who "tend to exploit and profit from their husband's passiveness and dependency."[1]

These stereotypes tend to be based on personal observations and have not been investigated empirically in a systematic fashion. Schultz, for instance, based his observations on a sample of four persons. It is also important to note that the foregoing stereotypes clearly place the cause for the violence within the victim, a phenomenon recently called "blaming the victim."[2]

This article (1) provides information about a population of battered women and their assailants, (2) suggests likely causes of domestic violence, (3) tries to dispel misunderstanding about the problem, and (4) indicates connections between characteristics of the affected population, causes of the problem, and the resulting need for services. The situation has gone beyond the point where professionals in mental health and social service can continue to ignore the problem.

Selection of Sample

In April 1975 the Ann Arbor, Michigan, chapter of the National Organization for Women (NOW) developed a Wife Assault Task Force and began to collect information about local domestic violence in the hope of providing free services to abused women, using volunteers from the community. In January 1976 that hope was realized and the NOW Domestic Violence Project began to offer the following services to battered women: emergency housing, short-term peer counseling by volunteers, legal advice and referral, financial assistance, 24–hour crisis phone coverage, and referral to appropriate social service and mental health agencies. Over 260 victims and their children were served in an 18–month period. This figure is surprisingly high in view of the feminist affiliation of the project. It undoubtedly reflects the desperation of these clients and the inability of existing community resources to meet their need for service. The study reported in this article was based on the 101 cases in the NOW project for which information was most complete.

Limitations of the Data   The group of women interviewed in the study cannot be considered representative of all women who are physically abused by their husbands or other men with whom they have primary relationships. Rather, generalizations can only be made to a population of abused women who appeal for assistance to a volunteer nonprofessional women's organization. Substantial amounts of data are missing for certain variables, especially those pertaining to the assailants. When this is true, the number of cases on which the relevant statement is based is indicated. In addition, the data regarding assailants were collected from victims—some of whom were in a state of disequilibrium at the time of the interview—and thus cannot be considered completely valid and unbiased.

Findings

It is hoped that the findings of this study will contribute to the slight knowledge about domestic violence. In many cases the data support hypotheses set forth in the literature or corroborate previous research findings, and this suggests that the data of the study are reasonably valid.

Demographic Characteristics   The total sample consisted of 101 women who were victims of assault. These women were referred to the project from a wide range of sources: 32 percent by social service agencies, 20 percent by the criminal justice system (police, judges, legal aid societies, and so on), 10 percent by friends, 10 percent by the media, and the remainder by miscellaneous sources.
The majority (60 percent) were married at the time of the interview; 22 percent were separated or divorced from the assailant (dispelling the myth that merely moving away from the assailant will solve the problem), 13 percent were unmarried and living with assailant, and 5 percent were single and living apart from the assailant. Seventeen percent of the couples had been together less than one year; 28 percent, one to three years; 33 percent, four to ten years; and 22 percent, 11 or more years. Of the 75 couples for whom

information regarding their marital history was available, over half had previously been separated at least once.

An overwhelming majority of the women studied (86 percent) had children; the average number per respondent was 2.23, with only 4 women reporting 5 or more. Forty-five percent of these children were 5 years of age or less, 42 percent were 6 to 15 years of age, and 13 percent were 16 years of age or more. The women themselves were relatively young; 65 percent of them were between 21 and 30 years of age. Half the assailants fell into that age group. In general, the assailants were several years older than the respondents. The racial breakdown was as follows: victims, 72 percent white, 27 percent black, 1 percent Oriental; assailants, 63 percent white and 37 percent black. (Racial data unavailable for 11 assailants.) Of the couples for whom racial information was available, 10 percent consisted of a white woman and a black man, but there were none consisting of a black woman and a white man.

In terms of socioeconomic status, the data are revealing. One-third of the victims had not finished high school, while another 25 percent were high school graduates but had no further formal education; 34 percent had some college or vocational training; only 7 percent had graduated from college. A similar pattern existed among the 58 assailants about whom information was available: 33 percent were high school dropouts, 31 percent were high school graduates, 19 percent had some college training, and only 17 percent were college graduates.

It can be seen that the educational attainment of the assailants was quite low compared with that of the total male population in this age group in the United States, and looked at in the aggregate it appears that victims and assailants have approximately equal educational attainment. But the data are deceptive. They were analyzed by case because the literature indicated an inconsistency in status between victims and assailants, and a different pattern emerged.[3] It was discovered that although both victims and assailants tended to have little education, the woman had more education than her partner in 26 of the 58 couples for whom educational data were available (45 percent). In only 17 of these couples (29 percent) did the man's educational achievement surpass that of the woman. This is unusual, considering that the normative pattern is for men to have higher educational attainment on the average and within any one couple.

Employment data are equally revealing. Of the 43 percent of the victims employed outside the home, only three were employed in professional positions; the remainder worked in clerical, technical, or unskilled jobs. This is clearly reflected in the income data for victims: only seven respondents had independent annual incomes of $9,000 or more. The majority employed outside the home earned $6,000–$9,000 per year. Thirty-four percent earned less than $6,000 or were supported by Aid to Families with Dependent Children. Almost one-third of the assailants (29 percent) were unemployed. Of 64 who were employed, only 12 percent were professionals, whereas 36 percent did unskilled work, 38 percent held semi-skilled or technical jobs, and 14 percent were in business, sales, or miscellaneous jobs. The occupational distribution is again reflected in the income statistics: 63 percent earned less than $12,000 per year, with 37 percent earning less than $9,000; only 25 percent earned $15,000 or more. In summary, it can be seen that both victims and assailants, when they were employed, usually held low-status, low-skilled, low-paid jobs. This situation can be expected to bring about many problems because of difficulties in maintaining family income. Unfortunately, income data were available for only 46 assailants; it is not known how representative these data are.

Social Characteristics An equal proportion of victims and assailants (39 percent of each) had received some type of counseling prior to the incident that brought the victims to the NOW project; in 20 percent of those cases counseling had occurred in an inpatient setting. About one-third of the victims had observed violence between their own parents, while one-half of the assailants had observed such violence as children.

A marked disparity between victims and assailants is noted with respect to alcohol and drug abuse. Only a small proportion of the victims admitted to being substance abusers (alcohol, 10 percent; drugs, 5 percent), whereas the victims reported substance abuse to be much more prevalent among their assailants (alcohol, 60 percent; drugs, 21 percent). In addition, victims reported that 27 percent of 92 assailants were child abusers and that 44 percent of 73 assailants had criminal records. Admittedly, the validity of data reported by the victims is somewhat questionable, but these data suggest that the assailants constitute a far more deviant population than do the victims.

Incidence of Assault Seventy-one respondents provided information regarding the frequency of violence experienced during the past year. For 25 percent of the women, incidents of violence had occurred with their partners only once or twice. Half had been assaulted three to eight times, 14 percent had been assaulted monthly, and 11 percent more frequently than once per month. Victims reported that alcohol was involved in two-thirds of the incidents which brought them to the project, whereas drugs were involved in 12 percent of the cases. In one-half the incidents it was reported that a weapon was involved; 60 percent of the weapons were household objects (for example, a shoe, an electric sander, a hockey stick); 25 percent of the weapons were guns; 16 percent, knives. Half the respondents stated that at some point they had tried to defend themselves against the attacks. Of those who attempted self-defense, 77 percent reported that this increased the intensity of the attack; 21 percent, that it had no effect; and only 2 percent (one respondent), that it decreased the intensity. In almost half the cases the victim was hurt severely enough to require medical attention.

What are victims of domestic violence likely to do after an assault? Information about this is especially important for those contemplating intervention for battered women. Accordingly, respondents were asked what they had done after the most recent assault incident. Up to two responses were coded for each respondent. Results are reported in Table 1.

It can be seen from the table that victims appear to be largely concerned with their own protection immediately after the assault and that 36 percent relied mainly on the police to provide this protection. Only 4 percent sought assistance from social service or mental health agencies. Other than the police, battered women appear to rely mainly on informal networks for obtaining sympathy and assistance, or they do not seek help at all.

It is well known among those who work closely with the criminal justice system that the police spend a substantial portion of their time (up to half, according to Saunders), responding to what police officers call "domestics."[4] Given the amount of interaction occurring between battered women and police agencies, how do victims view the quality of police response? It would appear, as shown in Table 2, that the respondents in this sample viewed the response of the police at least somewhat favorably. Table 2 reveals that only 25 percent gave outright negative evaluations ("not

TABLE 1. ACTIONS TAKEN BY RESPONDENTS AFTER BEING ASSAULTED (N = 154)[a]

Action Taken	Percentage of Responses
Consulted police	36
Consulted women's group	16
Consulted friend	14
Consulted family member	12
No action taken	6
Consulted social service or mental health agency	4
Consulted religious adviser	2
Other	10

[a]Many respondents gave more than one answer, and up to two responses were coded for each respondent.

TABLE 2. POLICE RESPONSE TO DOMESTIC VIOLENCE AS PERCEIVED BY VICTIMS (N = 77)[a]

Type of Police Response	Percentage of Responses
Concerned and helpful	36
Not helpful at all	20
Provided protection	13
Referred elsewhere	13
Concerned, but not helpful	13
Hostile	4
Primarily concerned with own safety	1

[a]Up to two responses were coded for each of 57 respondents who stated they had called the police in the recent past in response to domestic violence.

helpful at all," "hostile," or "concerned primarily with own safety"). On the other hand, there is obviously room for improvement in the response of police.

Discovering the causes of domestic violence presents an intriguing problem. Table 3 provides some leads to those causes. If bad temper is ignored for the moment, the message comes across clearly—from the perceptions of victims themselves—that financial and interpersonal stresses lead to domestic violence. This differs markedly from the view that the causes of family violence are intraphysic and therefore primarily require strategies of psychotherapeutic intervention.

Further Observations

A number of important observations can be made about the sample that were not reflected in the data already described. These observations were made during the year the author spent working directly with victims and as a consultant to the project. First, the one trait that seemed to characterize all victims was their devastatingly low self-concept. A factor contributing to this was that many had never worked outside the home. The second striking characteristic was the degree of isolation that most of these women experienced. Many had virtually no close friends or relatives with whom to share the pain and fear in their lives; others

TABLE 3. CAUSES OF DOMESTIC ASSAULT AS PERCEIVED BY VICTIMS (N = 215)[a]

Causes	Percentage or Responses
Money	35
Jealousy	21
Bad temper	15
Sex	7
Children	5
Household care	4
Pregnancy	4
Assailant's job frustration	2
Other	6

[a]Up to three responses were coded for each respondent; the mean number of responses per respondent was 2.30.

had depleted such resources and had found that sisters, mothers, friends, and others no longer wanted to hear about their plight.

Another observation concerns the children who are reared in homes characterized by periodic violence between domestic partners. It is often said that both the victims and their assailants (who should also be viewed as victims—victims of their own past and of their socialization) frequently grew up in homes in which they themselves were beaten severely or in which they saw violence between their parents. The modeling effects of aggression and violence had been well documented by social learning theorists and developmental psychologists. It is known, for example, that one does not have to be rewarded directly for aggressive behavior to learn aggression as a problem-solving strategy. Simply observing aggressive behavior occur without punishment is sufficient for learning such behavior.[5] This clearly suggests that children growing up in violent homes, especially boys, are far more likely to learn such patterns of behavior and to use them when frustrated than are children who do not observe domestic violence in their homes.

The following personal anecdote illustrates the link between observing and performing acts of aggression and violence. The author worked with a client who had been badly beaten by her husband. The victim's 14-year-old son had come home in the middle of the most recent, although by no means the first, attack. The son (who, incidentally, was often beaten so badly by his father that he was covered with bruises) immediately began to defend his mother by attacking his father with a hockey stick. The parents subsequently separated and the home situation improved. But about a year later, whenever the mother disciplined the boy verbally, he would respond by attacking her physically—and this was the same son who had defended her against physical attacks by her husband.

Another observation relates to the victims' intense attachment to and concern for their children. Often this contributed to their fear of leaving the assailant and living independently. Many knew they did not have the education or the skills to support their families adequately on their own. Assailants fed into this fear by threatening to desert the family and not provide financial support and by threatening to prove that the victim was an unfit mother so the children would be removed from her custody. While the latter threat might not seem realistic to persons with education and an understanding of how the justice system works, it fed into such deep-seated fears of many victims that they reacted as if it were a realistic threat. As a result, it often deterred them from taking the necessary steps to escape from the situation.

Sources of Violence

This author subscribes to what may be called the social structural view of family violence.[6] Persons holding this view believe that the sources of violence do not lie inside the individual (that is, in mental illness) or in certain subcultures (for example, "the subculture of violence"); rather, they maintain that the sources of family violence are complex structural circumstances creating environmental stresses that are distributed unevenly across the social structure. Poverty is one such environmental stress, and the respondents in this study clearly identified it as a source of stress and resulting violence.

How is it that environmental stress—in particular, stress arising from economic pressures—can lead to violence in a setting that should be supportive and harmonious? A number of social scientists have suggested that the linkage is related to the social and economic resources of family members and to intrafamily roles.[7] As Steinmetz and Straus state:

> When the social system does not provide a family member with sufficient resources to maintain his or her position in the family, violence will tend to be used by those who can do so.[8]

It is obvious that learning—especially learning violence as a response to stress, anger, or frustration—also plays a critical role in the etiology of family violence.

The normative pattern in American families has been for the husband to play the dominant role with respect to decision-making, the allocation of resources, and so on. But to maintain this superior position, certain conditions must be met in the domain of status. Thus for the husband to be dominant, he should have superior talent (as illustrated, for example, by his occupation and educational attainment) and superior resources (income) vis-á-vis his spouse. What happens when the wife, the supposed subordinate, has certain resources or talents superior to those of her husband? The paradigm outlined above predicts violence under such circumstances if there is accompanying structural stress and a history of learned violence as a response to frustration.

Are data available to support such a paradigm? O'Brien studied a sample of 150 divorcing couples and found that 25 had admitted to a history of overt violence.[9] He found that the status of a much higher proportion of the 25 couples was inconsistent (for example, the wife's educational achievement was higher than her husband's) than that of the nonviolent divorcing couples in the remainder of the sample.

A similar pattern was found in the data of this study, although overall educational attainment among both victims and assailants was low. When the status inconsistencies in these data are combined with the existing high level of unemployment (almost one-third of those for whom data were available), the possibility of an explosive situation can be predicted. When legitimate resources are not available as a power base, then violence—the "ultimate resource"—may be the result.[10] These data suggest that it was often the result in this sample. The hypothesis "that male power is associated with violence when the husband is low in resources" is supported by these data.[11]

Alcoholism and Violence

The use of alcohol among the violent men described in this report has been little mentioned. Professionals and nonprofessionals across the country who have worked with battered women can attest to its prevalence. Many victims incorrectly identify alcohol abuse itself as the major problem. Alcohol abuse is, in fact, a symptom of structural stress and frustration, but it serves to exacerbate rather than alleviate the problem. Many battered women state that when their husbands or partners are not drinking, these men are able to function normally and fulfill their role responsibilities adequately (for example, the victims often say that the men are good fathers and providers). Many women have been beaten by their partners only when the men were inebriated. Thus it would appear that alcohol use is not the cause of domestic violence, but rather that alcohol breaks down inhibitions, allowing many men to injure a woman who would not normally do so because of strong normative inhibitions against such behavior.

Alcohol abuse has been recognized as a serious national concern. Substantial resources have been committed to resolving the problem and its consequences. One potential consequence of alcohol abuse is domestic violence. Given the high proportion of assailants who are said to have problems with alcohol, it might be concluded that men who are alcohol abusers comprise a high-risk population for domestic violence. If this is the case, one means of intervention on behalf of battered women might be through existing programs for treating alcoholism. In trying to help families resolve their conflicts before they become unmanageable, systematic inquiries might perhaps be made regarding family disagreements and how they are resolved.

Leaving the Assailants

It is often assumed that because the victims of domestic assault do not leave the situation, they must enjoy the battering or need to be treated in such a way. When this assumption is examined closely, it can be seen that nothing is further from the truth. In fact, much evidence suggests that physically leaving the situation may not even solve the problem. Many divorced women (22 percent of the women in this sample were divorced or separated) continue to be abused by husbands who actively seek them out. Furthermore, there are realistic reasons why abused women continue to remain in dangerous situations, some of which Gelles has suggested.[12]

Clear patterns were found in the decisions women made after having been assaulted. It was discovered that the more resources a women had (for example, a job), the more likely she was to seek outside intervention. The frequency and severity of the violence were other factors related to the seeking of outside intervention and the type of intervention sought. Severe and frequent attacks of violence were more likely to lead a women to seek outside help. Women who had been exposed to violence as children—either as observers or recipients—were more likely to remain in the abusive situation. It appears that exposure to family violence at a young age may serve to desensitize girls to its effects and may lead them to expect violent behavior in a marital situation. However, Gelles found that the best predictor of a divorce or separation obtained by an abused wife was the level of family violence in the current family situation.[13]

Few women in the sample sought assistance from local social service or mental health agencies. This may reflect the low socioeconomic status of the sample, but it seems more likely to be an accurate reflection of the fact that established agencies in most communities do not provide the services most needed by assaulted women: emergency housing, financial assistance, legal advocacy, and emotional support. And if these services cannot be provided quickly—in some cases immediately—they are of little use to this client population. Furthermore, such services cannot be effectively provided in an agency office on a one-hour-a-week basis. Victims of domestic violence, if they are to make the changes necessary to leave an abusive situation, require a great amount of time and support. However, help need not be provided solely by professional workers. Nonprofessionals can fill the role adequately as long as they receive sufficient training, do not try to make decisions for the client, and do not label the client as deviant. Victims who choose to stay in their situation and hope to improve it also need support. But if the assailant's environment, either external or internal, does not change in a meaningful way, the prognosis for the improvement of the victim's situation is not favorable.

One type of intervention that could be attempted would be to reduce the status inconsistency between victims and assailants by improving the men's potential to support their families.[14] This, however, would reinforce the status already ascribed to men in the family domain. Intervention—in addition to enhancing the opportunities of men to support their families—should also move toward helping women support themselves and their families, especially women who are rearing children as single parents. An effort in this direction can be seen in a bill recently introduced into Congress by Yvonne Braithwaite Burke titled the "Equal Opportunity for Displaced Homemakers Act." The bill would provide for job counseling, training, and placement, as well as the creation of jobs in both the public and private sectors of the economy, for middle-aged homemakers who depended on their husbands for support until confronted with divorce or widowhood.[15] Since such women have no marketable skills, their prospects for becoming self-supporting are slim. The focus of this congressional bill is on utilizing past skills and experiences rather than merely developing new skills. Former victims of domestic violence who lack formal training or skills are being used effectively across the country as peer counselors who assist other battered women. This illustrates how displaced homemakers could be used to help others as well as support themselves and their families.

Although improving both men's and women's ability to provide for their families is important, the roots of domestic violence go beyond financial insecurity. This can be inferred from the fact that some battered women come from homes in which financial resources are not a central problem.

As long as men believe that responding to stress and frustration with aggression or physical violence is acceptable behavior, the problem of the battered woman will continue to exist. Thus in addition to improving the ability of men and women to support themselves and their families, efforts should be made to eradicate the beliefs that (1) men's status must and should be higher than women's, (2) men who are not dominant and are not physically more powerful than women are in some way not masculine and not adequate, and (3) physical power and coercion are valid means of solving disputes in the family or in any other interpersonal relationships. Until these fundamental changes in attitude have become widely accepted, helping professionals must try to reach out to a victimized population too long ignored. They must recognize that battered women are not women who are mentally ill, but rather are troubled women in need of emotional support as well as tangible assistance.

Notes

1. Leroy G. Schultz, "The Wife Assaulter," *Corrective Psychiatry and Journal of Social Therapy*, 6 (February 1960), pp. 103–111.
2. William Ryan, *Blaming the Victim* (New York: Pantheon Books, 1971).
3. Craig M. Allen and Murray A. Straus, "Resources, Power and Husband-Wife Violence," paper presented at The Annual Meeting of the National Council on Family Relations, August 1975; and John E. O'Brien, "Violence in Divorce-Prone Families," *Journal of Marriage and the Family*, 31 (November 1969), pp. 692–698.
4. Daniel G. Saunders, "Marital Violence: Dimensions of the Problem and Modes of Intervention." Paper presented at the Spring Social Work Symposium, Madison, Wisconsin, April 1976.
5. Albert Bandura, *Aggression: A Social Learning Analysis* (Englewood Cliffs, N.J.: Prentice-Hall, 1973).
6. Richard J. Gelles, *The Violent Home* (Beverly Hills, Calif.: Sage Publications, 1972).
7. O'Brien, op. cit.: and Suzanne K. Steinmetz and Murray A. Straus, "General Introduction: Social Myth and Social System in the Study of Intrafamily Violence," in Steinmetz and Straus, eds., *Violence in the Family* (New York: Harper & Row, 1974).
8. Steinmetz and Straus, op. cit., p. 9.
9. O'Brien, op. cit.
10. Allen and Straus, op. cit.
11. Ibid.

12. Richard J. Gelles, "Abused Wives: Why Do They Stay?" *Journal of Marriage and the Family*, 38 (November 1976), pp. 659–668.
13. Ibid.
14. O'Brien, op. cit.
15. Jane McClure, "Equal Opportunity for Displaced Homemakers Act: The Need for Comprehensive Legislative Reform." Unpublished manuscript, Ann Arbor, Michigan, 1976.

Critical Needs of Older People

ANN GLENANE FLYNN

In the past few years, demographic studies have alerted us to the development of new population trends which may transform the entire country. Based on this data the "Graying of America"[1] has been announced, and experts have forcasted major changes in the demographic structure of the population.

Since 1900 the older population has been increasing at a rapid rate, much more so than the rate of younger people. In 1900, the elderly, those 65 years of age and older, represented 4% of the population, in 1970 this rate increased to 10% of the population. It is expected that given a continued low birth rate the percentage of older people in the population will rise to 11.7% by the year 2000 A.D.[2] Around the turn of the century the number of people reaching 65 years of age is expected to taper off, reflecting the low birth rates during the depression and World War II. After this period projections based on U.S. Census data show that the elderly will comprise 13.1% of the population in the year 2020, and 15.4% in 2050 A.D.[3]

Advances in medical knowledge and a higher standard of living have made the "graying of America" possible. It is now not only possible, but probable that a greater number of people will live well beyond the age of 65. In 1970 a person 65 years of age could expect to live an additional 15.2 years.[4] This shift in the age composition of the population has implications of enormous economic, political, and social change. Not the least is the increased

225

need and demand for different types of human services, particularly in the areas of health and social service programs.

Although the elderly are a diverse segment of the population, they still encounter needs and problems peculiar to them as a group. The 1970 White House Conference identified the areas of health, income, housing and transportation as being of crucial importance to older Americans.

Problems in these areas are closely interrelated, to the extent, that to consider one need as more important than another is not only difficult but invites contention. Nevertheless, a strong argument can be made that health i.e., mental and physical health is probably the most critical area affecting an older person's well being.

The elderly are the major consumers of health services, although only 10% of the population they account for approximately 28% of the national expenditures for personal health care.[5] Of the elderly living in the community, 86% suffer from at least one chronic illness. It is unfortunate then that Medicare which was designed to provide health care for older people does not recognize the most common conditions requiring health care. Medicare excludes payment for chronic care unless there is an acute exacerbation of the chronic condition (Butler).[6] Medicare coverage for mental illnesses is equally as dismal, even though statistical evidence shows that the incidence of mental illness increases with age.

It is this author's belief that older people have a right to remain integrated in society for as long as possible, and that attempts should be made towards normalizing the aging process as much as we can, given our present limited understanding of what constitutes normal aging. To this end efforts and services should be directed towards assisting the non-institutionalized elderly by providing them with services which allow for the continuity of care for the chronically ill in the community and for the delivering of appropriate mental health services.

The purpose of these comments is to discuss particular situations which arise with regular frequency and seem to be of critical importance in determining whether or not an older person remains in his home, or is placed in an institutional setting.

Those situations involve the availability of on going home health services and the availability of resources that enable one to deal with behavioral changes seen in many elderly people.

Home Health Services

Although Medicare has done much to relieve older people of the major burden of medical expenses from acute illnesses as mentioned previously it has been ineffective in addressing health needs arising from chronic illnesses. Home health care benefits, under Medicare, Part A and Part B needs to be reevaluated and remedied. Revisions could not only improve the quality of life for countless numbers of older people, but would at the same time help keep down the costs of institutionalization.

A situation demonstrating the need for on going home health services arises when an older person, after a hospitalization is discharged to his home and receives home health benefits under Medicare Part A. Once on the road to recovery, it is discovered that the home health benefits which are needed to maintain functioning at home will soon expire.

Services could be continued either under Medicare Part B,[7] if one has subscribed to it or, under Supplementary Security Income (SSI) via Medicaid, if one is eligible. Many are ineligible and not infrequently it is only by a few dollars a month. Unfortunately those few dollars, which make them ineligible for SSI and subsequent Medicaid coverage are not sufficient to purchase needed home health services on a private basis. The purchasing of home health services on a private basis (1978) approximates $4.75 an hour. In most cases one must employ the health aide for at least 4 hours a day, therefore, minimal daily costs for the purchase of these services is $19.00.

In situations like this, many elderly who had been maintained satisfactorily in a community, receiving only home health services from Medicare must then consider institutional placement such as a residence or home for the aged or a nursing home. Ironically the ultimate costs of placement will most likely exceed the cost of providing home health services; given the limited savings of most older people, institutional costs and expected remaining years of life.

The case of Mr. D. illustrates this point:

Mr. D. a 76 year old man resides in New York City, and is recovering from a Cardiovascular Accident (C.V.A.), for which he was hospitalized several months ago. The C.V.A. resulted in a paralysis of the left side of his body. His right knee is arthritic, consequently he is almost completely non-ambulatory. He lives with his daughter Mrs. T., her husband, who is also disabled from a C.V.A. (of several years ago) and their three children, all of whom are in school.

Mrs. T. works as a secretary in a nearby school. The income from her job is needed in maintaining the family. Mr. T. wants to be employed, but is unable to find appropriate employment. Mrs. T's job not only provides needed income for her family, but serves as a healthy diversion in maintaining her mental health.

Following Mr. D's hospitalization, home care provides Mr. D. with a home health aide 5 days a week— 4 hours a day. Because of home health services, Mr. D's general health is maintained, he is alert, coherent, appears happy, and although limited, is functioning as a relatively normal human being.

Mrs. T. has been notified that the home health benefits are about to expire, Mr. D. does not subscribe to Medicare Part B. Even if it were financially possible for him to subscribe to the insurance plan, social security regulations state that he is not permitted to apply until January of the next year and would not be eligible to receive any benefits until July 1st, of that year — close to a year and a half from the time the services are needed.

For a 76 year old man — this is not a viable alternative. Inquiries as to eligibility for Medicaid, which provides home health services, reveal he receives $260.00 a month in social security benefits, which, because he lives with his daughter exceeds medicaid eligibility. Unfortunately, the difference is not enough to pay for a home health aide on a private basis or a less frequent basis, for example — 3 days a week instead of 5 days a week. Since Mrs. T. must work, and there is no one to care for Mr. D. he will be institutionalized.

Institutional expenses will be paid for by Mr. D. until his resources (up to $1500.00) are exhausted, at which time he qualifies for assistance.

Since his resources are minimal they will be used up in a relatively short time. When on assistance his placement will be borne by tax monies. If his condition requires placement in a skilled nursing facility, annual costs will be approximately $16,000, if a health related facility is indicated, annual costs will approximate $9,000. Annual costs for home health services for Mr. D. would be about $5,000 a year [based on 1978 costs].

Mr. D's case illustrates the short sightedness of our present model in delivering health care. His situation is not uncommon, and he is representative of a growing population of elderly who fall in between the slats, so to speak, of our current fragmented health care system. Not a few elderly faced with this decision refuse placement in a communal facility and attempt to make it on their own. When this is done without the presence of family or concerned friends in the background, they often rely on the good will of who ever happens to be in the immediate environment, e.g., landlord, neighbor, etc. Sometimes this works out, for a while at least. More often, such situations break down in a short time resulting in hospitalization and subsequent institutional placement. Changes in existing policy would go a long way in resolving some of the health care problems older people face.

The main purpose of the 1970 White House Conference was to develop a national policy for the elderly. While it fell short of its main goal, the conference was instrumental in bringing an elderly population to public attention. In addition, programs have been initiated that address identified needs. It remains for the 1980 White House Conference to, among other things, continue to work toward a national policy on aging, formulate policy recommendations, develop needed strategy and a plan of implementation.

Mental Health Needs

The delivery of mental health services to older people, on the other hand, seems a more complex situation. The scarcity of available services means that for those with the financial means as well as those without financial means or with very limited resources, appropriate effective mental health services are hard to find — in most situations they may not exist at all. Services that exist do not always reflect what is known or should be known by professionals about aging and the aging process. The delivery of mental health services to the elderly is indeed a challenging task — many of the elderly one sees in the community demonstrate the need for various kinds of mental health services ranging from supportive care to immediate treatment of acute emotional states. Proper intervention at the appropriate time is needed in order to rescue countless numbers of elderly from being marked with the wastebasket diagnosis of "senility," which means they are provided with treatment which is nothing more than custodial care, and have hardly anything more to expect than a vegetative existence. Unfortunately all too often those engaged in the delivery of mental health services seem to have disposition rather than therapy and services as their goal in treating old people.

The area of mental health care and the state of mental health services for older people today, seems to be a crucial, but critically weak link in the total system of care for older people.

A case report from a human service agency illustrates this point:

> A concerned friend called on behalf of Miss M., who lives alone and is getting "forgetful." Miss M. lives alone in an older section of the city. She has lived there a number of years with a housekeeper/companion who recently died. A staff member visits her and finds the apartment dirty, cluttered and with very little food in sight. She is apparently malnourished and somewhat confused, suspicious of callers and generally resistive to questions of any kind. Immediate needs are attended to by bringing in some food staples. Frequent repeated visits are required in order to begin to deal with her resistance and establish trust. She absolutely refuses to discuss financial affairs. It becomes obvious that she is becoming more suspicious and has paranoid ideas. Attempts to bring her to medical services are unsuccessful and bringing medical services to her is not feasible. If an ambulance is called, she will more than likely refuse to go. There are no known family members. Although she refuses to discuss financial matters, there are indications from her friend (who called originally) that she does have some resources. Plans are under way for appointment of a conservator,[8] but that takes time and does not help the present situation. Subsequent home visits find her confused, agitated, and very paranoid. One afternoon with much difficulty she is brought to the psychiatric division of the emergency room in a municipal hospital. Here she is thought to be "senile." No treatment is given and since it is against hospital policy to admit old patients with these symptoms, she is discharged — at 10 p.m. Still confused and agitated, this "senile" woman who lives alone is sent home with a prescription for Thorazine.
>
> Soon after, she was admitted to the psychiatric unit of a private voluntary hospital. Here with medication her agitation decreased, her mental state improved as did her nutrition and personal hygiene. However, this was an acute care unit and long term care was recommended. From here she was discharged to a nearby nursing home. Staff members visited Miss M. in the nursing home and found her sitting, tied to a chair, obviously sedated, eyes crusted and attempting to dislodge herself from the chair. In an attempt to make her more comfortable in the chair, it was noted that her feet were bare and her only body covering was a dress.

Discussions with staff and management indicated that custodial care and sedation was and would be the extent of her care. All of Miss M's resources will be used for the "care" she is now receiving. After her funds are depleted, public assistance will pay the nursing home costs.

It is unlikely that she will return to the community. If more effective and comprehensive mental health services were available, as well as a more responsible placement, it is entirely possible that she would not be in the nursing home in the first place.

Miss M's case points out the virtual non-existance of effective and appropriate mental health services (short and long term). In this case several professionals came in contact with this person, and although some valiantly tried they were unable to substantially improve the quality of her life; the situation also points out that the good intentions of individuals, however important they may be, are not enough to assure delivery of needed care. The delivery system itself needs to be redressed.

Attending to the mental and physical needs of old people requires special knowledge as to the numerous ways illness manifests itself in an older patient. An elderly patient with an acute illness may not present the usual signs and symptoms that are seen in a younger patient.

Generally, confused states are accepted as par for the course when one is older, delusional states are tolerated until they infringe on another and/or become unmanageable. When an older person manifests these symptoms, and goes untreated precious time is lost. Time that with proper treatment probably could prevent irreversible damage. Functional mental disorders are ignored, and since organic reversible brain syndromes are not recognized for what they are, they remain untreated, and consequently progress to where they are an irreversible chronic brain condition. Butler states:

> The failure to diagnose and treat reversible brain syndromes is so unnecessary and yet so widespread that I would caution families of older persons to question doctors involved in cases about this.[9]

His proposal that those working with and treating the elderly should not be eligible for medicare reimbursement unless they have had special training in this area seems warranted.[10]

The concept of (acute) Reversible Brain Syndrome began appearing in the literature during the 1930s, yet signs of an appreciation for an implementation of this concept in the treatment of the elderly is of rather recent origin, and is still a long way from being a universal concept of practice among physicians.[11] When the physical condition or illness which underlies Reversible Brain Syndrome is treated, the brain pathology and behavioral symptoms associated with its occurrence are reversed.

During the past thirty years there has been an enormous number of studies done, mostly descriptive research studies, which examined various aspects of aging. We are far from knowing all there is to know about the process of aging and older people, and although some are critical of the relevance of much of the accumulated scientific data, clearly we now know more about aging than we knew thirty years ago.

Accumulated findings provide a substantial body of knowledge about aging, which imply improved functional states and more satisfying expectations for older people. It is now reasonable to expect that given good health, an older person can continue to function intellectually, albeit, at a modified rate.[12] We know manifestations of emotional disturbances and behavioral changes are not necessarily a sign of "senility." Old age has more stress and anxiety-evoking situations and less anxiety reducing opportunities, consequently the elderly are very vulnerable to functional disorders.[13] On the other hand such symptoms may be indicative of (acute) Reversible Brain Syndrome masking or accompanying underlying physical illness.

The need for mental health services for the elderly is critical. These services should include preventive care, correct interpretations of symptoms, early intervention and availability of appropriate treatment. Current practices in mental health in no way reflects these needs for what is now known about aging and mental integrity. It is time we begin to implement present knowledge and direct resources towards the delivery of primary mental health care to the elderly population, as well as, improving other levels of mental health services for the elderly.

The interdependence and close relationship of mental and physical health, particularly in older people, can no longer be ignored. Consequently, this concept ought to be a major consideration in the direction of all mental health services as well as in the training of those who work with older people.

Good mental health is somewhat difficult to define. It may be viewed as one's capacity to cope, survive, grow and ultimately thrive with life's situations. In that respect, mental health is closely related to successful aging. Successful aging reflects a state of mental health that is effective and working for that particular person. To paraphrase George Maddox — successful aging means experiencing vitality, creativity, significant accomplishments and social distinctions; for those elderly who are impaired and where such expectations are not real, successful aging involves improving one's capacity to function.[14]

We now know that senility is not inevitable, in many cases it could be prevented; in situations where chronic brain syndrome is a reality, much can be done to maintain levels of functioning and prevent further regression. It is possible to see that the parameters of functioning for an older person range from vitality, creativity, and accomplishment to maximum functional capacity.

Notes

1. "The Graying of America", *Newsweek*, February 28, 1977.
2. Herman Brotman, "Population Projections," *The Gerontologist*, XVII, No. 3 (1977), pp. 203–209.
3. Neal Cutler, "The Aging Population and Social Police", *Aging: Prospects and Issues*, R. Davis, ed., Los Angeles, Ethel Percy Andrus Gerontology Center, University of Southern California, (1977).
4. *Ibid.*, p. 107.
5. James Corman, "Health Services for the Elderly," *Social Policy, Social Ethics and the Aging Society*, B. Neugarten, R. Havinghurst, eds., Chicago, Committee on Human Development University of Chicago (1976).
6. R. Butler, *Why Survive? Being Old In America* (New York: Harper and Row, 1975), p. 208.
7. Current (1978) monthly costs for subscription to Medicare Health Insurance Part B approximates $8.20 per month.
8. The recodified New York State Mental Hygiene Law, which became effective January 1, 1973, incorporated in it Article 77 — Conservators. It provides a viable method of managing the affairs of aging persons with a minumum of legal complications. Source: Private unpublished agency report.
9. Butler, *op. cit.*, chapter 7.
10. *IBID*, p. 222.
11. R. Butler and M. Lewis, *Aging and Mental Health, Positive Psychosocial Approaches* (St. Louis, Mosley Co., 1977), chpt. 5.
12. L. Jarvik, C. Eisdorfer, J. Blum, *Intellectual Functioning in Adults* (New York: Springer Publishing Co., 1973), p. 65.
13. Muriel Oberleder, *Emotional Breakdown in Elderly People*, Unpublished paper.
14. Maddox, G. "Successful Aging: A Perspective", in *Successful Aging — A Conference Report*, E. Pfeiffer, ed., Durham, North Carolina: Duke University, 1974.

Suggested Readings

Atchley, Robert. *Social Forces in Later Life*. Belmont, California: Wadsworth Company, 1972.

Administration on Aging. *Words on Aging: A Bibliography*. Washington, D.C.: U.S. Dept. of Health, Education and Welfare.

Baltes, P.B., K.W. Schaie. "Aging and I.d: the Myth of the Twilight Years." *Psychology Today*, VII (1974), pp. 35–40.

Barney, Jane Lockwood. "Community Presence as a key to Quality of Life in Nursing Homes." *American Journal of Public Health*, LXIV, March, 1974, pp. 265–268.

Beauvoir, Simone de. *The Coming of Age*. New York: Warner Books, 1973.

Botwinick, J. *Aging and Behavior*. New York: Springer Publishing Company, 1973.

Brotman, Herman B. "The Fastest Growing Minority: The Aging." *American Journal of Public Health*, LXIV, March, 1974, pp. 249–252.

Brown, Mollie, ed. *Readings in Gerontology*. 2nd ed. St. Louis: The C.B. Mosby Company, 1978.

Butler, Robert N., M.D. and Myrna I. Lewis, A.C.S.W. *Aging and Mental Health: Positive Psychosocial Approaches*. 2nd ed. St. Louis: The C.B. Mosby Company, 1977.

Carp, Francis. *Retirement*. New York: Behaviorial Publications Inc., 1972.

Davis, Richard H. ed. *Aging: Prospects and Issues*. University of Southern California: Ethel Percy Andrus Gerontology Center, 1977.

Erlich, Ira F. and Phyllis F. Erhlich. "A Service Delivery Model for the Aged at a Communal Level." *The Gerontologist*, XIV. June 1974, pp. 241–244.

Flasher, Bruce A., Victor J. Engandela and Roalda T. Alderman. "A Model for a Geriatric Transfer Service." *American Journal of Public Health*, LXIV. February 1974, pp. 129–135.

Gaitz, Charles M. "Barriers to the Delivery of Psychiatric Services to the Elderly." *The Gerontologist*, 14. June 1974, pp. 210–214.

Gerbner, George, ed. "Myths of Old Age: A Symposium of Images, Activities, and Environments." *Journal of Communication*, XXIV. Autumn 1974, p. 4.

Gerontological Society. Projects Division. "The Practitioner and the Elderly." *Working With Older People*, I. Arlington, Va.: U.S. Dept. of H.E.W. Devision of Health Care Services, March 1969.

Gerontological Society. Projects Division. "Biological, Psychological, and Sociological Aspects of Aging." *Working With Older People*, II. Arlington, Va.: U.S. Dept. of H.E.W. Division of Health Care Services, March 1969.

Gerontological Society. Projects Division. *The Aging Person: Needs and Services*, III. Arlington, Va.: U.S. Dept. of H.E.W. Division of Health Care Services, March 1969.

Gerontological Society. Projects Division. *Clinical Aspects of Aging*, IV. Arlington, Va.: U.S. Dept. of H.E.W. Division of Health Care Services, March 1969.

Goldfarb, A. "Predicting Mortality In The Institutional Aged: A Seven Year Follow Up." *Archives of General Psychiatry*, XXI. 1969, pp. 172–176.

Kart, C., E. Metress, and J. Metress. *Aging and Health: Biologic and Social Perspective*. Reading, Mass.: Addison-Wesley Publishing Co., 1978.

Katzman, R., R. Terry, and K. Bick. *Alzheimers Disease: Senile Dementia and Related Disorders*. New York: Raven Press, 1975.

Kubler-Ross, Elizabeth. *On Death and Dying*. New York: Macmillan Company, 1969.

Kubler-Ross, Elizabeth. *Questions and Answers on Death and Dying*. New York: Collier Books, 1974.

La Fontaine, Jean. "Anthropology" in *A Handbook for the Study of Suicide*. S. Perlin, ed. New York: Oxford University Press, 1975.

Lieberman, M.A. "Psychological Correlates of Impending Death." *Journal of Gerontology*, XX, 1965, pp. 181–190.

Lowry, Louis. "The Senior Center - A Major Community Today and Tomorrow." *Perspective on Aging*, III, 2. March-April 1974, pp. 5–9.

Menninger, K.A. *Man Against Himself*. New York: Harcourt, Brace & World, 1938.

Moss, Bertram B. and Mary Ellen Lavery. "Review of a New Community Health Care Evaluation and Service Center." *The Gerontologist*, XIV. June 1974, pp. 207–209.

Oberleder, Muriel. "Emotional Breakdowns in Elderly People." *Hospital and Community Psychiatry*, XX. No. 7. July 1969, pp. 191–196.

Palmore, E.B. "Physical, Mental and Social Factors in Predicting Longevity." *The Geronotologist*, IX, 1969, pp. 103–108.
Pfeiffer, Eric ed. *Successful Aging: A Conference Report.* Durham, North Carolina: Duke University Center for the Study of Aging and Human Development, 1974.
Raviv, Sheila E. "Working Effectively with Older People." *Prespective On Aging*, III, 2. March-April 1974, pp. 10–12.
Robinson, Nancy, et al. *Costs of Homemaker-Home Health Aide and Alternative Forms of Service: A Survey of the Literature.* New York: National Council for Health Aide Services, 1974.
Santori, Anthony F. and Herbert Diamond. "The Role of a Community Mental Health Center in Developing Services to the Aging: The Older Adult Project." *The Gerontologist.* XIV, June 1974, pp. 201–206.
Segerberg, Osborn J. *The Immortality Factor.* New York: Dutton, 1974.
Shanas, Ethel. "Health Status of Older People: Cross National Implications." *American Journal of Public Health*, LXIV, March 1974, pp. 261–264.
Siegel, Esther K. "Medicare: Does It Really Serve the Elderly?" *Perspective On Aging.* III, 2. March-April 1974, pp. 13–17.
Townsend, Claire. *Old Age: The Last Segregation.* New York: Grossman Publishers, 1971.
Whitehead, J.A. *Psychiatric Disorders in Old Age.* New York: Springer Company, 1974.
Woodruff, Desna S., James Burin. *Aging, Scientific Perspectives and Social Issues.* New York: D. Van Nostrand Co., 1975.
Youmans, E. Grant. "Age Group, Health and Attitudes." *The Gerontologist*, XIV. June 1974, pp. 249–254.
Youmans, E., M. Yarrow. "Aging and Social Adaptation: A Longitudinal Study of Healthy Old Men." In *Human Aging II, An Eleven Year Follow Up Biomedical and Behavioral Study.* Granick, S., R. Patterson, eds. Rockville, Md.: National Institute of Mental Health, 1974.

Aging

LEO MCLAUGHLIN

On July 30, 1977, I became officially old. As if I had been awarded a degree or sentenced to death, I became old by statute and a ward of the Social Security Administration.

I told myself all too often that this new legal status did not make any difference. The age 65 cutoff had been nonsense for more than half a century. It had started in Germany about 1885 during a period marked by social reforms. Bismarck (aged 70 and old enough to know better) selected 65 as an appropriate commencement of old age. In 1918, the magic number was adopted in the United States. But today 65 ". . . corresponds in terms of today's life and health expectancies to age 78 or 80."[1] I have not needed the evidence Peter F. Drucker used to justify that statement, a statement many social scientists and physicians have begun to echo. Old by statute, I have my intuition: my legal status changes nothing. I can still walk, talk, think, and create. I am not really old; properly motivated, I can crawl on my belly like a reptile.

I protest too much. I am affected by my own reactions to my legal status. It is not merely the legal status. I admit to a knack for blaming others for any and every unhappy situation, and I'll take a crack at the Image Makers in politics, business, and Media. How well they have worked! They have given me all those disgusting pictures of old people.

Now in my old age, an extraordinary event: I am being honest with myself. Without the Image Makers, I would still have had a problem because, all by myself, most of my life, even now except when I'm being careful, I thought and think of old people as wrecks who crawl or squat together. Most of my life, I have had something akin to respect for the geniuses who spent time and money devising solutions to problems created by our pre-conceived notion of what old people must be. No need had I of Image Makers to make me join all those who commit this first crime against the old. And from this basic crime came all the residual crimes: commercial exploitation, social ostracism (exile in nursing homes or to colonies for "Seniors,") political manipulation, emotional destruction in the name of efficiency or psychological consulting. I did not fight against any of these crimes. The best that I can say for myself is that I did not promote all of them.

I never needed the Image Makers to persuade me to believe that old people have only their past. I developed my own images from small sights seen and preserved by prejudice as I moved from adolescence to statutory old age. Some of my recent images are:

> —the white head barely visible behind the steering wheel of a car meandering along a highway at 25 miles an hour;
> —the lump of body slouched in a nursing home chair, drooling;
> —the frail, helpless body carried from an airplane, seeming to proclaim, silently, eloquently, that the old have no present, no future. The old have a past lost in memory. The old keep vigil for their own death.

I, and I am not alone, am influenced by what I think other people think of me. I know what I thought of the helpless old. I cannot help thinking that what I thought of the old will now be thought of me. And my thoughts will play a large part in making me what I am and what I am to be. If I think that others think that I am helpless, senile, insane, I move closer to helplessness, senility, insanity. It does not really matter if other people don't think these things: what matters is what I think they think. And this nonsense of being officially old plays a part. Without a court action, I shall not be proclaimed senile. But, by statute, I have joined a minority. The vast majority of people who have been legally declared senile come from that minority.

Whether or not we old people think consciously of all this, most of us are affected by it. Old people have been around always and, in different ways, in different cultures, have always been problems. In the United States today, for many reasons, we are a big problem, growing ever bigger. If we were not such a major issue, the bureaucrats and the experts would not bother us, and we old people would not have to cope with so many non-problems. As Americans fascinated with bigness, we forget that bigness creates problems unrelated to the essential problem. Thus when the old were relatively few in number, it was possible to look at Eben Flood[2] and to consider what should be done about him personally. Now that the old are numerous enough to be a major social concern, we make boxes for everybody who is old and there must be a box into which a contemporary Eben can be made to fit. He damn well better, sayeth the system.

There is another element which has helped shape our image of old people: for centuries, western culture has fostered the tradition that old people are helpless and useless. At another time, another place, I may try to prove that statement but now I shall merely cite from Act II, Scene 7 of *As You Like It* where Shakespeare has Jaques describe the last two stages of life:

The sixth age shifts
Into the lean and slipper'd pantaloon,
With spectacles on nose and pouch on side,
His youthful hose well saved, a world too wide
For his shrunk shank; and his big manly voice,
Turning again toward childish treble, pipes
And whistles in his sound. Last scene of all,
That ends this strange eventful history,
Is second childishness and mere oblivion,
Sans teeth, sans eyes, sans taste, sans everything.

I memorized that speech when I was in High School: Jaques and an entire educational experience set me on a path which now, at long last, I want to leave. This may be one challenge of being old: to see old age as it is, as it may be, rather than as it is blindly assumed to be.

There are many different ways in which people react to being old. I have decided to react by emphasizing the challenges which now face me.

Of its nature, a challenge supposes danger: while there is something to be gained, there is invariably something to be lost.

As soon as I decide to accept challenges, I accept as a fact that I have something to lose. This involves a major change in my attitude: with Jaques, I had believed that the old were "sans everything" — with nothing to lose. The things which I have to lose fall into two groups:

First, I can lose my material possessions. I do not want to deny the importance of what I have. However, if I overemphasize their importance, I can lose myself.

Second, and to my mind far more important, I can lose myself as a person capable of growing in wisdom and grace. If you like, forget the "wisdom and grace," forget that I can lose the ability to make money, to become famous. Remember only that I can lose the chance to grow, to become more fully myself. There is the essential, and if there were not the possibility of that loss, there could not be true tragedy in old age.

And what can I gain?

I do not want to talk about the superficial gains even though they may sometimes offer comfort and support. I want to think of the essential, of the fact that the last years of my life may be filled with growth, with wonder. I think that Einstein said in his old age: "If you can't experience wonder, you are as good as dead." I want my last years to be truly years of life, to be filled with the incredible mixture of tragedy and triumph, of despair and hope, of sadness and joy, which makes us human. I shall also keep vigil for my own death, not because I am helpless but because now, at long last, I realize the ever true, unchanged reality: my days have been numbered since birth.

The First Challenge — Leap of Faith   From the day I became officially old, I have been attempting to make this leap of faith. Nearly everyting I have said in the preceeding pages has been an attempt to deal with that need for faith in myself. First of all, and probably for the rest of my life, I shall have to cast out the images (if that sounds like casting out demons, the sound is not far from expressing the reality) which I have nurtured so confidently most of the years of my life. Second, since I have need of images, it is not enough merely to cast out images suggested by others. Someway, somehow, I must replace the long nurtured images with new images, be they ever so lean and hungry. Third, I must try to eliminate, or at least to weaken, the effect upon myself of what I think other people think of me. On one level, it is important to realize that most people are not thinking of me and that very few, if any, now look upon me as the classical helpless wreck — sans teeth and all the rest. On the more important level, it does not make any real difference if they think of me as hopelessly senile or mildly batty. As a child I joined in the refrain, "Sticks and stones will break my bones, but names will never hurt me." That was the refuge of children. I know that names can and have hurt me deeply. I am not going to solve the problem by returning to the tribal chant of my childhood. I must live with the fact that I shall be hurt. If I accept that, I can live with the hurt.

Over the months, I have made a start in making this leap of faith. First I moved, so slowly, gingerly, onto the spring board. An inching out — half an inch out, a foot back. How did I ever get this far? Almost to the end of the board. A little hop — a bigger hop — straight up — not far up — straight back to the board. Far from willing, cringing, terrified to leap out into the unknown. I am the unknown.

All my life I have feared that I would dive into an empty pool. No one can tell me to look, to touch the water: there isn't any pool to see, there isn't any water to touch. This is truly a leap of faith. Perhaps, in the final analysis, I have to believe in God or in a Supreme Being. Right here and now, in the simplistic analysis, there is no "perhaps" at all: I must believe in myself.

If I don't believe in myself, the bureaucrats will have me believe in them, and to reward me for my simple faith, they already have a box prepared for me. Statistically speaking, I should fit nicely. But I have never fitted into the boxes made for others, rarely into the boxes made for me. I shall not fit into the box made for the average person. I have always insisted — whenever I wasn't mistaking common images for reality — that the average person is no one. The average person is a construct of the statisticians' imagination. And statisticians are not supposed to have imagination.

I have to have faith in myself — not because I am right, but because the consequences of not making the leap are worse than standing there at the end of the board, shivering, cold, helpless, terrified. I have to have faith in myself because only with that faith do I have something to lose. If I have nothing to lose, I cannot win. If I have nothing to lose, I am already dead.

Sadly, I cannot make one leap of faith which will last for the rest of my days. I leap and return, leap and return, again and again —

lasting as long as the current "I" lasts. And in never knowing, not always believing, can I ever come to know myself.

The Second Challenge — Money   I am the unknown. Product of the American culture, I have at times attempted to find myself in the money I made or did not make. Others evaluated my worth by how much I had.

In this frame of reference, I am easily known. I am the money I make. In this same frame of reference, I am forced to retire. One day, I am making money. The next day, I am making nothing, I am contributing nothing. I live on Social Security benefits and on my pension. I am known for what I do not do, for what I do not make.

I do not like to think of the power of that negation: you can go on almost endlessly listing the things I might do, even the things I did. In the face of all the things I might do, all the things I have done, the stark reality is that I do nothing. I am retired. I play. I enjoy what the Image Makers sometimes call my "Golden Years."

If in the past I have made a great deal of money and exercised power wisely or unwisely, I may be known as "Chairperson of the Board." I don't have to worry about money. My nephews who kicked me upstairs (as I kicked my Father years ago) do not try to rob me. They wanted and got the power and they bear with me as long as I vote my stock the way they want. They make sure of that and then they try not to pay any attention to me. The fact is that I am an embarrassment. "There is no fool," they say, "like a rich old fool."

If I never made a great deal of money, or if I spent the money I made not wisely but too quickly, and I am brought to the nursing home with less than enough money to pay the minimum, I am known for what I do not have. And the orderlies no longer expect a tip from me and they do not bear with me. "There is no fool," they say, "like a poor old fool."

I can lose myself totally in this maze. With or without money, I can become unknowable to myself. I am unknowable if I want not to know myself or if there is nothing to know. I am also unknowable if there is too much to know.

Rich or poor, I am not what I have or what I do not have. Rich or poor, I can be lost in the maze. Rich or poor, I do not have to be lost in the maze. It is possible — so very difficult but still possible — for me to reach for myself beneath the value of what I have or the loss of value in what I do not have. I have to be interested in what I am, in what I can still be. Without my own interest in myself, there isn't any hope for me. With my interest in myself, I may make the next great break: I may become interested in others not for what they have but for what they are. Money has not turned off all the visions. Nor has old age. In old age, yes at every age, but perhaps particularly in old age, we lose the great vision: I am. And until the day I die, full of wonder, there will be more to know about me — the unknown.

The Third Challenge — To Know   With all the modern experts at my disposal, I am rather ashamed of myself for going back to Socrates for still another repetition of his command:

Know thyself.

Those two words seem to contain the beginning and the end. In youth and in old age, the command is the same. And it can be carried out as well in old age as in youth. And it needs to be carried out in youth and in old age.

If I know myself, I know that there is a relationship — strange and appealing — between my body and the part of me which is not my body. I do not know the nature of that relationship: it took me years to understand the simple fact that there is a relationship. In my old age, the relationship takes on special qualities: perhaps my final existence when I am no longer body — for the body will no longer exist — will be marked not by the spirit talking to the body — but as the relationship. It is the relationship which continues to exist because two realities were so closely related as my body to my spirit. The body rots; without the body, the spirit is not quite the same. The relationship — that which exists because the body and the spirit were related — will always be. The relationship exists so fully that it never ceases to be.

Know thyself.

Before I can know the relationship, I must first know my body. Then I must try to know my spirit.

If I know my body, I know how to take care of it. I know what I must do to keep it well. With the knowing, if it is truly knowing, comes the self discipline — the control — necessary to carry out what I know.

They say that since I'm old I'm not supposed to have control.

I, who am old, say that I have control because I am old.

My years have taught me something: I have learned to accept responsibilities for my own decisions, for my own actions. I hate to say how long it took me to become mature, to grow up.

I try to know my spirit. In the best spirit of Socrates, I can only say that I know that I do not know. I know that there is so much more to know and for all my days I shall be at the beginning. It is so wonderful to be old and to be able to begin.

There was never a magic moment when I began to grow. There has not been a dark moment when I stopped growing. I know that I can, at one and the same time, begin and continue to grow. It is wonderful to be old and to be able to continue to grow. It is more than that: for my life, I must continue to grow.

In this process which lasts as long as I live, I come to know myself more intimately when I begin to create. What I create comes from my deepest being. It — the essence — has been there all my life. Perhaps only in old age will I have the skill, the control, the knowledge of self which will allow me to give it life.

Know thyself.

The Last Challenge — Love   Even when I was young, I loved the poem by William Butler Yeats entitled "When You are Old"

When you are old and gray and full of sleep,
And nodding by the fire, take down this book,
And slowly read, and dream of the soft look
Your eyes had once, and of their shadows deep;

How many loved your moments of glad grace,
And loved your beauty with love false or true,
But one man loved the pilgrim soul in you,
And loved the sorrows of your changing face;

And bending down beside the glowing bars,
Murmur, a little sad, from us fled love;

He paced upon the mountains far above;
And hid his face amid a crowd of stars.

In old age, I love the poem even more. Yeats was twenty-seven
when he wrote it. I wish I had known as much at twenty-seven. I
hope I know as much in old age. And perhaps I know a little more:
old age is not made up only of memories. Oh yes, the beautiful and
ugly memories are part of me. But there is so much more: there is the
beautiful, full of wonder, now. Above all, Love has not fled: Love
has grown more magnificent with every passing day. Because I
know my Love, insofar as I know my Love,

I know myself.

Notes

1. Peter F. Drucker, "Thinking About Retirement Policy", *The Wall Street Journal*,
September 15, 1977.
2. For a valuable interlude, reread Edwin Arlington Robinson's poem, "Mr. Flood's
Party."

Alcohol and Alcoholism

ROGER SHIPLEY

Understanding Alcohol and Its Effects

Considering the long experience of man with alcohol, it is surprising how many experienced drinkers are relatively ignorant of the way their favorite beverages affect them, for better and for worse. The same applies to their non-drinking families and friends who may be concerned about why the drinker behaves as he does.

The fact is that until recent years when drinking problems forced public concern, there was little factual alcohol and health information available. There was a library on how to mix exotic drinks, but not much about what happens after the drinking starts.

A grasp of the known facts about the effects of alcohol on the body—both short-term and long-term—is essential to the person who wants to drink responsibly, and to those who want to understand the social custom of drinking, problem drinking, and alcoholism.

Short-Term Effects Most people drink alcoholic beverages to get feelings of pleasure as well as relief from tension. No doubt this is the reason for the popularity of alcohol as a social beverage. Drinking is such a familiar part of our lifestyle that it is hard to realize that alcohol is a drug—every bit as active in the body as prescription drugs that are usually taken as pills in carefully regulated dosages.

247

Alcohol's primary effects are in the central nervous system, the brain, although the whole body is affected. The familiar signs of drunkenness, such as slurred speech and unsteady gait, are not due to the direct action of alcohol on the tongue or legs, but by its effects on the parts of the brain which control their activities.

How Alcohol Goes to Work   Alcohol can act as a stimulant at low doses, and as a brain depressant at higher doses. The speed with which alcohol brings drunkenness, and drunken behavior, depends upon the rate of its absorption into the blood stream and (importantly) on the drinking history of the individual, what he wants and expects to happen.

Unlike other foods, alcohol does not have to be digested slowly before reaching the blood stream. It is immediately absorbed into the blood, having passed directly through the walls of the stomach and small intestine. The blood rapidly carries it to the brain.

Alcohol is metabolized, or burned and broken down, in the body at a fairly constant rate. As a person drinks faster than the alcohol can be burned, the drug accumulates in his body, resulting in higher and higher loads of alcohol in the blood.

The larger the person, the greater the amount required to attain a given concentration of alcohol. In a 150-pound man, alcohol is burned at about the rate of one drink per hour.

The typical drink—three-fourths ounce of alcohol—is provided by:

* a "shot" of spirits (1 ½ oz. of 50-percent alcohol—100-proof whiskey or vodka),
* a glass of fortified wine (3 ½ oz. of 30-percent alcohol),
* a larger glass of table wine (5 oz. of 14-percent alcohol),
* a pint of beer (16 oz. of 4 ½ percent alcohol).

Drinking at the rate of one drink an hour will result in little, if any, accumulation of alcohol in the blood.

Even the first few sips of an alcoholic beverage, however, may cause changes in mood and behavior. These may be helped along by what the individual has learned to expect from previous drinking experiences.

Blood Alcohol and Behavior   The first consistent sizable changes in mood and behavior appear at blood alcohol levels of approximately 0.05 percent—that is 1 part alcohol to 2,000 parts blood. Thought, judgment, and restraint may be affected at this level which would result from a 150-pound man taking two drinks in succession. He feels carefree, released from many of his ordinary tensions and inhibitions—he loosens up. It is mainly to achieve this pleasant state that people drink in moderation.

As more alcohol enters the blood, the depressant or "short-circuiting" action of alcohol involves more functions of the brain. At a level of 0.10 percent (1 part to 1,000) voluntary motor actions—hand and arm movements, walking, sometimes speech—become plainly clumsy.

At 0.20 percent (1 part to 500), the controls by the entire motor area of the brain are measurably impaired; that part of the brain which guides emotional behavior is also affected. The person staggers or he may want to lie down; he may be easily angered, or boisterous, or weep. He is "drunk."

At a concentration of 0.30 percent (1 part to 300), the deeper areas of the brain concerned with response to stimulus and understanding are dulled. At this level a person is confused, or may lapse into stupor. Although aware, he has poor understanding of what he hears or sees.

With 0.40 or 0.50 percent alcohol in the blood (1 part to 250 or 200), he is out of the world; he is in coma. Still higher levels of alcohol in the blood block the centers of the lower brain which control breathing and heart beat, and death comes.

This progression of effects is not unique to alcohol. It can be produced by other hypnotic sedative drugs, such as barbiturates, ether, and chloral hydrate.

Blood-alcohol levels have important legal implications. In most states, an individual with a blood-alcohol level of 0.05 percent or less is legally presumed to be sober and in condition to drive a motor vehicle. A person with a level of 0.10 percent or 0.08 percent is legally presumed to be intoxicated or "under the influence" in some states, while in others the 0.15 percent level means legal impairment.

Chronic Heavy Drinking Drinking large amounts of alcohol over long periods of time seems to change the sensitivity of the brain to the effects of alcohol. This means that larger amounts of alcohol are required to produce the same effects. This adaptation is called "tolerance." It shows up in the chronic use of all addictive drugs and is believed to be the basis of "addition" or "dependence."

The effects of alcohol on the moderate or heavy drinker, and on the alcohol-dependent person, are different. Instead of the pleasant, relaxing effects usually experienced by the normal drinker, alcoholic persons may become progressively more tense and anxious while drinking.

The alcohol-dependent person shows extraordinary adaptation to alcohol. He must take relatively huge amounts to produce the changes in feelings and behavior which he previously attained with smaller quantities. Moreover, his capacity to drink very large quantities without losing control of his actions also marks him as different from the moderate or heavy drinker. Over some period of time the alcoholic person may drink a fifth of whiskey a day without showing signs of drunkenness. He may perform accurately complex tasks at blood alcohol levels several times as great at those that would incapacitate moderate to heavy drinkers. Later, in the chronic stage, tolerance decreases markedly until he may become drunk on relatively small amounts of alcohol.

At present, it is not known what accounts for the dramatic "behavioral tolerance" of the alcohol-dependent person to alcohol. It was once thought that "tolerance" came from differences in the rate of alcohol metabolism. It has been shown, however, that normal drinkers and alcoholic persons do not differ much in their overall rate of alcohol metabolism. This argues that the adaptive changes must occur in the brain rather than in the liver.

Another way in which the moderate or heavy drinker differs from the alcoholic person is that the abrupt removal of alcohol can produce severe mental and bodily distress in the alcoholic person. Whereas the normal drinker may experience the passing misery of the "hangover," the alcohol-dependent person may have severe trembling, hallucinations, confusion, convulsions, and delirium— the alcohol withdrawal syndrome. The average person would have difficulty distinguishing between the common alcohol withdrawal syndrome involving the "shakes," sweating, nausea, and anxiety, and the more severe and potentially fatal condition known as delirium tremens. Both require immediate medical attention.

Effects of Alcohol on Sensation and Perception   Even low doses of alcohol reduce sensitivity to taste and odors. Alcohol has little effect on the sense of touch, but dulls sensitivity to pain.

Sharpness of vision seems relatively unaffected by alcohol. At high doses of alcohol, however, there is a decrease in ability to discriminate between lights of different intensities, and a narrowing of the visual field. The latter effect ("tunnel vision") may be particularly dangerous in automobile driving. Resistance to glare is impaired so that the eye requires longer to readjust after exposure to bright lights. Sensitivity to certain colors, especially red, appears to decrease.

In general, the senses are resistant to alcohol, but the changes that do occur are detrimental.

Effects of Alcohol on Motor Performance   Tests of muscular control or coordination show greater detrimental effects than on sensory capabilities. Intoxicating doses of alcohol impair most types of performance. A sensitive indicator of alcohol effect is the "standing steadiness" test. Alcohol increases swaying, especially if the eyes are closed. Coordination is also adversely affected by alcohol, as in tracing a moving object.

People differ in their susceptibility to the effects of alcohol on motor performance, especially at blood alcohol levels of 0.10 percent and below. Although sufficient alcohol impairs anyone's performance, anxious or determined people are better able to bring their performance up to its normal level.

Effects of Alcohol on Emotions   The direct action of alcohol on the body, coupled with its ability to relax feelings of self-criticism and inhibition, produce the "high" associated with alcohol use. This is found useful in social drinking situations as people mingle, each recognizing that the others are also less responsible for what they do and say. It has been suggested that the way people behave when they are drunk is determined by what their social group makes of and teaches them concerning the state of drunkenness.

Some studies show that alcohol tends to decrease fear and increase likelihood that an individual will accept risks. For example, when a group of bus drivers were given several drinks, they were more likely to try to drive their buses through spaces that were too narrow—and seemingly more willing to risk failure—than when they were sober. The judgment and skill impairment was not predictable on the basis of amount consumed: some drivers were more affected by two whiskeys than others were by six.

Reaction time is measured by the rapidity with which a subject makes a simple movement, such as pressing a button in response to a sound or visual signal. Below a blood alcohol level of 0.07 percent, reaction time varies little. Between 0.08 and 0.10 percent, reaction time slows measurably. Higher levels consistently produce larger performance failures. A much greater effect of alcohol on reaction time is found when attention is divided, as when the subject is at the same time engaged in another task.

Other tests measuring both speed and accuracy suggest that alcohol has a greater effect on accuracy and consistency then on speed. A person who has had several drinks tends to "breeze through" a complex test but makes more errors than he normally would and is more erratic in his responses. Many subjects, however, feel their performance has improved and refuse to believe when shown the poor results.

Effects of Alcohol on Sexuality   Alcohol's capacity to release inhibitions is connected in the public mind with the observation that after drinking, some people tend to show an increase amorousness. This has given rise to an assumption that alcohol promotes or improves sexual activity.

Tests have revealed consistently that large doses of alcohol frustrate sexual performance. Studies of alcoholic persons have revealed that their sex life was disturbed, deficient, and ineffectual. Impotence may result, sometimes reversible with the return of sobriety.

It appears that in nonalcoholic persons, a few drinks dull the sense of restraint and, by helping to overcome lack of confidence or feelings of guilt about sex, facilitate sexual activity. A subtle truth, however, was expressed by Shakespeare: Drink "provokes the desire, but it takes away the performance."

Effects of Alcohol on Sleep   The effects of alcohol on sleep are known to anyone who has gone to bed after having had too much to drink, only to toss and turn and awaken the following morning feeling headachy and fatigued. Taking several drinks before bedtime has been found to decrease the amount of REM (rapid eye movement) or dreaming sleep. The consequences of being deprived of REM sleep are impaired concentration and memory, as well as anxiety, tiredness, and irritability.

Mixing Other Drugs and Alcohol In recent years, hundreds of new drugs have been introduced to the public. They include drugs for inducing sleep, tranquilization, sedation, and for relief of pain, motion sickness, or head cold and allergy symptoms. Too numerous to name, they include narcotics, barbiturates and other hypnotic-sedative drugs, tranquilizers, antihistamines, and volatile solvents. Some of these drugs act on the same brain areas as alcohol does.

When used simultaenously with alcohol, these drugs can grossly exaggerate the usual responses expected from alcohol or from the drug alone. This is due to the additive or combined effects exerted by alcohol and the other drugs on the central nervous system. For example, alcohol and barbiturates when combined multiply each other's effects. Taking both drugs in close order can be particularly dangerous and may result in death. The use of any drug that has a depressant effect on the central nervous system in combination with alcohol represents an extra hazard to health and safety and, in some cases, to life itself.

Sobering Up The speed of alcohol absorption affects the rate at which one becomes drunk; in reverse, the speed of alcohol metabolism affects the rate at which one becomes sober again. Once in the bloodstream and carried throughout the body, alcohol undergoes metabolic changes and eventually is reduced to carbon dioxide and water. Most of these processes take place in the liver, although from 2 to 5 percent of the alcohol is excreted chemically unchanged in urine, breath, and sweat.

As a general rule, it will take as many hours as the number of drinks consumed to sober up completely. Drinking black coffee, taking a cold shower, or breathing pure oxygen will not hasten the process.

Search for some method to speed up the rate of alcohol metabolism, and thus provide quick sobriety, has been unsuccessful. All one can do is wait, and let the liver do its work.

A familiar after-effect of overindulgence is the hangover—the morning-after misery of fatigue, nausea, upset stomach, anxiety, and headache. The hangover is common and unpleasant, but rarely dangerous. Although the hangover has been blamed on mixing drinks, it can be produced by any alcoholic beverage, or by pure alcohol. The exact cause is unknown.

There is no scientific evidence to support the curative claims of popular hangover remedies such as coffee, raw egg, oysters, chili pepper, steak sauce, "alkalizers," vitamins, "the hair of the dog," or such drugs as barbiturates, amphetamines, or insulin. Doctors usually prescribe aspirin, bed rest, and solid feed as soon as possible.

Hangovers can be prevented by drinking slowly, with food in the stomach, under relaxed social circumstances, with sufficient self-discipline to avoid drunkenness.

What Determines Drinking Behavior? As suggested above, the rate at which alcohol is absorbed into the bloodstream and its effects on behavior are influenced by several interacting factors.

On the physical side, a person's weight, how fast he drinks, whether he has eaten, his drinking history and body chemistry, and the kind of beverage (and mixer) used are all influential.

On the psychological side, the drinking situation, the drinker's mood, his attitudes, and his previous experience with alcohol will all contribute to his reactions to drinking.

1. **Speed of drinking.** The more rapidly an alcoholic beverage is swallowed, the higher will be the peak blood-alcohol level.
2. **Body weight.** The greater the weight of the body muscle (but not body fat) the lower will be the blood-alcohol concentration from a given amount of alcohol.
3. **Presence of food in the stomach.** Eating while drinking retards the absorption of alcohol, especially in the form of spirits or wine. If alcohol is taken with a substantial meal, peak blood-alcohol concentrations may be reduced by as much as 50 percent.
4. **Drinking history and body chemistry.** Individuals with a long history of drinking develop "tolerance" and require far more alcohol to get "high" than an inexperienced drinker. Each person has an individual pattern of physiological functioning which may affect his reactions to alcohol. For example, in some conditions, such as that marked by the "dumping syndrome," the stomach empties more rapidly than is normal, and alcohol seems to be absorbed more quickly. The emptying time may be either

slowed or speeded by anger, fear, stress, nausea, and the condition of the stomach tissues.

5. **Type of beverage.** In all the major alcoholic beverages—beer, table wines, cocktail or dessert wines, liqueurs or cordials, and distilled spirits—the significant ingredient is identical: alcohol. In addition, these beverages contain other chemical constituents. Some come from the original grains, grapes, and other fruits. Others are produced during the chemical processes of fermentation, distillation, or storage. Some are added as flavoring or coloring. These nonalcoholic "congeners" contribute to the effects of certain beverages, either directly affecting the body, or affecting the rates at which alcohol is absorbed into the blood and oxidized.

Diluting an alcoholic beverage with another liquid, such as water, helps to slow absorption, but mixing with carbonated mixers can increase the absorption rate.

Long-Term Effects Drinking alcohol in moderation apparently does the body little permanent harm. But when taken in large doses over long periods of time, alcohol can prove disastrous, reducing both the quality and length of life. Damage to the heart, brain, liver, and other major organs may result.

Prolonged heavy drinking has long been known to be connected with various types of muscle diseases and tremors. One essential muscle affected by alcohol is the heart. Some recent research suggests that alcohol may be toxic to the heart, and to the lungs as well.

Liver damage especially may result from heavy drinking. Cirrhosis of the liver occurs about eight times as often among alcoholic individuals as among nonalcoholics. Yet it also occurs among nondrinkers, and its cause is still sought. Malnutrition has been blamed. Some investigations, however, have shown that very large amounts of alcohol may cause liver damage even in properly fed subjects.

When large quantities of alcohol are consumed, the gastrointestinal system can become irritated. Nausea, vomiting, and diarrhea are mild indications of trouble. Gastritis, ulcers, and pancreatitis often occur among alcoholic persons.

Heavy drinkers have long been known to have lowered resistance to pneumonia and other infectious diseases. Malnutrition is usually considered to be the cause. Recent research has shown, however, that lowered resistance may also occur in well-nourished heavy drinkers, and appears to result from a direct interference with immunity mechanisms. With blood-alcohol levels of 0.15 to 0.25 percent, the reduction of white blood cell mobilization was as great as that found in states of severe shock.

Heavy drinking over many years may result in serious mental disorders or permanent, irreversible damage to the brain or peripheral nervous system. Mental functions such as memory, judgment, and learning ability can deteriorate severely, and an individual's personality structure and grasp of reality may disintegrate as well.

Problem Drinking and Alcoholism: The Nature and Scope of the Challenge

A nationwide survey of American drinking practices showed that more than two-thirds of adults drink alcoholic beverages at least occasionally. Adding younger drinkers to this population gives about 100 million people who drink. The overwhelming majority of those who drink do so responsibly. But what of the others, far too many, whose drinking gets out of hand, endangering themselves and those around them?

What Are Problem Drinking and Alcoholism? Distinctions are sometimes made between people with drinking problems and those suffering from alcoholism—alcoholic persons being considered the more uncontrolled and injured group. However, in practice the two are often hard to distinguish, except in extreme cases of alcoholism; hence, hard and fast labeling is seldom done.

Within our society, problem drinking is usually recognized whenever anyone drinks to such an excess that he loses ability to control his actions and maintain a socially acceptable life adjustment. One authority describes a problem drinker as:

1. Anyone who must drink in order to function or "cope with life."
2. Anyone who by his own personal definition, or that of his family and friends, frequently drinks to a state of intoxication.
3. Anyone who goes to work intoxicated.
4. Anyone who is intoxicated and drives a car.
5. Anyone who sustains bodily injury requiring medical attention as a consequence of an intoxicated state.
6. Anyone who, under the influence of alcohol, does something he contends he would never do without alcohol.

Other "warning signs" that often indicate problem drinking are: the need to drink before facing certain situations, frequent drinking sprees, a steady increase in intake, solitary drinking, early morning drinking, and the occurrence of "blackouts." For a heavy drinker, a blackout is not "passing out" but a period of time in which he walks, talks, and acts, but does not remember. Such blackouts may be one of the early signs of the more serious form of alcoholism.

Definitions of Alcoholism   At present there is no definition of alcoholism that satisfies all. The following one is widely accepted:

> Alcoholism is a chronic disease, or disorder of behavior, characterized by the repeated drinking of alcoholic beverages to an extent that exceeds customary dietary use or ordinary compliance with the social drinking customs of the community, and which interferes with the drinker's health, interpersonal relations, or economic functioning. (Mark Keller in *Ann. Am. Acad. Polit. Soc. Sc.*, 315:1, 1958.)

Another is based on measures of behavior: (1) loss of control—the victim finds himself drinking when he intends not to drink, or drinking more than he planned; (2) presence of functional or structural damage—physiological, psychological, domestic, economic, or social; (3) use of alcohol as a kind of universal therapy, as a psychopharmacological substance through which the person tries to keep his life from coming apart.

Most definitions refer only to destructive dependency on alcohol. One definition which suggests the origins of alcoholism is that of Drs. Morris Chafetz and H. W. Demone, Jr.

We define alcoholism as a chronic behavioral disorder which is manifested by undue preoccupation with alcohol to the detriment of physical and mental health, by a loss of control when drinking has begun (although it may not be carried to the point of intoxication) and by a self-destructive attitude in dealing with personal relationships and life situations. Alcoholism, we believe, is the result of disturbance and deprivation in early infantile experience and the related alterations in basic physiochemical responsiveness; the identification by the alcoholic with significant figures who deal with life problems through the excessive use of alcohol; and a sociocultural milieu which causes ambivalence, conflict, and guilt in the use of alcohol. (*American Handbook of Psychiatry*.)

Whatever the definition used, it is generally agreed that there are about 12 million people in the United States with drinking and alcoholism problems.

Who and Where Are the Alcoholic Men and Women?   To many people, the notion of an alcoholic person means the skid row derelict. Yet investigation shows that the alcoholic men of skid row make up less than 5 percent of problem and alcoholic drinkers.

Most of the problem drinkers are employed or employable, family-centered people. More than 70 percent of them live in respectable neighborhoods, with their husbands and wives, send their children to school, belong to clubs, attend church, pay taxes, and continue to perform more or less effectively as businessmen, executives, housewives, farmers, salesmen, industrial workers, clerical workers, teachers, clergymen, and physicians.

Estimates vary, but it appears that about 80 percent of alcoholic individuals are men, and 20 percent are women. The proportion of women has been rising in recent years, perhaps due to a growing willingness of such women to seek treatment. They may therefore now be more visible rather than more numerous.

A survey found the percentage of problem drinkers was highest in the western states, and among males, residents of the larger cities, the divorced or unmarried, those with the least and those with the most education, and those with the lowest and highest job status.

Irresponsible Drinking

The Personal Price   If one considers only the personal cost of drinking problems, the price is high. The life expectancy of alcoholic drinkers is shorter by 10 to 12 years than that of the general public. The mortality rate is at least two and one-half times greater, and they suffer more than their share of violent deaths. Alcoholism appears as a cause of death on more than 13,000 death certificates yearly. Undoubtedly, alcohol and its abuse contribute to many deaths which are attributed to other causes.

Effects of alcoholism are not limited to the drinker alone. His family, his employer, and society at large are all harmed by his behavior, and all have a stake in helping to prevent the disease from becoming more severe. If one considers the ill effects of drinking problems on just the families of problem drinkers, at least 36 million Americans can be regarded as caught in the web of alcohol abuse. Unhappy marriages, broken homes, desertion, divorce, impoverished families, and deprived or displaced children are all parts of the toll. The cost to public and private helping agencies for support of families disabled by alcohol problems amounts to many millions of dollars a year.

The Drinking Driver Public shock over the thousands of deaths and hundreds of thousands of disabling injuries caused annually by drinking drivers has been a major reason for the current concern about alcohol abuse.

Highway deaths have been rising steadily until nearly 60,000 Americans are now killed yearly. It has been shown that alcohol is involved in half of the highway fatalities. Drivers with chronic drinking problems are responsible for about two-thirds of the alcohol-related deaths. Young drivers and social drinkers with a high blood-alcohol level at the time of the accident cause the remaining one-third. These figures say nothing about the 500,000 people who are injured, and possibly disabled, nor do they cover the immense costs in property damage, wage losses, medical expenses, and insurance costs.

Not only are alcohol-impaired drivers the cause of accidents; drunken pedestrians also contribute to the toll. A California study showed that 62 percent of the drivers and 40 percent of the pedestrians in fatal accidents had been drinking, and 53 percent of the drivers and 32 percent of the pedestrians had blood-alcohol levels about 0.10 percent.

Efforts to reduce driving while under the influence of alcohol include improved public education programs; uniform state laws to give police the right to test blood-alcohol levels of any suspected driver; reduction of the legal criterion of intoxication to 0.10 percent or lower; and improved traffic law enforcement.

Alcohol and Crime   For some drinkers, alcohol releases violent behavior that might be unlikely or even unthinkable in their sober state. Half of all homicides and one-third of all suicides are alcohol-related—accounting for about 11,700 deaths yearly. Alcohol is also frequently involved in assaults and offenses against children. A California study of more than 2,000 felons concluded that "problem drinkers were more likely to get in trouble with the law because of their behavior while drinking or because they needed money to continue drinking."

Alcohol figures in less violent criminal behavior as well. For example, almost half of the 5½ million arrests yearly in the United States are related to the misuse of alcohol. Drunkenness accounts for apprroximately 1,400,000 arrests, while disorderly conduct and vagrancy—used by many communities instead of the public drunkenness charge—account for 665,000 more. Intoxicated drivers make up the 335,000 remaining arrests. Cost to taxpayers for the arrest, trial, and keeping in jail of these persons has been estimated at more than $100 million a year.

The arrests include only a portion of a community's excessive drinkers; many are skid row people who are arrested, jailed, released, and arrested again, time after time. This is the so-called "revolving door" procedure found in most communities.

The Cost to Industry   More than half of the nation's alcoholics are employed. Employees with drinking problems are absent from work about 2½ times as frequently as the general work force. Their drinking may result in friction with co-workers, lowered morale, bad executive decisions, and poor customer and public relations for their employers. No doubt, drinking problems result in the loss of trained employees—particularly those experienced workers in their middle years with lengthy service—among the most valuable assets of any firm.

A loss of $10 billion yearly has been attributed to worktime lost through alcohol problems of employees in business, industry, civilians in government, and the military.

The Cost to the Nation The private act of drinking, when carried to excess, has consequences which affect and harm many others. Ultimately, society as a whole pays a high price. An economic cost to the nation of $15 billion per year has been attributed to problem drinking and alcoholism. This includes the $10 billion mentioned above in lost work time, as well as $2 billion in costs for health and welfare services provided for alcoholic persons and their families, and a cost of from $3 to $3.5 billion as a result of property damage, medical expenses, overhead costs of insurance, and wage losses.

The human cost cannot be measured.

The Origins of Alcoholism: Physiological, Psychological and Sociological Factors

For a long time, people with drinking problems were lumped together under the label "alcoholic." All were assumed to have the same illness. The search was for *the* cause of alcoholism.

As more was learned, it became clear that there are many kinds of drinking problems, many types of people who have them, and many reasons why they begin and continue to drink too much.

The search for a single cause of alcoholism has widened to include physiological, psychological, and sociological factors that might, singly or in combination, explain problem drinking by various types of individuals.

The Cooperative Commission on the Study of Alcoholism reported:

> An individual who (1) responds to beverage alcohol in a certain way, perhaps physiologically determined, by experiencing intense relief and relaxation, and who (2) has certain personality characteristics, such as difficulty in dealing with and overcoming depression, frustration, and anxiety, and who (3) is a member of a culture in which there is both pressure to drink and culturally induced guilt and confusion regarding what kinds of drinking behavior are appropriate, is more likely to develop trouble than most other persons. An intermingling of certain factors may be necessary for the development of problem drinking, and the relative importance of the different causal factors no doubt varies from one individual to another.

Physiological Factors   To date, neither chemicals in specific beverages nor physiological, nutritional, metabolic, nor genetic defects have been found which would explain alcoholism.

Alcoholism occurs frequently in children of alcoholic persons which suggests a hereditary basis. Yet it also occurs in the children of devout abstainers. And an early study showed that children of alcoholic parents placed in foster homes before the age of 10 were no more likely to become alcoholic individuals than children of nonalcoholic parents.

Vitamin or hormone deficiencies have been suggested as causes of alcoholism. Most of such deficiencies seen in individuals with advanced alcoholism appear to be results, rather than causes of excessive drinking.

There is no proof that alcoholic persons are generally allergic to alcohol itself or to other nonalcoholic components of alcoholic beverages.

Although it is frequently said that alcoholic individuals are unable to metabolize or eliminate alcohol as rapidly as normal individuals, research indicates that many actually metabolize it about 10 to 20 percent more rapidly when they are drinking heavily.

Interest in the physiological basis of alcohol dependence has grown in recent years. The current state of knowledge has been summed up:

> The nature of the addictive process, the developmental sequence of events and the central nervous system alterations which define the condition of alcohol addiction are unknown. Beyond the obvious requirement of ingestion of sufficient quantities of alcohol over a long enough period of time, the determinants of alcohol tolerance and dependence remain a matter of conjecture. The development of approaches to these very basic questions constitutes perhaps the major challenge to the biological scientist concerned with addiction.

Psychological Factors   Psychologists and psychiatrists have described alcoholic persons as neurotic, maladjusted, unable to relate effectively to others, sexually and emotionally immature, isolated, dependent, unable to withstand frustration or tension, poorly integrated, and marked by deep feelings of sinfulness and unworthiness. Some suggest that alcoholism is an attempt at a self-cure of an inner conflict, and might be called "suicide by ounces." There are no reliable studies to confirm these observations.

Many researchers have gathered data showing that alcoholic individuals often come from broken or unhappy homes, and have undergone serious emotional deprivation during their childhood. But many nonalcoholic men and women have these backgrounds and personality qualities. Some of the latter may suffer from a variety of mental illnesses; others lead reasonably normal lives.

If there is such a thing as an "alcoholic personality"—or a "prealcoholic personality"—its specifications are loosely defined and often contradictory.

Sociological Factors One of the most promising studies of the causes of alcoholism has been the comparison of drinking practices and alcohol problems with different cultures and societies. This is aimed at finding why alcoholism is widespread in some national, religious, and cultural groups but rare in others.

Groups with highest rates of alcoholism classed as "high incidence" groups include the northern French, the Americans— especially the Irish-American and Alaskan Indians, the Swedes, Swiss, Poles, and the northern Russians. Relatively low-incidence groups include the Italians, some Chinese groups, Jews, Greeks, Portuguese, Spaniards, and the southern French.

Differences between some of these cultures are seen within the United States. In one survey of problem drinkers in New York City (when the total population was about 10 percent Irish, 15 percent Italian, and 25 percent Jewish), 40 percent of the alcoholic persons were Irish, 1 percent Italian, and none Jewish. In a California study, in an area with large proportions of Irish, Italians, and Jewish residents, 21 percent of the alcoholic persons were Irish, 2 percent Italian, and 0.6 percent Jewish.

The low rates of alcoholism seen in some groups cannot be attributed to abstinence. Most Mormons and Moslems, for example, do not drink because of religious beliefs, and their alcoholism rates are low. But among the Italians, Greeks, Chinese, and Jews, a large percentage of the population drinks, and many use alcohol abundantly, yet their alcoholism rates are low, too. The per capita consumption of alcohol in Italy is second only to top-ranked France, but alcoholism rates among Italians are relatively low.

Drinking Customs Are Important One authority suggests that the rate of alcoholism is low in those groups in which the drinking customs, values, and sanctions are well established, known to and agreed upon by all, and consistent with the rest of the culture. By contrast, groups with mixed feelings about alcohol (such as the Anglo-Saxon Protestant group in America)—with no agreed-upon ground rules—tend to have high alcoholism rates.

This has been found among the few Mormons who do drink, among drinkers who feel forced to overindulge to prove their "manliness," and especially among children of parents with con- flicting attitudes—such as a father who accepts drinking and a mother who feels drinking is a sin.

In general, research has shown that among groups that use alcohol freely, the lowest incidence of alcoholism comes with certain habits and attitudes:

1. The children are exposed to alcohol early in life, within a strong family or religious group. Whatever the beverage, it is served in diluted and small quantities, with consequent low blood-alcohol levels.
2. The beverages commonly although not invariably used are those containing relatively large amounts of nonalcoholic components (wines and beers), which also give low blood-alcohol levels.
3. The beverage is considered mainly as a food and is usually consumed with meals, again with consequent low blood- alcohol levels.
4. Parents present a constant example of moderate drinking.
5. No moral importance is attached to drinking. It is con- sidered neither a virtue nor a sin.
6. Drinking is not viewed as proof of adulthood or virility.
7. Abstinence is socially acceptable. It is no more rude or ungracious to decline a drink than to decline a piece of cake.
8. Excessive drinking or intoxication is not socially ac- ceptable. It is not considered stylish, comic, or tolerable.
9. Alcohol is not a prime focus for an activity.
10. Finally, and perhaps most importantly, there is wide and usually complete agreement among members of the group on the "ground rules" of drinking.

Overcoming Alcoholism: Diagnosis and Treatment

Alcoholism is a treatable illness from which as many as two-thirds of its victims can recover. Yet there persists a number of myths and misunderstandings that make it difficult for alcoholic persons to seek and get the help they need.

We still think of alcoholism as a form of moral weakness, rather than an illness—a stigma which causes problem drinkers and their families to hide their "sins" rather than tell of their problems and seek treatment.

In addition, many people, laymen and medical personnel alike, still consider alcoholism to be untreatable, and regard the person with alcohol problems as unmanageable and unwilling to be helped. None of these assumptions is true.

The Chances of Recovery About 70 percent of alcoholic people are men and women who are still married and living with their families, still holding a job—often an important one—and still are accepted and reasonably respected members of their communities. For those of this group who seek treatment, the outlook is optimistic. It is quite possible for a person with drinking problems to learn to abstain completely, or to control his drinking most of the time.

The Rehabilitation Approach Recently, some therapists have been using a different basis for measurement of treatment outcome—rehabilitation. Success is considered achieved when the patient maintains or reestablishes a good family life and work record, and a respectable position in the community. Relapses may occur but do not mean that the problem drinker or the treatment effort has failed. A successful outcome can be expected in at least 60 percent, and some therapists have reported success in 70 to 80 percent of their cases. This depends on the personal characteristics of the patient; the competence of the therapist; the availability of treatment facilities; and the strong support of family, employer, and community.

"It is doubtful that any specific percentage figure has much meaning in itself," says Dr. Selden Bacon, director of the Center of Alcohol Studies at Rutgers University. "What has a great deal of meaning is the fact that tens of thousands of such cases have shown striking improvement over many years."

For the remaining part of the alcoholic population—the skid row alcoholics and the 10 percent who are psychotic alcoholics, usually in state mental hospitals—the prognosis is less optimistic. Less than 10 to 12 percent can achieve full recovery.

Treatment Adapted to Patient   There is no evidence that any particular type of therapist—physician, clergyman, Alcoholics Anonymous member, psychiatrist, psychologist or social worker—will have better results than another. The chances of a successful outcome apparently depend more on the combination of right patient and right treatment. Different patients respond to different treatments. The earlier treatment is begun, the better are the prospects for success, although many have been treated successfully after many years of excessive drinking.

Diagnosing Alcoholism

Alcohol problems are often slow to be recognized by those who could treat them. Thus, the diagnosis of alcoholism is often made only when the illness is in its advanced stages—when the victim is unable to control his drinking, may no longer have an established family life or be able to hold a job, or when malnutrition or organic damage is already present.

Members of the medical profession now realize that since alcoholic individuals rarely admit, even to themselves, that they have drinking problems, their family physicians must make special efforts to discover the illness in its early stages.

Diagnosing the Alcoholic Person   Unfortunately, there is no simple diagnostic procedure for detecting alcoholism. Some of the factors involved in diagnosing an alcoholic person include:

1. *The quantity of alcohol consumed.* But quantity alone is an insufficient measure.
2. *The rate of consumption.* One pint of distilled spirits consumed during a 10-hour period causes different behavior than a pint consumed in 1 hour. Drunkenness depends on rate of consumption as well as quantity.
3. *Frequency of drinking episodes.* One who gets drunk three or four times a year is less liable to be labeled

alcoholic than someone who gets drunk every week. Frequency of drunkenness is one factor indicating alcoholism.

4. *The effect of drunkenness upon self and others.* A man who commits deviant sex acts or beats his wife while drunk is more likely to be labeled alcoholic than a man who quietly gets drunk and leaves others alone. That is, the effect of drunkenness on others, and the reaction of others to the drunkenness, determines if and how the individual is labeled alcoholic.

5. *Visibility to labeling agents.* The police, the courts, school personnel, welfare workers, employers and, in some situations, family, friends, and helping agents—psychiatrists, physicians, lawyers—are the key sources of alcoholic labeling.

6. *The social situation of the person.* There are different standards set by each class and status group in our society. How one does or does not conform to the standards of one's own group will determine whether a person will be labeled an alcoholic and, therefore, be reacted to as an alcoholic.

Help in sorting out particular characteristics of alcoholic persons can usually be obtained from one or more of the following: the family physician, clergyman, Alcoholics Anonymous, Al-Anon Family Group, alcoholism clinic, or alcoholism information and referral center, public health nurse, social worker, community mental health center, Veterans Administration or general hospital, health, welfare, or family service agency, some employers and labor unions, and local affiliates of the National Council on Alcoholism.

Treating Alcoholism

There are generally three steps in the treatment of alcoholism, although all persons may not need to take all three:

1. Managing acute episodes of intoxication to save life and overcome the immediate effects of excess alcohol.
2. Correcting the chronic health problems associated with alcoholism.
3. Changing the long-term behavior of alcoholic individuals so that destructive drinking patterns are not continued.

There are many different types of drinking problems and numerous kinds of treatment techniques available. The challenge is to identify the needs of the individual and to match them with the most appropriate therapy.

The Treatment Environment An individual may begin treatment during a spell of temporary sobriety, during a severe hangover, or during acute intoxication. For many it will be during the drying out or withdrawal stage.

An acutely ill alcoholic person, or the nonalcoholic individual who is acutely intoxicated, should be given care under medical supervision. A general hospital ward is considered best for preliminary treatment. A few general hospitals have long offered such care, but the majority are still reluctant to accept alcoholic men and women as patients.

The position of most hospital officials has been attributed to hostile feelings evoked by the so-called "typical alcoholic patient," who at admission is often disheveled, disturbing, and demanding.

A favored patient might be admitted but only if he or she paid for a private room and 24-hour private nursing care. Other patients, unable to afford such care, may be sent to the "drunk tank" of the local jail, the psychiatric ward of a state hospital, or the emergency ward of a local hospital. Most emergency wards are concerned primarily with sobering the patient, treating obvious wounds, and discharging him as quickly as possible.

Changing Hospital Attitudes San Francisco's Mount Zion hospital proved this technique was outmoded when they decided to accept alcoholic men and women simply as sick people needing hospital care. These patients were placed in open wards and treated by physicians, nurses, and other personnel who had been trained in the use of new drugs and were ready to treat them as patients who were ill. It quickly became evident that other patients were not disturbed, hospital routines were not upset, and most of the alcoholic persons were willing to undertake followup therapy.

A study at Massachusetts General Hospital has shown that many people with drinking problems who appear unwilling to accept treatment on a long-term basis will indeed follow through in treatment if they are met from arrival in the emergency ward with understanding, sympathy, and attention.

ALCOHOL AND ALCOHOLISM   269

Although the success at Mount Zion and Massachusetts General have been repeated at other hospitals, and leaders of the American Medical Association and the American Hospital Association have urged hospitals throughout the country to follow this lead, many are still unwilling to accept alcoholic people as ordinary patients. Change, where it comes, usually is in response to demands from the community.

Physiological Treatment

In practice, there are six physiological conditions which must be recognized and treated if an alcoholic patient is to get appropriate care. These include: (1) acute alcohol intoxication or severe drunkenness, (2) alcohol withdrawal symptoms short of delirium tremens, (3) delirium tremens itself, (4) diseases often associated with alcoholism, such as cirrhosis and polyneuropathy, (5) neurological and psychiatric conditions such as alcoholic encephalopathies, and (6) the long-term problem of addiction or dependency.

Tranquilizers are often used in the treatment of acute intoxication. These have been effective in reducing the trembling, anxiety, sleeplessness, nausea, and general discomfort which occur when an alcoholic person stops drinking. Among the tranquilizers used are chlorpromazine, promazine hydrochloride, and chlordiazepoxide. The latter drug has been found safe and often effective in preventing delirium tremens and convulsions during withdrawal.

Delirium Tremens Delirium tremens (DT's) is a serious and sometimes fatal condition, in which the patients are confused, trembling, feverish, and sometimes convulsive. They have terrifying hallucinations. About 5 percent of alcoholic people in hospitals, and perhaps 20 to 25 percent who suffer the DT's alone and unattended, die as a result. Tranquilizers, intensive nursing care, control of the food intake and fluid electrolyte balance, are important treatment aids.

It appears that delirium tremens is not simply a direct toxic effect of alcohol on the brain. In fact, it usually occurs after withdrawal—in persons who have stayed drunk for many days or weeks.

New Medical Findings   Recent research has helped in medical management of acute intoxication and withdrawal. For example, it was observed that some alcoholic people brought to the hospital in a state of coma may not have high blood-alcohol levels but do have low blood-sugar levels. Apparently, a large dose of alcohol taken after fasting 24 hours or more can produce a rapid drop in blood-sugar and, in fact, can cause hypoglycemic coma similar to that produced by an overdose of insulin.

Research has also shown that, contrary to long-held opinion, patients during withdrawal are not always dehydrated, and do not necessarily require intravenous fluids. In fact, overhydration may be the problem, because alcoholic drinkers often consume large amounts of other liquids while on a binge.

The Tranquilizer "Bridge"   Once over the acute stages of intoxication or withdrawal, the alcoholic patient starting long-range treatment may require a kind of drug "bridge" over the difficult early days or weeks.

Physicians commonly prescribe minor tranquilizers, such as meprobamate, to produce relaxation and to reduce the tensions which many alcoholic persons believe to have triggered their drinking bouts. Patients are cautioned to beware of switching dependence from alcohol to tranquilizers.

Aversion and Deterrent Agents   Other physicians use "aversion" therapy—administering an alcoholic beverage and at the same time a powerful nausea-producing agent like emetin or apomorphine. Repeated treatments are intended to develop a conditioned reflex loathing for alcohol in any form.

More widely known and used are the so-called "deterrent agents" such as disulfiram (Antabuse) and citrated calcium cyanamide (Temposil). A patient regularly taking one of these finds that if he drinks any alcohol, a pounding headache, flushing, nausea, and other unpleasant symptoms will result.

Physicians screen patients carefully to decide which treatment is most appropriate for a given individual. The "aversion" methods of treatment require close medical supervision and informed consent of the patient.

Psychological and Social Therapy

Drug therapy can provide important, although temporary, relief for many patients. However, for most patients, it can help only as the introduction to treatment which attempts to get at the factors underlying the alcoholic person's drinking.

Psychotherapy Helps Many Experience has shown that long-lasting results can be achieved for many patients primarily through psychotherapy. Psychotherapy covers various kinds of self-examination, counselling, and guidance. A trained professional works with—rather than on—patients, alone or in groups, to help them change their feelings, attitudes, and behavior toward more rewarding patterns of living.

The psychotherapeutic approach usually starts out with gaining acceptance—by the patient himself and, perhaps, his family—of the alcoholic person as one who is sick but not evil, immoral, or weak. And there must be genuine acceptance by the patient of the idea that he needs help. Once this is done, the therapist attempts to understand some of the patient's underlying tensions as well as his more troublesome life problems. He tries to solve those problems that can be readily handled, and to find a means—other than drinking—which will enable the patient to live with those problems that cannot be solved.

Preaching Doesn't Work Most successful therapists say that pleading, exhortations, telling the patient how to live his life, or urging him to use more willpower, are usually useless and may be destructive. They stress the need for creating a warm, concerned relationship with the patient.

Psychotherapy for alcoholic patients differs somewhat from that used with other patients. It tends to be directed more to action, focusing on the immediate life situation of the patient and his or her drinking problem. Many therapists bring members of the patient's family into the therapy program. Research has shown that the family may include another member, perhaps more emotionally disturbed than the patient, who may be partly responsible for the alcoholic person's drinking.

How Long in Treatment?   Usually patients find that sobering up means they must face a backlog of personal, family, financial, and social problems. They may need help to work out these problems. Many therapists argue that treatment cannot be conducted on a hit-or-miss, intermittent basis, or restricted to straightening out occasional drinking episodes. They suggest frequent sessions during the first weeks or months, and then sessions at longer intervals as the patient progresses.

On the other hand, doctors at the Cleveland Center on Alcoholism claimed after 5 years of experience with nearly 2,000 patients that a substantial portion could be given significant help in from one to five therapeutic sessions. Not advocated for all, this short-term therapy was found to be most effective with those with good family ties and a determination to get well, who could with help face their situation quickly.

Some therapists claim that individual treatment on a one-to-one basis is the most successful. Others prefer group therapy, especially when a group of patients is treated simultaneously by a team of therapists.

Voluntary Helpers   The discussion of treatment resources has so far centered on the role of the medical and allied professions in helping the alcoholic person. Yet there are many organizations and agencies, staffed largely by nonmedical personnel, which provide help to countless thousands of alcoholic persons, and aid them in reestablishing better relations with their families, employers, and community.

Alcoholics Anonymous   One of the major voluntary helpers is the fellowship of Alcoholics Anonymous. AA is described as a loosely knit, voluntary fellowship of alcoholic individuals gathered together for the sole purpose of helping themselves and each other to get sober and stay sober. It has also been pictured as serving its members first as a way back to life, and then as a way of living. It has about 425,000 members in about 13,000 groups in the United States. There are perhaps 600,000 to 650,000 alcoholic men and women participating in AA all over the world. However, despite its scope, even AA reaches only a limited number of those who need help, when the approximately 9 million alcoholic and problem drinkers in our country are considered.

Important to the AA approach is an admission by the alcoholic person of his lack of power over alcohol. He finds his life unmanageable and his situation intolerable. For some, this realization may come when they have lost everything and everyone. For others, it may occur when they are first arrested by the police, or warned by their employer. At this point, "the individual must decide to turn over his life and his will to a power greater than his own." Much of the program has a spiritual, but nonsectarian basis.

During the early years of AA, some members insisted that "only an alcoholic can understand an alcoholic," and there was little cooperation between AA workers and physicians, clergymen, and social workers. As they have come to know one another better, most AA members no longer hold this view, and cooperation with professional therapists has been increasing. Conversely, professionals strongly encourage membership in AA as part of the treatment programs for alcoholic people in detoxification centers, general and psychiatric hospitals, clinics, and prisons.

Al-Anon and Alateen Serve Families Other organizations stimulated by the example of Alcoholics Anonymous have been effective in involving family members and helping them. Al-Anon, an organization of spouses and other relatives of alcoholic patients, is available whether or not the alcoholic family member is in AA or part of some other rehabilitation procedure. The value of membership is to learn that one is not alone in this predicament and to take advantage of others' trial-and-error attempts at better adjustment. Alateen is a parallel organization for the teenage children of an alcoholic parent. These organizations are listed in most telephone directories.

Many professionals emphasize that, valuable and widely accessible as it is, AA should not be considered as a complete form of treatment for all alcoholic individuals; rather, it should be viewed for many as a support to and not a substitute for various forms of therapy.

Alcohol's Effects Tied to Chemical A team of physicians has discovered a major chemical difference between alcoholics and other people that may explain how continued heavy drinking damages body organs and perhaps why some people become addicted to alcohol.

The team found that a powerful chemical, acetaldehyde, reaches higher levels in alcoholics than in other people even when both groups have the same level of alcohol in their blood.

Acetaldehyde is a breakdown product of alcohol. It is known to be toxic to heart muscle and liver cells. It has also been shown to interact with nervous system hormones to produce drugs called alkaloids, which interfere with nerve functions.

Alcoholics often develop cirrhosis of the liver, diseases of the heart muscle and brain damage.

Thus, the finding indicates that alcohol itself may not be the "bad actor" in alcoholism; rather, acetaldehyde may be responsible for alcohol's effects.

If further studies bear this out, they may lead to ways preventing alcohol-induced damage and perhaps of identifying alcoholism-prone individuals and preventing the disease itself.

It is not yet known, whether the higher levels of acetaldehyde are a factor in alcoholism because after a relatively small intake of alcohol, it reaches a plateau—or maximum level—in the blood, and further drinking does not increase this level.

In the studies, the person in the tests were given alcohol intravenously, allowing precise control over the amount of alcohol in the blood. Simultaneous measurements were made of alcohol and acetaldehyde levels for eight to ten hours thereafter.

They showed that the acetaldehyde levels in the blood of the alcoholics reached a plateau that was 62 percent higher than the plateau of the normal person.

Acetaldehyde is the substance that is responsible for the effectiveness of Antabuse in treating alcoholics.

Antabuse blocks the breakdown of acetaldehyde, and when a person who is taking the drug drinks alcohol, there is a sudden, dramatic increase in acetaldehyde in his blood, far beyond the normal plateau this chemical reaches. This causes an extremely unpleasant reaction, including nausea, a drop in blood pressure, sweating and flushing.

Differences in the level or action of acetaldehyde may also explain ethnic variations in sensitivity to alcohol. A study in Boston three years ago showed that people of Oriental descent, among whom alcoholism is extremely uncommon, respond with a rapid intense flushing of the face and symptoms of mild intoxication to amounts of alcohol that have no apparent effect on whites.

Liquor and Livers What causes alcoholics to develop cirrhosis and other frequently fatal liver diseases? Many doctors, noting the tendency of alcoholics to drink more than they eat, believe that poor nutrition plays a key role. But two researchers now claim that it is drink alone that does the damage. A four-year study has convinced them that even in the well nourished, alcohol can be lethal to the liver.

Drs. Emanuel Rubin and Charles Lieber selected baboons for their study because the primates live as long as fifteen years, far longer than most other laboratory animals, and have livers that are similar to man's. The researchers put twenty-six baboons on high-protein, high-vitamin diets, but for thirteen of the animals substituted ethanol, a grain alcohol, for much of the carbohydrate portion of the dietary requirements. The alcohol provided the animals with fully half their caloric intake.

The baboons responded to the booze—equivalent to about a fifth per day for a man—just as humans would. They became intoxicated and ultimately, dependent upon drink. Two of the animals became so addicted to alcohol that they experienced withdrawal symptoms, including what seemed to be delirium tremens, or DT's when off the bottle.

But the most significant result of the study was the destruction of the myth that alcoholic liver damage is the result of a bad diet rather than booze. All of the animals who were kept on the drinker's diet for anywhere from nine months to four years developed some form of alcoholic liver damage. Seven of the baboons developed fatty livers, and four contracted alcoholic hepatitis. Two animals, kept on the bottle for four years, developed cirrhosis, the progressive and severe hardening and contraction of the liver.

The study provided other insights into alcoholism, which Rubin and Lieber consider to be one of man's worst "environmental" ailments. Because pure alcohol was used exclusively, it became evident that the toxic effects were the result of the alcohol itself and not, as some researchers have suggested, caused by any of the impurities or additives found in beer, wine or hard liquor. Concludes Rubin: "You can't protect yourself against alcoholic damage by eating well; what counts is the total amount of alcohol you drink."

United States Drinking Reels to New High—The Gallup Poll The proportion of adults who drink is at the highest point recorded in thirty-five years of regular Gallup audits of American's drinking habits.

In the latest survey, 68 percent (or a projected ninety-five million Americans, eighteen and older) say they have occasion to use alcoholic beverages. Among persons in the highest income group ($20,000 per year and over), the proportion of drinkers is nearly nine in ten.

The percentage of drinkers is up four points from the previous measurement, taken in 1969, and continues a general upward trend since 1958 when the lowest figure to date (55 percent) was recorded.

TABLE 1. 1974 AUDIT OF DRINKERS BY GROUPS

	Use Alcoholic Beverages %
National	68
Men	76
Women	61
Under 30 years	79
30–49 years	75
50 years and older	54
$20,000 and over	88
$15,000–19,999	78
$10,000–14,999	64
$7,000–9,999	58
$5,000–6,999	57
Under $5,000	46
East	78
Midwest	75
South	51
West	70
Professional and business	85
Clerical and sales	78
Manual laborers	71
College trained	83
High school	70
Grade school	45
Protestants	61
Catholics	83

The latest survey also shows nearly one-fourth of drinkers—one-fifth of the total sample—admitting they sometimes drink to excess. In addition, one person in eight in the survey (12 percent) reveals that liquor has been a cause of trouble in his family.

These survey findings are recorded at a time of growing concern in the nation over alcoholism and excessive drinking, believed to be related to half of the nation's traffic fatalities, one-half of the homicides, and one-third of the suicides.

Table 1 gives the full results, showing the highest proportion of drinkers to be among men, younger persons, higher income groups, persons living outside the South, professional and business people, persons with a college background and Catholics

In the 1945 survey, conducted shortly after the end of World War II, a near all-time high of 67 percent reported they drank. The same proportion was found in 1946. The figure subsequently trended downward and stabilized around 60 percent in the early and middle 50s.

In the recession year of 1958, the figure dropped to 55 percent, but subsequent surveys have shown an upward trend.

Since 1939, the increase in the proportion of women drinkers (up 16 points) has been twice that for men (up 7 points since the first audit in 1939).

Many of the nation's largest employers, concerned about financial losses because of alcoholic personnel, are instituting programs designed to identify employees with drinking problems and see that they get treatment.

Bibliography

Clinebell, Howard: *Understanding and Counseling the Alcoholic.* Nashville, 1968, Abingdon.

Hafen, Brent: *Alcohol: The Crutch that Cripples.* St. Paul, 1977, West Publishing Co.

Fort, Joel: *Alcohol: Our Biggest Drug Problem.* New York, New York, 1973, McGraw-Hill Co.

Kinney, Jean and Gwen Leaton: *Loosening the Grip, A Handbook of Alcohol Information.* St. Louis, 1978, C.V. Mosby Co.

Miles, Samuel, ed.: *Learning About Alcohol*. Washington, D.C., 1974, American Association for Health, Physical Education and Recreation.

Smart, Reginald: *The New Drinkers*. Toronto, Canada, 1976, Addiction Research Foundation of Ontario.

Smart, Reginald: *Alcohol and Health — New Knowledge*. Rockville, 1974, National Institute on Alcohol Abuse and Alcoholism.

Smart, Reginald: *Facts About Alcohol and Alcoholism*. Rockville, 1976, National Institute on Alcohol Abuse and Alcoholism.

Smart, Reginald: *The Health Consequences of Smoking*. Atlanta, 1976, U.S. Dept. of HEW, Center for Disease Control.

Smart, Reginald: *Twelve Steps and Twelve Traditions*. New York, New York, 1953, Alcoholics Anonymous World Services, Inc.

Drug Use and Abuse

ROGER SHIPLEY

Perspective

The Drug Culture. What is it? Where did it come from? How long will it last? What are its effects? The experts are actively seeking answers to these questions and more.

Although mankind has been ingesting various natural substances specifically for their pleasure-giving qualities since before the beginning of recorded history the Drug Culture, as generally referred to today, is a recent phenomenon.

When we speak of the Drug Culture, we usually refer to the pervasive use of psycho-active substances by a large segment of our society who rely upon them and actively seek their pleasurable sensations. We refer to the art, music and poetry—which are by-products of this activity. We refer to the demeanor, the dress, and the life style of those who depend on drugs as part of their every-day existence.

Since many compulsive drug abusers exhibit similar behavioral patterns and can be defined by their special mode of life within our society, we can validly identify them as members of a sub-culture, or if you will, the Drug Culture.

Who belongs to this special group? Recent studies indicate that representatives of all races, classes and ethnic groups are represented. Also included are some rich, but many poor, some educated, some illiterate, some with superior intelligence, some

279

near the imbecilic level, male and female, some middle aged, very few old, very many young.

Anybody can join the Drug Culture. All one has to do is become excessively dependent on alcohol, marihuana, tobacco, opium, barbiturates, amphetamines, or a host of other pleasure-giving substances which are alien and toxic to our bodies when misused.

Man's capacity for chemical self-indulgence has its roots in the earliest antiquity.

Over 2,500 years ago, Theognis wrote in his Maxims that "Wine is wont to show the mind of man." Homer, Plato, and Aristotle all wrote about the effects of noxious substances on human behavior, and an ancient Sumerian tablet described an herb, thought to be opium, as "the joy plant." However, only recently have we begun to witness the widespread use of drugs permeating all levels of society without attachment to religious or symbolic systems, ingested solely for their effect upon the senses, the Drug Culture.

The first modern record of widespread drug abuse is found in the chronicles of opium addicts in China in the 18th and 19th Centuries. So much opium was imported into China in the early 1800s that addiction grew to epidemic proportions. In 1839, the Chinese emperor appointed an energetic administrator to halt the spread of opium addiction. All foreign vessels were forbidden to carry opium into the country. When the law was violated, the ships' crews would be detained until the contraband was surrendered. This action curtailed foreign profits and was a blow to the prestige of many European countries, especially England, the largest exporter. The importation of opium continued unabated until 1911 when England and China finally signed a treaty banning further traffic in opium.

In the United States, addiction to opium was recognized before the Revolutionary War. The eating of opium was common among many of the lower and middle classes. In 1842, *Knickerbocker Magazine* carried an article by William Blair entitled "Opium Eater in America."

At the turn of the 19th century, a German pharmacist isolated the opium alkaloid that he named morphine after Morpheus, the Greek god of dreams. Morphine addiction soon became a recognized problem of its own, particularly with its uncontrolled use in military medicine during the American Civil War. Internationally, addiction among soldiers became so widespread during the latter half of the century that it soon became known as the "soldiers disease." The invention of the hypodermic syringe which made it possible to inject morphine directly into the bloodstream was originally thought to prohibit addiction since the drug did not pass through the stomach. Accordingly, the public reacted favorably by purchasing syringes and morphine on a do-it-yourself basis.

In 1874, a further modification of morphine was chemically developed in England. It was called heroin. By the beginning of this century, with reports that heroin was ten times more potent than morphine or codeine, a chemical company in Germany began commercial production of heroin. It was first believed that heroin would cure addiction to morphine, but it was soon learned that heroin was more highly addictive than any hitherto known substance.

In 1875, San Francisco became the first American city to pass an antiopiate law in reaction to demands for protective legislation against the "opium dens" in Chinatown.

At about the same time, cocaine was isolated from the leaves of a coca shrub which for hundreds of years had been sacred to the Incas.

The first global effort to control the spread of addictive drugs was the International Opium Commission, convened in Shanghai in 1909. Three more conventions met before 1915 to establish even tighter international controls, for by then, the detrimental effects of drug abuse were generally recognized. The League of Nations absorbed drug control activities after World War I, and in 1931, signatories of the League agreed to the limiting of manufacture and the regulation of distribution of narcotic drugs. The United States, through the Harrison Narcotic Act of 1914, had already enacted legislation in this regard, but it was not until 1930 that a Federal Bureau of Narcotics was established.

For hundreds of years peyote was used in Mexico, and at the turn of this century, use of the plant spread to several Indian tribes in the United States. The active ingredient of peyote is the alkaloid mescaline, which was named after the Mescalero Apaches who had developed religious rites involving the use of the drug. In order to protect their unique form of worship from restrictive legislation, several tribes of North American Indians joined to form the Native American Church in 1918. They argued that Peyotism is truly a religion whose followers believe that God put a form of his Holy

Spirit into the plant. The worshipers eat the sacramental peyote in the same way as bread and wine are consumed in certain Christian religions. Peyote has hallucinogenic properties as does LSD, a synthetic chemical which was accidentally discovered in Germany in 1943. After World War II, the United Nations adopted a narcotic protocol placing authority for the control of addictive drugs in the hands of the World Health Organization.

In India, a sticky and aromatic resin extracted from a hemp plant has been cultivated as a drug for countless generations. In Arabia, the same drug is called hashish. In the United States, the leaves of this plant are smoked as marihuana. Mexican laborers introduced marihuana smoking into our southern states within this century. New Orleans soon became the focal point of marihuana use but within the last 25 years, it has spread throughout the United States.

Some claim that the roots of the present Drug Culture were laid down during the early part of this century when chemists first discovered their ability to synthesize drugs. Today, among the most widely abused drugs are the manmade substances used as sedatives and stimulants. In 1903, the synthetic barbiturates were introduced into medicine as central nervous system depressants. This group of chemicals lends themselves to almost infinite variation, and some 1,500 or more derivatives of barbituric acid have been synthesized over the past 50 years. In 1949, approximately one of every four poisoning cases in United States hospitals was due to acute intoxication from barbiturates and they caused more deaths than any other type of poisoning.

A further potential for drug abuse became available in 1927 when a California pharmacologist synthesized amphetamine, which seemed to give the user extra energy and alertness. The amphetamines soon became known as "pep pills."

Today, members of the Drug Culture make use of all these substances and many more. Contemporary man now has the ability not only to pollute the atmosphere in a variety of ways, but his body as well, and to many Americans, the Drug Culture is now as normal a part of American life as cigarette smoking and the cocktail hour. Modern communications and advertising have helped spread the underlying theory of the Drug Culture, namely, that there now exists a substance to satisfy every desire.

We are exhorted dozens of times a day, on radio and TV, in newspapers and magazines, in hand-outs and on billboards—to take a little pill, capsule, tonic or tablet for the blues, blahs, and bloats.

But the problems of the Drug Culture come really not from the controlled medicinal use of these often life-sustaining substances, but in their abuse!

Most physicians and pharmacologists readily agree on the toxic and detrimental effect of drugs on our systems, but opinions among experts and laymen alike concerning the social and legal aspects of drug abuse are often conflicting and contradictory. Much of this confusion results from varying interpretations of data and the issue is often confounded by questionable statistics and a scarcity of hard facts. The real truth is that at this time, no one really knows the full extent of drug abuse in the United States.

Discussion of drug abuse often becomes argumentative and passionate. One school takes the view that our entire society is dependent on drugs in one form or another. They point to the widespread use of coffee, tea and even cola drinks to prove that almost everyone indulges in pleasure-giving substances at one time or another. Very often the proponents of this view take very liberal legal and social positions regarding the control and distribution of drugs. They often opt for the legalization of marihuana and other nonnarcotic substances and point out carefully that drug use is really an individual matter. They insist that each person reacts differently to the ingestion of drugs and argue that a substance can be at one and the same time used as a drug by one person but as a medicine, tonic, beverage or intoxicant by another.

But a majority of older Americans, according to a recent Gallup survey indicating drug abuse the third most important social question in the country, feels that a real distinction can and should be made between coffee, tea and tobacco on the one hand, and mind and mood altering drugs on the other.

Most people realize that a wide gulf exists between man's new-found ability for self abuse, made possible by the synthesis of new and dangerous drugs, and his long history of indulgence in pleasure-giving substances. They point to hard medical and social evidence of the destructive effects of contemporary drug abuse on man in particular and on society in general.

Very few have difficulty in distinguishing between tea and cocaine or coffee and morphine, and while many find withdrawal from cigarette smoking difficult and unpleasant, they, nevertheless are aware of the difference between that and withdrawal from heroin.

Many observers of the Drug Culture make a distinction between "hard" and "soft" drugs, meaning the difference between the most dangerous narcotic drugs like heroin and morphine and nonnarcotic substances like tobacco and marihuana. Some experts create a middle category between those two extremes into which they include alcohol and certain stimulants and sedatives, while others merely make a distinction between drugs which are physically addictive and those which are not. Many pharmacologists feel that narcotic drugs are only physically addictive, meaning that upon withdrawal of the drug, the addict suffers physical symptoms. But a good number of psychiatrists and other scientists support the view that drug addiction can also be primarily psychological in nature. They claim that many drug abusers depend upon drugs to escape the realities of life and to postpone emotional and personal problems.

When it comes to a discussion of the causes of drug abuse, experts and theorists abound from every discipline and there are as many opinions as there are people willing to talk about it.

Many claim the Drug Culture is a result of the change in values we have witnessed in recent years. The moral climate has changed, they claim, and permissiveness is the order of the day. Drug abusers are seen as self-indulgent persons who demand immediate gratification.

Others claim that drug abuse is a phenomenon reflecting the malaise of a sick society, that drug abusers are in fact challenging authority and society itself.

Sociologists tell us that peer group pressure plays an important role in starting a youngster on the road to drug abuse as does boredom, frustration, ennui and alienation.

Many believe that drug use can alone produce relief from the pressures and stresses of life and that it can alleviate hopelessness. Drugs are supposedly taken to cure loneliness, indicate rebellion, imitate others, for mere curiosity, for spiritual satisfaction, as part of adolescent experimentation, as an adventure into the forbidden and unknown, and taken by some merely out of habit.

Abusers report that under the influence of drugs they are happy, sad, exhilarated, fearful, aggressive, benign, sleepy or active. Drugs are reported to produce wonderful sensations, terrible experiences, religious insights, or panic and severe illness.

All this can be very confusing to the layman attempting to formulate an opinion of his own, but even after a cursory investigation several general conclusions do become apparent.

First, that we are indeed experiencing a unique phase in man's use of drugs, one that can aptly be termed a Drug Culture.

Second, that the use and abuse of drugs ultimately depend on the general perception of their pleasure-giving qualities. No one claims to purposely take drugs because they make the user feel bad.

And thirdly, that there exists a wide divergence of opinion concerning the extent, causes and effects of drug usage.

However, even when confronted with this diversity of opinion, an observer should be able to formulate one final conclusion: While it is true that the degree of sensation, reaction, capacity and tolerance for drugs varies from one individual to another, it is also equally true that a mind or mood altered artificially by drugs is substantially different from that prior to usage. Most abusers take drugs specifically for that reason, to make themselves feel different. In that quest, the abuser's compulsive desire for drugs can become so intense that he often suffers loss of self control. When that happens, when an individual becomes so dependent upon drugs that his own free will is no longer operative, then it seems that he has not only failed to achieve his goal of freedom but has instead become a prisoner in a new form of enslavement.

Abuse of Illegal Drugs   The use of illegal drugs, or of drugs acquired illegally, is another kind of abuse of particular concern. Illegal drugs, such as marijuana, LSD, and heroin, have almost no medically accepted application; their importation into the United States and the manufacture, sale, or possession of any of them within the country are prohibited by law.

Penalties for violations of the law include stringent fines and lengthy prison terms. But there are estimated to be 600,000 to 800,000 heroin addicts in the United States, and there is every reason to believe that the use of marijuana is extremely widespread; these facts indicate that the law is not particularly effective. Legal drugs that produce a "high"—morphine, codein, barbiturates, amphetamines, and tranquilizers—are frequently obtained illegally. They reach the market by various means: from illegal laboratories operating clandestinely; through use of forged prescription blanks; through the collusion of unscrupulous doctors and pharmacists; and through thefts from pharmaceutical companies.

Mixing of Drugs. A frequent practice among drug abusers is deliberate mixing of the drugs they intend to use. The contents of a barbiturate capsule may be dissolved in a solution of alcohol for intravenous injection; more commonly, the mixture of alcohol and barbiturate is taken orally. In such a mixture, alcohol is a potentiator; that is, it intensifies the effect of the barbiturate. When injected, the combination has a deteriorating effect on muscle tissues and may contribute to the formation of abscesses. Beyond that, since both barbiturates and alcohol depress the central nervous system, a potent mixture of the two may cause the collapse of one or more systemic functions. If that collapse should occur in the respiratory control center of the brain, breathing will cease, and the user will suffocate and die. A sizable overdose of barbiturates alone will produce this same effect, and that accounts for some 3,000 suicidal and accidental deaths in the United States each year. It is also likely that many deaths attributed to heroin overdose alone actually result from the mixture of heroin and alcohol in the body. The mixing of drugs is not unusual in ordinary experiences. People often take both aspirin and cough syrup containing codeine to treat a cough and cold. Where more potent drugs are concerned, particularly those that affect the central nervous system, the results of such mixing can be extremely dangerous.

The scope of drug abuse is an ever-widening one as the number of new drugs keeps increasing. An inherent danger in the improper use of these drugs is the development of drug dependence best described in terms of drug addiction or habituation. The World Health Organization has defined these terms as follows:

Drug Addiction is a state of periodic or chronic intoxication produced by the repeated consumption of a drug (natural or synthetic). Its characteristics include:

1. an overpowering desire or need (compulsion) to continue taking the drug and to obtain it by any means;
2. a tendency to increase the dose;
3. a psychic (psychological) and generally a physical dependence on the effects of the drug;
4. an effect detrimental to the individual and to society.

Drug Habituation (habit) is a condition resulting from the repeated administration of a drug. Its characteristics include:

1. a desire (but not compulsion) to continue taking the drug for the sense of improved well being that it engenders;

2. little or no tendency to increase the dose;
3. some degree of psychic dependence on the effect of the drug, but absence of physical dependence and hence of an abstinence syndrome;
4. a detrimental effect, if any, primarily to the individual.

It is significant to note that a number of drugs that were hailed as safe when first discovered and introduced were later found to be addictive, strongly habituating, or harmful in other ways. Drugs demand a respect for their beneficial effects when properly used and for the dangers they present to health and life itself when abused. A healthy respect for drugs is not present in our society as indicated by increased drug dependence, drug misuse, and drug-related deaths.

Drug Factors *Pharmacological properties.* So far we know little about drugs and about the human nervous system, so it is not possible to say precisely how a certain drug acts on a human organism. We can, however, describe the *general* properties of some drugs. For example, some drugs are classified according to which part of the body they affect. Drugs that stimulate the central nervous system are called CNS stimulants. Other drugs are classified according to their chemical makeup, such as opioids or cannabis products.

Dose-response function. Increasing the dose of a drug changes the way a drug affects people. This property is called the dose-response function. It is wrong to think, however, that increasing the dose simply intensifies the first effect. It may produce an opposite effect, as in the familiar case of the person who becomes friendly after one cocktail and belligerent and hostile after several.

Time-action function. The effects of a drug are greatest when tissue concentrations of the drug are changing the fastest, especially if they are increasing. A constant drug level, even if it is high, is likely to change the user's experience or behavior. Immediately after a person takes a drink, the alcohol begins to be absorbed into the digestive tract, and the level of alcohol in the blood begins to rise rapidly. As the alcohol is *metabolized,* the blood alcohol level gradually falls. Intoxication is much greater when the level is rising than when it is falling, even though there may actually be somewhat less alcohol in the blood.

Cumulative effects. Psychoactive drugs may over time cause physiological alterations in the body that change the effects of a drug. For example, people who use marijuana all the time often report more intense *subjective* reactions to a given dose of marijuana than occasional users. When habitual and occasional alcohol users take the same amount of alcohol, the habitual user is less affected.

Method of use. Swallowing a drug usually produces stronger effects than sniffing or inhaling the same drug, although this fact does not hold for drugs such as opium that are poorly absorbed from the digestive tract. Injecting a drug generally produces stronger effects than swallowing the same drug.

Physical differences in individual users. Even when the drug factors are the same for two individuals, they may respond quite differently. Weight can make a difference. The effect of a drug on a 100 pound person will be twice as great as the effect of the same amount on a 200 pound person. Other causes of differing responses include general health and various subtle *biochemical* states. Interactions between drugs, including many prescription drugs and over-the-counter drugs, can also have unpredictable effects.

Psychological and social factors. With large drug doses, *pharmacological* factors, the chemical properties of the drug itself, tend to have the strongest influence on a user's response. With small doses, psychological and social factors seem more important. These factors or variables, are called the setting. The *setting* means the physical and social environment surrounding the drug use. The *set* refers to how the user expects to react. Experiments have been conducted in which some subjects smoked small quantities of marijuana, while others (unknowingly) smoked a substance that smelled and tasted like marijuana but was not. The intensity of the *high* the subjects experienced was not related to whether or not they had actually smoked marijuana. Clearly the setting and the set had greater effects on the smokers than the drug itself.

The Drug Abuser

Although much is known about the effects of drugs with abuse potential, the user himself remains an enigma. Slum conditions, easy access to drugs, peddlers, and organized crime have been blamed for the problem. While any of these factors may contribute, no single cause nor single set of conditions clearly leads to drug dependency, for it occurs in all social and economic classes.

The key to the riddle may well lie within the abuser and any one of many sets or conditions. Drug dependency cannot develop without a chemical agent. Yet, while millions are exposed to drugs by reason of medical need, relatively few of these people turn to a life of drugs. It is true that in metropolitan areas, there are invariably found groups of "hard-core" users and a large proportion of the young persons who use drugs in the ghetto areas. Even though drugs may be available on street corners in metropolitan areas, only a small percentage of individuals exposed join the ranks of abusers.

For the most part, hard-core addicts suffer from certain types of emotional instability which may or may not have been apparent prior to initial drug abuse experience. Occasional cases may have a background (often undiagnosed) of psychiatric disorders. Some psychiatrists have said that addicts have an inherent inability to develop meaningful interpersonal relationships. Others have said that addicts are persons who are unwilling to face the responsibility of maturity. Adolescent addicts may have suffered childhood deprivation or overprotectiveness. Or, they simply may not be able to cope with the physical and emotional changes accompanying this period. It is significant that many addicts have their first drug experience in their teens.

The transition from childhood to adulthood is seldom smooth, and many individuals are not emotionally equipped to meet the demands they face. The early and middle teens bring a loosening of family ties, a diminution of parental authority, increasing responsibility and sexual maturing. Beset with anxiety, frustration, fear of failure, inner conflicts, and doubts, the adolescent may find that amphetamines and marihuana promote conversation and sociability; barbiturates relieve anxiety; hallucinogens heighten sensations; and narcotics provide relief and escape. Drug abuse may provide the entree to an "in group" or be a way of affirming independence by defying authority and convention.

In general, drug abusers fall into four main groups. The first group employs drugs for a specific or "situational" purpose. Examples: the student who uses amphetamines to keep awake at exam time; the housewife who uses anti-obesity pills for additional energy to get through household chores; the salesman who uses amphetamines to keep awake while driving all night to an early morning appointment. Such individuals may or may not exhibit psychological dependence.

The second group consists of "spree" users, usually of college or high school age. Drugs are used for "kicks" or just the experience. There may be some degree of psychological dependence, but little or no physical dependence because of the sporadic and mixed pattern of use. Some spree users may only try drugs once or twice and decide there are better things in life. Drug sprees constitute a defiance of convention, an adventurous daring experience, or a means of having fun. Unlike "hard-core" abusers, who often pursue their habits alone or in pairs, spree users usually take drugs in groups or at social functions.

The third is the "hard-core" addict. His activities revolve almost entirely around drug experience and securing supplies. He exhibits strong psychological dependence on the drug, often reinforced by physical dependence when certain drugs are being used. Typically, the hard-core addict began drug abuse on a spree basis. He has been on drugs for some time and presently feels that he cannot function without drug support.

A new type of drug abuser has emerged in the past few years that makes up the fourth group—the "hippies." These drug users tend to believe that the systems of today are either antiquated or wrong, and a new way of life should be found. Drugs are an integral part of the hippie life, and they could be considered the same as the "hard-core" abusers. The major difference is that most hippies do not come from the slum areas, but from middle or upper-middle income families, and their educational level is far above that of the ghetto dweller.

Obviously, there is much overlapping of these groups, and a spree or situational user may deteriorate to the hard-core group, or become enmeshed in the hippie philosophy. The transition occurs when the interaction between drug effects and a personality causes a loss of control over drug use. To the user, the drug becomes a means of solving or avoiding life's problems.

Slum sections of large metropolitan areas still account for the largest number of known heroin abusers. But frustration, immaturity, and the emotional deprivation are not peculiar to depressed neighborhoods, and the misuse of a variety of drugs by middle and upper economic class individuals is being recognized with increasing frequency. Drug dependence is not discriminating. A drug, an individual, an environment which predisposes use, and a personality deficiency are the key factors in its development.

Research has indicated that there are several predisposing characteristics of young drug abusers. The following profile is characteristic of many drug users:

1. No religious affiliation or nonpracticing.
2. Lower grades are most likely a variable.
3. No involvement in sports activities.
4. Low self-esteem.
5. Broken homes.
6. Less ambition for future.
7. Increased parental permissiveness towards licit drugs.
8. Parental use of drugs.
9. Use of cigarettes and alcohol early in life.

Of course some of these characteristics could be caused by drugs instead of leading to them. Some researchers have coined the term "addictive personality" which means that certain individuals are predisposed to relying on a crutch. These individuals will become dependent on any drug that they utilize and they are likely to progress towards more addicting drugs. As these individuals abuse one drug they eventually will seek a better high and a more addictive drug. The "addictive personality" could have some validity since many people abuse drugs, but only a small proportion will seek more addictive drugs and become physically addicted to them.

Researchers have also found that the reasons people experiment with drugs are curiosity and a pleasure seeking desire. Most people continue using nonaddicting drugs simply for the pleasurable feeling. Peer pressure, escape, boredom, and creativity influence some drug users, but the majority are simply seeking a pleasurable feeling. Even if the drug does not provide pleasure, they may avoid some discomfort while high. In our society, people seek pleasure and try to avoid discomfort. This attitude is developed very early. As soon as a young child develops symptoms of an illness, many parents will begin medication (over-the-counter or previous prescriptions). Thus, for every little thing, young people are conditioned to take medication. As the person grows older, he then has the concept that a pill (drug) will cure any of his problems. Reinforcing the pill taking attitude are the various advertisements used to promote the concept that our ordinary, day-to-day anxieties constitute diseases that the advertisers product will relieve or cure. They offer escape from problems and pressures that once were rightly regarded as a normal everyday part of human experience. Such advertising promises panaceas for almost every stress and strain. Some researchers feel that such widespread promotion of drugs, their magical qualities, and the immediacy of their effects may be factors that encourage young people to experiment with their chosen array of drugs, whose effects are just as immediate, just as magical, and just as wonderful for them.

Drugs of Abuse

Narcotics   The term *narcotic*, which originally referred to a variety of substances inducing an altered state of consciousness, in current usage means opium, its derivatives, or synthetic substitutes that produce tolerance and dependence, both psychological and physical.

Narcotics are especially useful in the practice of medicine for the relief of intense pain; they are the most effective analgesics known. They are also used as cough suppressants and as a remedy centuries old for diarrhea.

Relief of physical or psychic suffering through the use of narcotics may result in a short-lived state of euphoria. They also tend to induce drowsiness, apathy, lethargy, decreased physical activity, constipation, pinpoint pupils, and reduced vision. Except in cases of acute toxication, there is no loss of motor coordination or slurred speech as in the case of the depressants. A larger dose may induce sleep, but there is an increasing possibility of nausea, vomiting, and respiratory depression—the major toxic effect of the opiates.

The initial effects of narcotics are often unpleasant, leading many to conclude that those who persist in their use may have latent personality disturbances that antedate the physical and psychological dependence produced. To the extent that the response is felt to be pleasurable, its intensity may be expected to increase with the amount of the dose administered. Repeated use, however, will result in increasing tolerance; that is, the user must administer progressively larger doses to attain the desired effect, thereby reinforcing the compulsive behavior known as narcotics addiction.

Methods of administration include oral ingestion, sniffing or smoking, and the more direct—and correspondingly more rewarding—routes of subcutaneous ("skin popping"), intramuscular, and intravenous ("mainlining") injections. Since addicts tend to become preoccupied with the procuring and taking of drugs, they often neglect themselves and may suffer from malnutrition, infections, and unattended diseases or injuries. Among the hazards of addiction are contaminated drugs and needles as well as unsterile injection techniques, resulting commonly in abscesses, blood poisoning, hepatitis, and endocarditis.

Since there is no simple way to ascertain the purity of a drug that is sold on the street, the effects of illicit narcotics are unpredictable, compounding the dangers of overdose and death. A person suffering from a mild overdose may be stuporous or asleep. Larger doses may induce a coma and slow, shallow respiration. The skin becomes cold and clammy, the body limp, and the jaw relaxed. There is a danger that the tongue may fall back and block the air passageway. Convulsions may also occur. Death will follow if respiratory depression is sufficiently severe.

Physical dependence refers to an alteration in the normal functions of the body that necessitates the continued presence of a drug in order to prevent the withdrawal or abstinence syndrome characteristic of each class of addictive drugs. The intensity and character of the physical symptoms experienced during the withdrawal period are directly related to the amount of narcotic used each day and are characterized by states of increased excitability of those same bodily functions that have been depressed by the use of the drug.

With the deprivation of morphine or heroin, the first withdrawal signs are usually experienced shortly before the time of the next scheduled dose. Complaints, pleas, and demands by the addict are prominent, increasing in intensity and peaking from 36 to 72 hours after the last dose, then gradually subsiding. Symptoms such as watery eyes, runny nose, yawning, and perspiration appear about 8 to 12 hours after the last dose. Thereafter, the addict may fall into a restless sleep. As the abstinence syndrome progresses, restlessness, irritability, loss of appetite, insomnia, goose flesh, tremors, and finally violent yawning and severe sneezing occur. These symptoms reach their peak at 48 to 72 hours. The patient is weak and depressed with nausea and vomiting. Stomach cramps and diarrhea are common. Heart rate and blood pressure are elevated. Chills alternating with flushing and excessive sweating are also characteristic symptoms. Pains in the bones and muscles of the back and extremities occur as do muscle spasms and kicking movements, which may be the source of the expression "kicking the habit." At this time an individual may become suicidal. Without treatment the syndrome eventually runs its course and most of the symptoms will disappear in from 7 to 10 days. How long it takes to restore physiological and psychological equilibrium, however, is unpredictable. For a few weeks following withdrawal the addict will continue to think and talk about his use of drugs and be particularly susceptible to an urge to use them again.

The withdrawal syndrome may be avoided by reducing the dose of narcotic over a one-to-three-week period. Detoxification of an addict can be accomplished quite easily by substituting oral methadone for the illicit narcotic and gradually reducing the dose. However, the addict's entire pattern of life is built around drug taking and narcotic dependence is never entirely resolved by chemical withdrawal alone.

Infants born of addicted mothers may also be expected to experience withdrawal symptoms. Since narcotics pass the placenta, these babies are themselves physically dependent and possibly in a life-threatening condition. Therapy may be necessary to preserve the infant's life.

Narcotics of Natural Origin   The poppy *Papaver somniferum* is the primary source of the nonsynthetic narcotics. The milky fluid that oozes and is scraped from incisions made in the unripe seed pod is air dried to form raw opium.

Opium. The plant was grown in the Mediterranean region as early as 300 B.C. At various times it has been produced in Hungary, Yugoslavia, Turkey, India, Burma, China, and Mexico. There were no restrictions on the importation or use of opium in the United States until the early 1900s. Patent medicines in those days often contained opium without any warning label and many persons became physically dependent on medicines that were bought and sold without restriction. Today there are state, federal, and international laws governing the production and distribution of narcotic substances, and there is little abuse of opium in this country.

At least 25 organic substances can be extracted from opium. These are alkaloids of two general categories, each producing markedly different effects. The first, represented by morphine and codein, are used as analgesics and cough suppressants. The second, represented by papaverine (an intestinal relaxant) and noscapine (a cough suppressant), have no significant influence on the central nervous system and are not regulated under the CSA. About 240,000 kilograms of opium are legally imported into the United States annually. Although a small part of this amount is used to make antidiarrheal preparations such as paregoric, most of it is processed by U.S. pharmaceutical and chemical firms for the manufacture of morphine and codeine.

Morphine. The principal constituent of opium, ranging in concentration from 4 to 21 percent, morphine is one of the most effective drugs known for the relief of pain. It is marketed in the form of white crystals, hypodermic tablets, and injectable preparations. Its licit use is restricted primarily to hospitals. Morphine is odorless, tastes bitter, and darkens with age. It is administered subcutaneously, intramuscularly or intravenously, the latter method being the one most frequently resorted to by addicts. Tolerance and dependence develop rapidly in the user. Most of the morphine extracted from opium by the pharmaceutical industry is converted to codeine and semisynthetic narcotics. Since morphine remains in the dried opium poppy, it can also be produced from the so-called poppy straw process, which provides for the collection of the whole poppy pod rather than opium gum.

Codeine. This alkaloid is found in raw opium in concentrations ranging from 0.7 to 2.5 percent. It was first isolated in 1832 as an impurity in a batch of morphine. Although it occurs naturally, most codeine is produced from morphine. As compared with morphine, codeine produces less analgesia, sedation, and respiratory depression. It is widely distributed in products of two general types. Codeine for the relief of moderate pain may consist of codeine tablets or be combined with other products such as Empirin Compound or APC. Some examples of liquid codeine preparations for the relief of coughs (antitussives) are Robitussin AC, Cheracol, and elixir of terpin hydrate with codeine. Codeine is also manufactured to a lesser extent in injectable form for the relief of pain.

Thebaine. A minor constituent of opium, which may also be obtained from the species *Papaver bracteatum,* thebaine is chemically close to both codeine and morphine but produces stimulant rather than depressant effects. Although not in itself a drug of abuse, thebaine can be converted into therapeutically useful narcotic drugs subject to abuse, and it is therefore regulated under the CAS.

Semi-Synthetic Narcotics The following narcotics are among the more significant synthetic substances that have been derived by modification of the chemicals contained in opium.

Heroin. First synthesized from morphine in 1874, heroin was not extensively used in medicine until the beginning of this century. The Bayer Company in Germany first started commercial production of the new pain remedy in 1898. While it received widespread acceptance, the medical profession for years remained unaware of its potential for addiction. The first comprehensive control of heroin in the United States was established with the Harrison Narcotic Act of 1914. Pure heroin is a white powder with a bitter taste. Illicit heroin may vary in color from white to dark brown because of impurities left from the manufacturing process or the presence of diluents such as food coloring, cocoa, or brown sugar. Pure heroin is rarely sold on the street. A "bag"—slang for a single dosage unit of heroin—may weigh about 100 mg, usually containing less than 10 percent heroin. To increase the bulk of the material sold the addict, diluents are mixed with the heroin in ratios ranging from 9 to 1 to as much as 99 to 1. Sugar, starch, powdered milk, and quinine are among the diluents used.

Hydromorphone. Most commonly known as Dilaudid, hydromorphone is the second oldest semisynthetic derivative of morphine. Its analgesic effect is from 2 to 8 times that of morphine. It is shorter acting, more sedative, and less euphoriant than morphine. It is available both in tablets and in injectable form, the latter the most frequently used and abused.

Oxycodone. Oxycodone is synthesized from thebaine. It is similar to codeine, but more potent and with a higher dependence potential. It is effective orally and is marketed in combination with other drugs as Percodan for the relief of pain. Addicts take Percodan orally or dissolve tablets in water, filter out the insoluble material, and "mainline" the active drug.

Etorphine and Diprenorphine. Both substances are made from thebaine. Etorphine is more than a thousand times as potent as morphine in its analgesic, sedative and respiratory depressant effects. For human use its potency is a distinct disadvantage because of the danger of overdose. Etorphine hydrochloride (M99) is used by veterinarians to immobilize large wild animals. Diprenorphine hydrochloride (M50–50), acting as an antagonist, counteracts the effects of etorphine. The manufacture and distribution of both substances are strictly regulated under the CSA.

Synthetic Narcotics In contrast to pharmaceutical products derived directly or indirectly from narcotics of natural origin, synthetic narcotics may be chemically related to the opium alkaloids but are produced entirely within the laboratory. A continuing search for a product that will retain the analgesic properties of morphine without the consequent dangers of tolerance and dependence has yet to yield a drug that is not susceptible of abuse. The two that are most widely available are meperidine and methadone.

Meperidine (pethidine). The first synthetic narcotic, produced originally a generation ago, meperidine is chemically dissimilar to morphine but resembles it in its analgesic potency. Next to morphine it is probably the most widely used drug for the relief of intense pain. Available in pure form as well as in products containing other medicinal ingredients, it is administered either orally or by injection, the latter method the most widely abused.

Methadone. In response to a shortage of morphine during World War II, German chemists synthesized methadone. Although chemically unlike morphine or heroin, it produces many of the same effects. It is administered orally or by injection. Tolerance and physical dependence can develop. Withdrawal symptoms develop more slowly and are less severe than in withdrawal from morphine or heroin but may be more prolonged. Methadone was introduced in the United States in 1947 as an analgesic and distributed under such names as Amidone, Dolophine, and Methadon. Since the 1960s it has become widely used in detoxification of heroin addicts and in methadone maintenance programs. There are special restrictions imposed by the Federal Food, Drug, and Cosmetic Act as well as the CSA for both the manufacture and use of methadone.

Other synthetic narcotics in current medical use are levorphan (Levo-Dromoran), phenazocine (Prinadol), alphaprodine

(Nisentil), and anileridine (Leritine). All produce many of the same effects of morphine, but they differ primarily in their potency and duration of action. All have addiction liability.

Cannabis Sativa   *Cannabis sativa* L. is in wide distribution throughout the temperate and tropical regions of the world. The plant has been cultivated for centuries for the hemp fibers of the stem, the seeds which are used in feed mixtures, and the oil as an ingredient of paint, as well as for the biologically active substance contained in its leaves and flowering tops. The plant is grown extensively in Jamaica, Colombia, Mexico, Africa, India, and the Middle East. It is considered by most botanists to be a single species with many varieties.

The principal psychoactive substance in cannabis is thought to be delta-9-tetrahydrocannabinol (THC), a unique chemical found nowhere else in nature. THC is produced occasionally in the laboratory for purposes of research, but no synthetic THC has so far been found in the illicit traffic. In addition to delta-9-THC, cannabis contains other cannabinoids and chemicals, the biological effects of which have not yet been determined.

As a psychoactive drug, cannabis is usually smoked in the form of loosely rolled cigarettes ("joints"), although it may also be taken orally. It may be smoked alone or in the combination with other plant materials. Low doses tend to produce initial restlessness and an increased sense of well-being, followed by a dreamy, carefree state of relaxation; alteration of sensory perceptions, including an illusory expansion of time and space; a more vivid sense of touch, sight, smell, taste, and sound; hunger, especially a craving for sweets; together with subtle changes in thought formation and expression. Moderate doses may result in a state of intoxication that intensifies these reactions. The individual may experience rapidly changing emotions, shifting sensory imagery, a flight of fragmentary thoughts with disturbed associations, a dulling of attention, and impaired memory, accompanied by an altered sense of self-identity and commonly a sense of enhanced insight. Even at higher doses, however, this condition of intoxication may not be noticeable to an observer. High doses can result in distortions of body image, loss of personal identity, fantasies, and hallucinations. Very high doses may precipitate a toxic psychosis. This state will clear as the drug is eliminated from the body.

Despite preliminary reports to the contrary, there have been several papers in scientific journals since 1971 that document the dependence-producing properties of cannabis. The reported withdrawal syndrome is characterized by sleep loss and disturbance, irritability, restlessness, hyperactivity, decreased appetite, sweating, sudden weight loss, increased salivation, and increased introacular pressure. Although the amounts involved were usually large and not typical of prevailing patterns of use, the dangers of a withdrawal syndrome in at least some heavy users must be considered.

Three forms of cannabis are currently distributed on the illicit U.S. market, which, it should be noted, vary markedly in their psychoactive chemical content.

Marihuana. Marihuana, the popular name of the cannabis plant, also denotes the drug that is prepared by drying the leaves and flowering tops of the plant to make a tobaccolike material. Marihuana produced in the United States is considered inferior because of the low concentration of psychoactive ingredients, which varies between 0.2 and 2.0 percent. Marihuana of Mexican origin is known to be slightly stronger. The variety known as Jamaican ganja, which consists primarily of the flowers and bracts, has a TCH content of 4 to 8 percent.

Hashish. A drug-rich resinous secretion from the flowers of the cannabis plant, hashish is processed by drying to produce a drug several times as potent as marihuana. The resin from the flowers is richer in cannabinols than the leaves and tops, ranging in THC content from 5 to 12 percent.

Hashis Oil. A concentrate of cannabis, hashish oil is produced by a process of repeated extraction to yield a dark viscous liquid, samples of which have been found to contain from 20 to 60 percent THC. A drop or two of this liquid on a cigarette is equal in psychoactive effect to an entire marihuana cigarette.

Half of Americans Age 18 to 25 Said to Have Tried Marijuana   More than half of the Americans in the 18-to-25-year age group have tried marijuana at least once, according to a government report.

The report, stated that scientists were still uncertain about the drug's long-term effects on health and behavior.

Prepared by the National Institute on Drug Abuse, the report said that use of the drug appeared to be concentrated primarily in the 18–to–25–age bracket and was twice as common among males as females.

A survey made in 1972 indicated that 48 percent of that age group had tried marijuana. The figure rose to 53 percent in the latest survey, made in late 1974 and early 1975. One in four of those sampled said that they had used the drug within the last month.

The new report also cited a Gallup survey that put the percentage of college students who had tried the drug at 55 percent, a substantial increase from 1967, when only one in 20 said that he had used it.

In seven years, the institute's report said, what was once clearly statistically deviant behavior has become the norm for this age group. While in previous years use was correlated with level of education, the percentage now reporting marijuana use is virtually identical for high school dropouts, high school graduates and college graduates in similar age ranges.

Once a drug associated with the "counter-culture" and regarded as a symbol of opposition, marijuana has lost some of its anti-establishment symbolism. The drug also appears to be in common use with alcohol, rather than as an alternative to that other widely used "recreational" drug.

The report said, however, that marijuana had not become popular with persons in the older age groups, and that its use might diminish as the young adopted such adult roles as careers and marriage. However, the report said that any prediction regarding the future of the drug in American society must be hedged with caution.

The same caution was applied to most of the much-publicized health and behavioral effects of long-term use of marijuana.

In the past, medical reports from various sources have attributed all manner of ill-effects to prolonged use of marijuana. Among these were disruption of basic cellular function, hormonal imbalance, interference with the body's defense against infection and impairment of sperm production. All of these remain unproved, the report said, but at the same time, none have been conclusively disproved.

Charges of serious behavioral effects were similarly described as unresolved. Reported ill-effects have included mental illness, diminished intellectual performance and loss of interest in work and other conventional activities.

Interpretation of such reports has unfortunately been complicated by the lack of adequate control groups, poor research design, use of opium and other drugs, poor diagnostic criteria, nutritional deficiencies and other differing factors of life style, the document said.

It cited one study of admissions to a mental hospital showing a statistical correlation between use of marijuana and subsequent mental illness.

While there was a correlation between marijuana and subsequent psychiatric illness, the report said, it was less than with such casually unrelated variables as having danced and having drunk beer.

The report also cast doubt on such reported benefits of the drug as enhanced vision, hearing and sense of feel.

Marijuana Seen as Help in Cancer Treatments   Marijuana shows unusual promise in the treatment of cancer patients but the drug can create physical dependency among long-term, chronic users, according to a government report.

"This report does not give marijuana a clean bill of health, as some would hope," said Dr. Robert Dupont.

"Nor does it support the fear and irrationality that still characterize some of the public debate about marijuana," he said.

Instead, he said, it is a progress report on the effort to understand a challenging health problem with "immense social, political and economic implications."

Dupont said marijuana use is exceeded only by use of alcohol and tobacco.

The report said marijuana use has increased so significantly during the last two years that for the first time a majority of young persons aged 18 to 25—53 percent—have now tried the drug.

Marijuana shows unusual promise in reducing nausea and vomiting in cancer patients receiving chemotherapy, it said.

At the same time, it said a suspicion that long-term chronic marijuana smokers develop a tolerance to the drug—requiring increased amounts to achieve the same effect—is confirmed by recent evidence.

MDs Find Potential Benefits Along with Pot Dangers Prolonged marijuana use may be fraught with dangers scientists are yet only dimly aware of. But the drug may have therapeutic potential.

One of the most voluminous studies was performed by Dr. Sidney Cohen, who has been looking at the subject of marijuana for the past four years.

He recently completed a study of the effects of heavy marijuana use on male subjects from 21 to 35 years of age. Dr. Cohen lists some of his findings.

He found that work behavior is not significantly affected whether the subject is stoned or sober. Still, Dr. Cohen suspects that individuals who have smoked pot may not perform as well on complicated tasks.

It may be that doing a boring task while under the influence of a mild tranquilizer makes for better results.

He found that marijuana, like tobacco, irritates the bronchial tubes. Both substances contain coal tar, said to be a cancer producing agent.

But pot, unlike tobacco, also widens the bronchial tubes. Asthma is uncomfortable and dangerous because these tubes become constricted.

Possibly, hypothesizes Dr. Cohen, some form of marijuana could be used in the treatment of asthma.

In addition, heavy marijuana use does not cause the pupil of one's eyes to dilate. In the past, policemen have looked for dilated pupils as evidence of pot smoking and some courts in criminal trials have accepted this evidence to "prove" the suspect has been involved with marijuana.

Marijuana does, however, decrease inward pressure on the eyeball. People with glaucoma have elevated pressure on the eyeball; it may be that marijuana in some form may some day be used as a treatment for glaucoma.

Dr. Cohan, contradicting at least one other finding, reported that heavy marijuana use does not lead to impairment of the immunity of individuals to resist infections or cancer.

But he does indicate that male sex hormones are temporarily lowered by pot, though not enough, he continued, to be a reliable method of birth control.

This finding might spell trouble for two classes of people, each of whom rely on the production of these male hormones especially at certain stages of their lives. One class is young men who are just developing sexually. The other class is pregnant women.

An interesting finding concerns the right-left dichotomy of the brain. The left side is said to be the rational, logical side; the right the creative, intuitive side. Pot seems to shift the dominance from the left to the right.

Thus, many marijuana users allege smoking enhances their ability to paint or write poetry or symphonies.

"There might be something to this, but I'm not at all sure," said Dr. Cohen, emphasizing the preliminary aspect of this finding. "I suspect the sober mind is probably the best state for creativity."

Dr. Jack Mendelson spoke of what pot fans call the "munchies"— an increased appetite after smoking.

Indeed, his studies show a significant increase in both caloric intake and weight gain during continual pot smoking. With heavy users the increase is even more dramatic.

"Some of the weight gain might be due to water retention," he surmised. "But not all." The subjects were certainly eating a lot more.

Other findings indicated that when a habitual user went on the wagon, he frequently showed loss of appetite and consequent weight loss.

Studies carried out in Canada reveal pot puffing can adversely affect driving ability.

"At this point," said Dr. Ralph Hanstein, "We would have to say driving under the influence of cannabis, like alcohol, should be avoided." He conceded that pot, unlike alcohol, might have one beneficial effect in an auto situation: It might reduce aggressiveness in driving.

The experts agreed psychological effects of long-term use are less understood than the biological effects. For instance, just how habitual use may decrease reality perception in those who have stopped smoking is a worrisome, but unstudied aspect.

Stimulants

The consumption of chemical agents that stimulate the central nervous system is an accepted part of modern life. The two most prevalent stimulants are nicotine, contained in tobacco products, and caffeine, the active ingredient in coffee, tea, and some bottled beverages sold in every supermarket. When used in moderation they tend to have the effects of relief from fatigue and increased alertness.

There is also a broad range of stronger stimulants that may produce mood elevation and a heightened sense of well-being, but because of their dependence-producing potential are under regulatory control. The controlled stimulants are available on prescription, and they are also clandestinely manufactured in vast quantities for the illicit market. Chronic users tend to rely on stimulants to feel stronger, more confident, decisive, and self-possessed. They often follow a pattern of taking; "uppers" in the morning and "downers" such as alcohol or sleeping pills at night. Such chemical self-control, however, interferes with normal body processes and can lead to mental and physical illness.

Young people who resort to stimulants for their euphoric effects consume large doses sporadically, over weekends or at night, often going on to experiment with other drugs of abuse. The oral consumption of stimulants may result in a temporary sense of exhilaration, superabundant energy, hyperactivity, and extended wakefulness; it may also induce irritability, anxiety and apprehension. These effects are greatly intensified with administration by intravenous injection, which may produce a sudden sensation known as a "flash" or "rush." The protracted use of stimulants is followed, however, by a period of depression known as "crashing" that is invariably described as unpleasant. Since the depression can be easily counteracted by a further injection of stimulant, this abuse pattern becomes increasingly difficult to break. Heavy users may inject themselves every few hours, a process sometimes continued to the point of delirium, psychosis, or physical exhaustion.

Tolerance develops rapidly, increasing the probability of overdose. Larger doses also result in various mental aberrations, the early signs of which include repetitive grinding of the teeth, touching and picking the face and extremities, performing the same task over and over, a preoccupation with one's own thought processes, suspiciousness, and a feeling of being watched. Paranoia with auditory and visual hallucinations characterize the toxic syndrome resulting from continued high doses. Dizziness, tremor, agitation, hostility, panic, headache, flushed skin, chest pain with palpitations, excessive sweating, vomiting, and abdominal cramps are among the symptoms of a sublethal overdose. In the absence of medical intervention, high fever, convulsions, and cardiovascular collapse may precede the onset of death. Since death is due in part to the consequences of a marked increase in body temperature, it should be added that physical exertion and environmental temperature may greatly increase the hazards of stimulant use. Fatalities under conditions of extreme exertion have been reported among athletes who have taken stimulants in moderate amounts.

Whether or not these drugs produce *physical* dependence is still open to question. But there can be no doubt that the chronic high-dose users do not easily or soon return to normal if withdrawn from stimulants. Profound apathy and depression, fatigue, and disturbed sleep up to 20 hours a day characterize the immediate withdrawal syndrome, which may last for several days. A lingering impairment of perception and thought processes may also be present. So strong is the psychological dependence produced by the sustained use of stimulants that anxiety, an incapacitating tenseness, and suicidal tendencies may persist for weeks or months.

Cocaine. The principal active ingredient of the South American coca plant, cocaine is the strongest stimulant of natural origin. In the Andean highlands, where it has been cultivated since prehistoric times, the leaves of the plant are chewed for refreshment and relief from fatigue, much as North Americans once chewed tobacco. While most of the crop serves the needs of a domestic subsistence economy, some cocaine is legally exported to the United States. In this country the leaves—decocainized—yield flavoring extracts for cola beverages and the pure cocaine extract supplies a dwindling world market for medical purposes. Cocaine as a local anesthetic has been largely supplanted by synthetic substitutes, its medical applications now mainly restricted to ear, nose, and throat surgery. While the demand for licit cocaine has been going down, the supply of illicit cocaine in recent years has been rapidly rising. Virtually all the cocaine available in this country today is of illicit origin. It is sold on the street in the form of a white crystalline powder containing usually from 5 to 10 percent pure cocaine "cut" with other white powders such as procaine, lidocaine, and lactose. It is administered by sniffing or "snorting" and for heightened effect by intravenous injection, producing intense euphoria with increased heartbeat, blood pressure, body temperature, . . . a sense of increased muscular strength, talkativeness, and a reduction in the feeling of fatigue. The pupils become dilated. In larger doses, cocaine can produce fever, vomiting, convulsions, hallucinations and paranoid delusions. In cases of overdose, breathing and heart functions may be so depressed that death results.

Because of the intense stimulation received from this drug, most abusers voluntarily seek sedation, sometimes combining depressant drugs with cocaine. (A cocaine-heroin combination is called a "speedball.")

The cocaine abuser may feel a strong psychological dependence on the drug although physical dependence does not develop. When use is stopped, he may feel depressed, and hallucinations may persist.

Amphetamines. Amphetamine, dextroamphetamine, and methamphetamine are so closely related chemically that they can be differentiated from one another only in the laboratory. Amphetamine was first synthesized in 1887 and first used clinically in the mid-1930s to treat narcolepsy, a rare disorder resulting in an uncontrollable desire for sleep. After the introduction of the amphetamines into medical practice, the number of conditions for which they were prescribed multiplied, and so did the quantities made available. They were sold without prescription for a time in inhalers and other over-the-counter preparations. Abuse of the inhalers became popular among teenagers and prisoners. Housewives, students, and truck drivers were among those who used amphetamines orally in excessive amounts, and "speed freaks," who injected them, won notoriety in the drug culture for their bizarre and often violent behavior. Whereas a prescribed dose of methamphetamine is between 2.5 and 15 mg per day, those on a speed binge have been known to inject as much as 1,000 mg every two or three hours. Recognition of the deleterious effects of these drugs brought about a limitation of their medical use and a corresponding reduction in the availability of proprietary products containing them. Medical use of the amphetamines is now limited to narcolepsy, appetite control in cases of obesity, and hyperkinetic behavioral disorders in children. Despite the recent reappraisal of the amphetamines, which resemble cocaine in effects as well as potential for dependence, they remain in wide distribution on the illicit market.

Phenmetrazine (Preludin) *and Methylphenidate* (Ritalin). The effects, medical indications, patterns of abuse, and adverse effects of phenmetrazine (Preludin) and methylphenidate (Ritalin) compare closely with those of the other stimulants. The primary medical use of phenmetrazine is as an appetite suppressant and that of methylphenidate for treatment of hyperkinetic behavioral disorders in children. They have been subject to abuse in countries where freely available, as they are here in a few localities where there are medical practitioners who write prescriptions on demand. While the abuse of phenmetrazine involves both oral and intravenous use, most of that associated with methylphenidate results from injection after the drug in tablet form is dissolved in water. Complications arising from such use are common since the tablets contain insoluble materials which upon injection give rise to blood clots and abscesses, especially in the lungs.

Anorectic Drugs. In recent years a number of drugs have been manufactured and marketed to replace amphetamines as appetite suppressants. These so-called anorectic drugs include benzphetamine (Didrex, etc.), chlorphentermine (Pre-Sate, etc.), clortermine (Voranil), diethylpropion (Tenuate, Tepanil, etc.) fenfluramine (Pondimin), mazindol (Sanorex), phendimetrazine (Plegine, Bacarate, Melfiat, Statobex, Tanorex, etc.), and phentermine (Lonamin, Wilpo, etc.). They produce many of the effects of the amphetamines but are generally less potent. Abuse patterns of some of them have not yet been established, but all are controlled to prevent their becoming subject to abuse. Fenfluramine differs somewhat from the others in that at low doses it produces sedation; it is presently controlled in Schedule IV. The others, with the exception of diethylpropion and phentermine, are in Schedule III. (Diethylpropion and phentermine have been recommended for Schedule III, but pending the outcome of judicial proceedings remain in Schedule IV.)

Pemoline (Cylert). Early in 1975 pemoline was approved for marketing as a drug to be used in the treatment of hyperkinetic behavioral disorders in children. During its development it was said to enhance learning and increase memory—claims since found to be unwarranted. If taken in sufficient doses, it produces the general effects of a stimulant. It is in Schedule IV.

Depressants

Substances regulated under the CSA as depressants have a potential for abuse associated with both physical and psychological dependence.

Taken in amounts as prescribed by a physician, depressants can be beneficial in the symptomatic treatment of insomnia, relief of anxiety, irritability, and tension. In excessive amounts, however, they produce a state of intoxication that is remarkably similar to that of alcohol.

As in the case of alcohol, these effects may be expected to vary not only from person to person but from time to time in the same individual. Low doses produce mild sedation; higher doses, insofar as they relieve anxiety or stress, may produce a temporary state of euphoria, but they may also produce mood depression and apathy. In marked contrast to the effects of narcotics, however, intoxicating doses invariably result in impaired judgment, slurred speech, and an often unrealized loss of motor coordination. They may also induce drowsiness, sleep, stupor, coma, and possible death.

The abuse of depressants falls into several distinct patterns. Episodic intoxication is found most commonly in young adults or teenagers, whose source of supply may be the family medicine cabinet, the illicit market, theft, or illegal prescriptions. In addition to the dangers of disorientation, resulting in accidents on the highway or by an overdose, habitual users incur increasing risks of long-term involvement with drugs. Tolerance to depressants develops rapidly, extending the intake capacity while narrowing the range between an intoxicating and lethal dose. The person who is unaware of the dangers of increasing dependence will often seek prescriptions from several physicians concurrently, increasing the daily dose up to 10 or 20 times the recommended amount, nor will others recognize the person's problem until he or she exhibits confusion, decreased ability to work, or recurrent episodes of intoxication. Members of the drug subculture often use depressants as self-medication to soothe the "jangled nerves" brought on by the use of stimulants, to quell the anxiety of "flashbacks," or to ease their withdrawal from heroin. The dangers of depressants, it should be stressed, multiply when used in combination with other drugs or alcohol. Chronic intoxication by depressants is most common in middle age. Depressants also serve as a means of suicide, a pattern especially common among women.

The depressants, as will be shown, vary with respect to their lethal overdose potential. Moderate depressant overdose closely resembles alcoholic inebriation. The symptoms of severe depressant poisoning are coma, a cold and clammy skin, a weak and rapid pulse, and a slow or rapid but shallow respiration. Death will follow if the reduced respiration and low blood pressure are not counteracted by proper medical treatment.

Anyone who ceases to take or abruptly curtails the amount of a depressant on which he has become dependent will encounter symptoms of withdrawal more severe than in an otherwise comparable case of narcotics addiction. In its mildest form the abstinence syndrome is characterized by anxiety, agitation, and apprehension, accompanied by a loss of appetite, nausea, vomiting, a palpitating heart, excessive sweating, fainting, insomnia, tremulousness, and muscle spasms. If the individual is dependent on a large amount of the drug, delirium, psychotic behavior, or convulsions and even death may occur. In view of the severity of the withdrawal syndrome, it is recommended that withdrawal from depressants be supervised under the controlled conditions of a hospital. The withdrawal regimen will usually consist of the substitution of a long-acting barbiturate for the depressant used, followed by a gradual decreasing of the dose.

Among the depressants that most commonly give rise to the general conditions described above are chloral hydrate, a broad range of barbiturates, glutethimide, methaqualone, the benzodiazepines, and meprobamate.

Chloral Hydrate. The oldest of the hypnotic (sleep-inducing) drugs, chloral hydrate was first synthesized in 1862 and soon supplanted alcohol, opium, and cannabis preparations to induce sedation and sleep. Its popularity declined after the introduction of the barbiturates, but chloral hydrate is still widely used. It has a penetrating, slightly acrid odor, and a bitter caustic taste. Its depressant effect, as well as resulting tolerance and dependence, are comparable to those of alcohol, and withdrawal symptoms resemble delirium tremens. Chloral hydrate is marketed in the form of syrups and soft gelatin capsules. Cases of poisoning have occurred from mixing chloral hydrate with alcoholic drinks. Chloral hydrate is not a "street" drug of choice. Its main misuse is by older adults.

Barbiturates. Among the drugs most frequently prescribed to induce sedation and sleep by both physicians and veterinarians are the barbiturates. About 2,500 derivatives of barbituric acid have been synthesized, but of these only about 15 remain in widespread use. Small therapeutic doses tend to calm nervous conditions, and larger amounts cause sleep from 20 to 60 minutes after oral administration. As in the case of alcohol, some individuals may experience a sense of excitement before sedation takes effect. If dosage is increased, however, the effects of the barbiturates may progress through successive stages of sedation, sleep, and coma to death from respiratory arrest and cardiovascular complications.

Barbiturates are classified as ultrashort, short, intermediate and long-acting. The ultrashort-acting barbiturates produce anesthesia within one minute after intravenous administration. The rapid onset and brief duration of action practically preclude abuse of these drugs. Those in current medical use are buthalital (Transithal), hexobarbital (Evipal), methitural (Neraval), methohexital (Brevital), thiamylal (Surital), and thiopental (Pentothal).

Among the short-acting and intermediate-acting barbiturates are pentobarbital (Nembutal), secobarbital (Seconal), and amobarbital (Amytal)—three of the most widely used and abused drugs in the depressant category; the group also includes butabarbital (Butisol), butalbital (Lotusate), allobarbital (Dial), aprobarbital (Alurate), and vinbarbital (Delvinal). The onset time of action is from 15 to 40 minutes and duration of action is up to 6 hours. Physicians prescribe short-acting barbiturates for purposes of sedation. Veterinarians use pentobarbital for anesthesia and euthanasia. They may also be misused as suicide agents.

Long-acting barbiturates, which include barbital (Veronal), phenobarbital (Luminal), methylphenobarbital (Mebaral), and metharbital (Gemonil), have onset times of up to one hour and durations of action up to 16 hours. They are used medicinally as sedatives, hypnotics, and anticonvulsants; they may also be useful for gastrointestinal disorders and as preanesthetic medication. Their slow onset of action precludes the possibility of their use for episodic intoxication, and they are not ordinarily distributed on the illicit market. It should be emphasized, however, that all barbiturates result in a rapid buildup of tolerance, and dependence on them is widespread.

Glutethimide. When glutethimide (Doriden) was first introduced in 1954, it was believed to be a safe barbiturate substitute without an addiction potential. But experience has shown glutethimide to be another CNS depressant with no particular advantage over the barbiturates. The sedative effects of glutethimide begin about 30 minutes after oral administration and last for 4 to 8 hours. Glutethimide is marked as Doriden in 125, 250, and 500 mg tablets. Because the effects of this drug are of long duration, it is exceptionally difficult to reverse overdoses, which often result in death.

Methaqualone. Methaqualone is a synthetic sedative chemically unrelated to the barbiturates, glutethimide, or chloral hydrate. It has been widely abused because it was once mistakenly thought to be safe, nonaddictive, and to have aphrodisiac qualities. Actually, methaqualone has caused many cases of serious poisoning. It is administered orally. Large doses cause coma and may be accompanied by thrashing movements or convulsions. Continued heavy use of large doses leads to tolerance and dependence. Methaqualone has been marketed in the United States under various brand names such as Quaalude, Parest, Optimil, Somnafac, and Sopor. Mandrax is a European brand name for methaqualone in combination with an antihistamine.

Minor tranquilizers somehow insulate an individual from external stimuli that cause him anxiety and stress. It is generally believed that these drugs, which decrease excessive emotional behavior, act directly on the reticular formation and lower areas of the brain; but the exact sites of action have not been identified.

A large variety of these agents are on the market. Four of the most frequently used minor tranquilizers are *benzodiazepines* (Valium), *meprobamate* (Milltown and Equanil), *diphenylmethanes* (Phobex, Suavitil, and Atarax) and *chlordiazepoxide* (Librium and Librax).

The minor tranquilizers are potent antianxiety drugs and should be considered dangerous. There have been reports of both addiction to meprobamate and suicides. Thus, they are not so harmless as their advertising image and casual use by the general public might suggest.

Few of the minor tranquilizers are commonly used illegally, mainly because they do not produce any euphoric effect. But addiction to them can come from increased dosages over a long period of time. Consequently, in the addiction-prone personality, the progressive increase in self-administration of tranquilizers is a very real danger and would be termed drug abuse. When large dosages are taken for long periods of time, a sudden withdrawal may result in muscular twitching, convulsions, and other withdrawal symptoms. The dosages recommended by a physician may be maintained for extremely long periods of time without adverse effects.

Hallucinogens

The hallucinogenic drugs are substances, both natural and synthetic, that distort the perception of objective reality. They produce sensory illusions, making it difficult to distinguish between fact and fantasy. If taken in large doses, they cause hallucinations— the apparent perception of unreal sights and sounds. Under the influence of hallucinogens, a user may speak of "seeing" sounds and "hearing" colors. His sense of direction, distance, and time become disoriented. Restlessness and sleeplessness are common until the drug wears off. Recurrent use produces tolerance, inviting the use of greater amounts. The greatest hazard of the hallucinogens is that their effects are unpredictable each time they are taken. Toxic reactions that precipitate psychotic reactions and even death can occur. Persons in hallucinogenic states should be closely supervised—and upset as little as possible—to keep them from harming themselves and others. There is no documented withdrawal syndrome. The hallucinogens have therefore not been shown to produce physical dependence.

Peyote and Mescaline The primary active ingredient of the peyote cactus is the hallucinogen mescaline. It is derived from the buttons of this plant, which has been employed by Indians in Northern Mexico from the earliest recorded time as a part of traditional religious rites. Peyote is used in group settings to attain a trance necessary for tribal dances. The Native American Church, which uses peyote in religious ceremonies, has been exempted from certain provisions of the CSA. Usually ground into a powder, peyote is taken orally. Mescaline can also be produced synthetically. A dose of 350 to 500 mg of mescaline produces illusions and hallucinations from 5 to 12 hours.

Psilocybin and Psilocyn Also derived from plants, psilocybin and psilocyn are obtained from certain mushrooms grown primarily in Mexico. Like mescaline, they have been used in Indian rites for centuries. They are taken orally. Their effects are similar to those of mescaline, except that a smaller dose of 4 to 8 mg is ample. The experience lasts for about six hours.

LSD (LSD-25, lysergide) LSD is an abbreviation of the German expression for lysergic acid diethylamide. It is a semi-synthetic compound produced from lysergic acid, a natural substance found in a fungus or rye. It was first synthesized in 1938. Its psychotomimetic effects were discovered in 1943 when a chemist accidentally took some LSD. As he began to experience the effects now known as a "trip", he noticed a sense of vertigo and restlessness; objects and other workers in the laboratory appeared to undergo optical changes; light was intensified, and bizarre visions with bright colors appeared. This condition lasted for about two hours.

For psychedelic "trip," 100 to 250 micrograms of LSD are used in a diluted solution or mixed with other substances. Drops of the solution are usually taken on a lump of sugar or on blotting paper. Along with the mental changes described earlier, physical reactions may include dilated pupils, lowered temperature, nausea, "goose bumps," profuse perspiration, increased blood sugar, and rapid heartbeat. "Flashbacks" after pharmacological effects have worn off have also been reported.

DOM (STP, 4-methyl-2, 5-dimethoxyamphetamine) DOM was first synthesized in 1964 as one of a series of psychoactive drugs referred to as "psychotomimetic amphetamines." These chemicals produce many of the effects of amphetamines but have the added capability of producing hallucinations. They are chemically related to both mescaline and the amphetamines. Under the popular street name of STP (standing for "serenity, tranquility, and peace"), the drug first won acceptance on the West Coast, where for a time it was legal, inexpensive, and reputed to produce longer and safer hallucinogenic experiences. It is estimated that the drug is from 30 to 50 times less potent than LSD and a hundred times more potent than mescaline. DOM is now under the regulatory controls of the CSA.

DMT and DET (dimethyltryptamine and diethyltryptamine) - DMT is found in the seeds of certain plants indigenous to the West Indies and parts of South America. In Haiti the pulverized seeds have been used for centuries as a snuff, producing a state of mind which the inhabitants believe enable them to communicate with their gods. It can also be produced synthetically. DET is chemically related to DMT, but has not yet been found in plant life. They are administered by smoking one of the chemicals with tobacco, marijuana, or other plant materials. Both illicit substances produce strong, short-lived hallucinogenic effects.

MDA and MMDA   Chemically, MDA and MMDA are related to the amphetamines, mescaline, and DOM (STP). They are controlled as hallucinogens; they also produce some stimulation and a sense of well-being. The MDA sold on the street is synthesized illicitly and sold in powder, tablet, or liquid form. It is usually taken orally but may be "snorted" through the nose or injected intravenously. The MDA experience is reported to be devoid of the visual and auditory distortions which mark that of LSD.

Phencyclidine (PCP)   Phencyclidine, developed in the 1950s, is now licitly manufactured as a veterinary anesthetic under the trade name Sernylan. Since 1967 it has also been produced in clandestine laboratories, frequently in dangerously contaminated forms. The prevailing patterns of street-level abuse are by oral ingestion of tablets or capsules, containing the drug in powder form both alone and in combination with other drugs, and by smoking the drug after it has been sprinkled on parsley, marihuana, or some form of tobacco. It is sometimes sold to unsuspecting consumers as LSD, THC, or mescaline. Reported experiences under the influence of phencyclidine are mainly nondescript or unpleasant. In low doses the experience usually proceeds in three successive stages: changes in body image, sometimes accompanied by feelings of depersonalization; perceptual distortions, infrequently evidenced as visual or auditory hallucinations; and feelings of apathy or estrangement. The experience often includes drowsiness, inability to verbalize, and feelings of emptiness or "nothingness." Reports of difficulty in thinking, poor concentration, and preoccupation with death are common. Many users have reacted to its use with an acute psychotic episode. Common signs of phencyclidine use include flushing and profuse sweating. Analgesia, involuntary eye movements, muscular incoordination, double vision, dizziness, nausea, and vomiting may also be present.

Volatile Substances   Many volatile liquids produce an intoxicated state when inhaled. Young children and adolescents have experimented with this method of distorting consciousness; others have become habituated to the effects of some inhalant. At present, the use of commercial solvents, of which airplane glue is the most popular, may be on the decline. Use of aerosols from spray cans, however, appears to be increasing. The magnitude of the problem is difficult to determine. In large cities a few thousand cases come to the attention of the school or enforcement authorities each year.

A wide variety of industrial solvents, anesthetics, and other chemicals produce intoxication or coma. They can be divided into three groups:

1. Commercial Solvents. Toluene, xylene, benzene, naphtha, hexane, acetone, trichlorethylene, carbon tetrachloride, and many other volatile solvents are found in model airplane glue, plastic cements, paint thinner, gasoline, cleaning fluids, nail polish remover, and cigarette lighter fluid.

2. Aerosols. The propellants in many household and commercial aerosol sprays are gases containing chlorinated or fluorinated hydrocarbons. Aerosols that have been abused include insecticides, deodorants, glass chillers, and hair sprays.

3. Anesthetics. Infrequently, chloroform, ether and nitrous oxide (laughing gas) have been misused in recent years. Nitrous oxide is available commercially as a tracer gas to detect pipe leaks, as a cream whip propellant, and to reduce preignition in racing cars.

Liquid is poured on a rag or into a plastic bag and the fumes are inhaled. Aerosols may be directly breathed in. A tube can be attached to a nitrous oxide cylinder, and one end placed in the mouth.

A number of factors enter into young people's involvement in chronic sniffing of volatile chemicals. The chemicals are readily available in the kitchen, the laundry, the store, and the garage. Not infrequently, the "gang" exerts considerable pressure for everyone to indulge. Studies of persistent sniffers indicate that most of the youngsters were emotionally disturbed or had been involved in antisocial activities. Some were excessively shy; others were very tense or depressed. A poor ability to deal with the ordinary frustrations of life has been suggested as a reason for becoming inebriated with volatile substances. Difficulty in expressing certain emotions, anger, for example, is suggested as another reason for use of the solvents.

Impulsive, destructive behavior may be unleashed. In addition, the repetitive use of these chemicals is a substitute for dealing with life's problems, and therefore may retard emotional maturation.

Certain volatile chemicals have specific toxic properties. Carbon tetrachloride can cause irreversible kidney and liver damage.

Gasoline and naphtha in high concentrations can cause serious heart complications and bone marrow depression. In addition, the lead in gasoline can cause lead poisoning. Toluene is a kidney irritant and can affect the bone marrow and the liver. The aerosols have been known to cause death by freezing the larynx and causing it to contract, or by inducing heart arrest. Repeated use of chloroform and trichloroethylene can result in liver damage. The impurities in commercial solvents and chemicals added to aerosols can be poisonous over and above the substance in which they are dissolved.

Any inhalant which reduces the blood supply to an organ requiring considerable oxygen, such as the brain, will be associated with tissue damage.

For the individual involved, an attempt to bring order and control into his life is necessary. Group therapy may provide the support and interpersonal involvement required to achieve this. A period of time away from an environment where solvent usage is customary may be needed.

The immediate physical effects consist of irritation of the tissues in contact with the solvent, nausea, dizziness, shakiness, and muscle spasms. Weight loss may develop with prolonged periods of inhalation. The psychic effects may include a "high" dreamlike state, drunkenness, sleepiness, disorientation, hallucinations, delusions, and stupor. Occasionally, the individual may manifest excitement, impulsive behavior, and overactivity. Most of the events occurring during the intoxication are not recalled. The state lasts for minutes or an hour or two, depending on the dosage.

Most sniffers have a history of delinquent activity. In some instances this existed before their first contact with drugs. In others, shoplifting, truancy, and curfew violations seem to be associated with the habit.

Poor school performance and accident proneness are directly related to the persistent use of volatile organic solvents.

Tolerance to the effects of the various inhalants occurs, and a desire to repeat the experience is absent in some, but overwhelming in others. Physical dependence and withdrawal symptoms are negligible.

All the inhalants share the hazard of inducing an intoxicated state in which judgment and motor functioning are impaired. Accidents, some fatal, have repeatedly occurred. Suffocation is the major cause of death. Typically, this occurs when the user becomes unconscious with the apparatus used still covering his nose and mouth.

Sniffers tend to be young, generally between eight and eighteen years of age. Most come from impoverished, deprived families with broken or chaotic homes. In particular, the father is either absent or incapable of forming any positive relationship with his children. During the past few years, some middleclass youngsters have become involved. In general, this is an urban problem except for gasoline inhaling which also occurs in rural areas. Most habitual users are male. Prisoners who have access to intoxicating inhalants also tend to use them to become drunk.

The problem is not solely an American one. Japan and other countries have numbers of juveniles who indulge in inhaling such organic solvents as lacquer thinner, gasoline fumes, or volatile cements.

The Infinite Resilience of Drug Abuse

Public issues come and go, and surprisingly, one that has gone quietly is drug abuse.

Many drug administrators have, in the last few years, publicly proclaimed that the corner has been turned on drug abuse, particularly heroin addiction. The pronouncement had some basis in fact, especially in 1973 and early 1974. Drug-related deaths leveled off or dropped from the highs of previous years in most major cities. New York and Washington reported unused openings in drug programs in which a six-month wait had not been unusual. And finally, the expenditure of hundreds of millions of federal law-enforcement dollars on severing the European heroin connection was rewarded with a significant drop in the quality of street level heroin, considered an important factor in motivating addicts to seek treatment.

There were those who did not interpret the same facts with optimism. Addicts weren't reforming, they argued, they were only getting smarter. Faced with a supply shortage, they turned instead to barbiturates, legally produced in pill form by the billions, or to methadone, which they could get simply by enlisting in a methadone program. Speed freaks who were caught short when federal regulations on amphetamines were tightened, were simply switching to cocaine, a potent though not physically addictive substance whose South American supply lines seem to be beyond federal government interdiction. Drug dabblers on high school and college campuses may have turned away from psychedelics and narcotics, but they were turning instead to the nation's primary narcotic, alcohol.

Recent statistics indicate it may have been the critics who were closer to the mark:

- In cities where heroin-related deaths had gone down, methadone deaths doubled and tripled. Methadone advocates argued that such deaths were caused by abuse of methadone bought on the black market, but federal drug abuse officials have tried and failed to uncover a major source for street methadone other than methadone clinics and their patients.
- The two-year shortage of heroin seems to be over. The purity of street level heroin, down to as low as 2 to 3 percent in 1973, is said to be climbing again. The head of a Washington treatment center reports street levels as high as 7 percent and there are similar reports in New York.
- Federal officials fear a major new source of heroin: Mexico. United States Government efforts have finally slowed the Turkish-French flow to a trickle, but now brown Mexican heroin is slipping through a border that over the years has been notoriously porous.
- Federal statistics show that cocaine seizures have increased sevenfold since 1969. New York City undercover policemen report that they are making more cocaine buys on the street than heroin buys. Cocaine ranks behind only marijuana and alcohol as the college students' drug of choice; in 1972, the Commission on Marijuana and Drug Abuse reported that 10.4 percent had tried it at least once, and federal officials say that number has now grown to at least 15 percent.

Drug abuse, and programs to prevent or overcome it, cost the country more than $10 billion a year. Of that amount $791 million goes for federal prevention programs alone, a sum that makes plain society regard drug abuse as a vital issue, politically and socially. Two questions arise: why the concern, and why does drug abuse continue despite that huge effort and expenditure?

In answer to the first, the drug problem has always been seen as more than a health problem. Most americans hold drug abuse and drug abusers responsible for the sharp rise in the crime rate over the last decade. Addicts, in the public mind, become thieves, muggers, and senseless killers.

Recent studies contradict that image. They show that most criminal addicts were criminals before they were addicts, and that most addict criminals are arrested for property crimes, and not violent crimes. But many drug programs were conceived, and funded, before those studies. When several pilot programs using methadone as a substitute for heroin produced successful results, worried politicians and administrators saw methadone as the answer to heroin addiction; and methadone programs became the primary method of treatment in many cities.

Why have these programs not lived up to their promise? The pilots strictly regulated the dispensation of methadone; they also provided other forms of therapy and counseling for their patients. Faced with the problems of delivering treatment to a much larger population, many methadone programs were soon shortcutting, and even cutting out such controls.

There is another factor. The substitution of one addictive substance for another has never solved addiction problems. Heroin, after all, was originally introduced as a medical substitute for morphine.

Methadone does not create the same problems as heroin because it effectively blocks the heroin high, and because its effect on the body lasts a lot longer. There is no frenetic urge for a dose, and so a methadone addict finds it easier to hold down a job or keep his family together. But attempts to detoxify methadone patients have met with a high recidivism rate: many detoxified addicts simply continued to buy methadone on the street, or started shooting heroin again. Others have developed serious drinking problems, or barbiturate habits. More ominously, there is a growing number who have become addicted to methadone who have never experimented with heroin.

Drug Treatment—Historical Background

During the nineteenth century, treatment for drug abusers was generally handled by private physicians and usually involved simply helping the patient through withdrawal. The widespread medical use of morphine, an alkaloid of opium, for relief of pain during the Civil War resulted in morphine addiction among thousands of soldiers. Many of these "medical addicts" were successfully withdrawn from morphine when it was no longer needed for pain relief, but many others continued compulsive use of the drug. The easy availability of opium in the form of patent medicines resulted in addiction among thousands of other people—many of them rural housewives.

Heroin, a semisynthetic derivative of morphine, was developed in 1898 as a potent pain-killer and cough suppressant which was believed to be nonaddictive. Because heroin relieved morphine withdrawal symptoms, it was advertised as a cure for morphine addiction. Several years passed before medical authorities discovered that heroin was as addictive as morphine.

In the late 1800s most physicians regarded drug addiction as a physical disease which would be cured by gradually reducing use of the drug (withdrawal). The psychological element of addiction was largely ignored and, because there was very little followup on patients after treatment, the significance of the problem of relapse was not recognized. The problem of drug addiction did not become a public health issue until the early years of the 20th century when the public became increasingly aware of the link between narcotics and organized crime, as well as the growing incidence of drug addiction among physicians.

The Harrison Act, passed in 1914, restricted the distribution of opiates and cocaine to registered physicians and dentists for use only in the course of professional practice. After this legislation, physicians were deluged with addicted patients seeking drugs. The Federal Government interpreted the law as prohibiting doctors from prescribing maintenance doses to addicts, and as a result numerous indictments were brought against honest physicians who believed that maintenance was the only useful treatment for dependence, as well as the notorious "script" doctors who indiscriminately prescribed large doses of opiates. After 1919, when legitimate sources of narcotics were no longer available, thousands of addicts, particularly those in the larger cities, turned to the illegal market.

To deal with this new problem the Federal Government encouraged large cities to establish temporary clinics for maintenance of dependent persons on doses of opiates with the idea of gradually reducing the dosage and eventually withdrawing the drug. Of the 44 clinics which were established, some claimed success in gradually withdrawing patients, others merely provided maintenance, and several became notoriously careless in their distribution of opiates. The poor performance of some of the clinics along with the condenmation of outpatient maintenance by the American Medical Association led the Federal Government to withdraw its support. The last of the clinics had closed by 1925.

In the following few years, the emphasis on prohibition appeared to solve part of the problem of drug abuse, particularly the danger of medical dependence which had resulted from prescribed drugs and patent medicines. However, a new pattern of drug abuse had begun to emerge in the larger cities. The declining population of mostly middle-aged medical dependents was beginning to be replaced by a new group of young male users who preferred heroin to morphine. From 1925 to 1935, treatment for drug abusers was virtually nonexistent. By that time the medical community was well aware of the extremely high relapse rate among chronic users, and a mood of discouragement prevailed.

Because the Federal prisons were receiving large numbers of drug addicts, in 1929 Congress authorized the establishment of two drug abuse treatment hospitals, primarily as a means of segregating the opiate-dependents from other prisoners. The first Federal drug abuse treatment clinic opened in Lexington, Kentucky, in 1935, and the second opened in Forth Worth, Texas, three years later. Although the clinics were designed primarily for incarceration of Federal prisoners who were drug addicts, voluntary patients were accepted and they soon made up the majority of patients. The clinics withdrew patients using decreasing doses of morphine, followed by a period of inpatient treatment which was supposed to last several months. Voluntary patients were free to leave whenever they wished, however, and most of them did not stay to complete the full treatment period. Followup studies showed that a substantial majority of those patients relapsed to drug use.

The Federal clinics at Lexington and Forth Worth were the only major drug abuse treatment facilities in the country until 1952, when the State of New York opened Riverside Hospital for juveniles in response to the alarming increase in drug addiction among teenagers in New York City. Treatment involved hospitalization for a period of 18 months or more, followed by a period of outpatient care. Because the hospital had actual custody of the juveniles for up to 3 years, most of the patients completed the full treatment regime. Several years later, however, a study showed that approximately 95 percent of the patients relapsed after treatment, and Riverside was closed in 1963.

The explosion of drug addiction in the urban slums in the 1950s and 1960s led to a search for more effective treatment methods. Synanon, founded in 1959 by a former alcoholic named Charles Dederich, was the first of a line of residential treatment programs called therapeutic communities. These programs emphasized the psychological element of drug addiction and attempted to modify the addict's character through group therapy and reinforcement of good behavior. The communities were not designed to treat large numbers of people at one time, and many who entered the programs dropped out after a short period. However, the novelty of the method and the dramatic success of the few who remained in the communities attracted the attention of the public. The therapeutic community and group therapy were soon recognized as important methods of treatment.

In 1961 and 1962, California and New York established statewide treatment programs for drug addicts. The programs were modeled after Lexington but were expected to be more successful because aftercare was compulsory. Treatment involved withdrawal, psychiatric care, and group therapy, beginning with a period of mandatory hospitalization. After several years, the results of both programs were disappointing. As in the case of Lexington and Riverside, the programs were believed to have very high patient relapse rates.

In 1964, Marie Nyswander and Vincent Dole began an experimental drug maintenance program in New York using methadone, a synthetic opiate substitute. Hospitalized patients were gradually stabilized on a high daily dose of methadone. After stabilization, the patients were released and required to return to the clinic daily for their methadone dose. They also received individualized counseling and support services. All the patients stayed in the program voluntarily, and most showed dramatic improvements in social functioning, in terms of employment or enrollment in school. Encouraged by this success, Doctors Dole and Nyswander expanded the program and enrolled about 4,000 patients over the next 3 years. In 1967, an independent evaluation of the program showed that 80 percent of the patients had remained in the program and showed significant improvements in social functioning. The Federal Government then permitted the establishment of other experimental methadone maintenance programs. Subsequent experiments showed that initial hospitalization was unnecessary, a factor which greatly reduced the expense of the programs. Methadone programs then proliferated across the country, and by 1972 methadone had become one of the most widely used treatment methods.

At about the same time that methadone experimental programs were beginning in 1965, researchers at Lexington began to experiment with the use of narcotic antagonists—drugs which counteract the effects of opiates without being addictive themselves. The antagonists had already proved to be clinically useful in treating cases of narcotic overdose and in detecting opiate dependent individuals. The main problems with using antagonists in the treatment of addiction proved to be their short duration of action and some unpleasant side effects, which discouraged, rather than encouraged, addicts to continue in treatment.

In 1966, while methadone maintenance was still in the experimental stages, the Narcotic Addict Rehabilitation Act (NARA) (P.L. 89–793) was passed by Congress. Title I of the Act authorized diversion to treatment before conviction for a restricted class of Federal offenders. Title II provided for treatment as a sentencing alternative for a slightly larger class. Title III provided for voluntary and involuntary civil commitment to Federal treatment facilities in localities where no adequate State treatment facilities existed. Title I of NARA has been little used, apparently because of a lack of interest by U.S. District Attorneys and the restrictions on eligibility. Title II has been used to a greater extent but strict eligibility standards also prohibited its widespread use. However, as a result of Title II, the Bureau of Prisons has initiated a number of innovative treatment programs for a wider variety of drug-dependent offenders. Title III served primarily as a mechanism through which the Federal treatment facilities were made available to States and local communities where no adequate facilities existed. In terms of current funding priorities, Title IV was the most important part of the Narcotic Addict Rehabilitation Act. Under Title IV, the Federal Government began to provide financial and technical assistance to states and cities for the development of drug abuse treatment programs. Two other pieces of Federal legislation authorizing additional aid to state and local treatment programs followed during the next 5 years.

The Comprehensive Drug Abuse Prevention and Control Act of 1970 (P.L. 91–513) further expanded community assistance programs to include all types of drug-dependent persons and drug abusers as well as opiate-dependents. In addition to providing financial support for community-based treatment programs, in recent years the Federal Government has encouraged the development of programs which offer more than one method of treatment, referred to as multi-modality programs. The Drug Abuse Office and Treatment Act of 1972 (P.L. 92–255) provided greatly increased Federal resources to develop community-based, multi-modality treatment centers throughout the United States. The Federal Government has also encouraged treatment programs to judge patient "success" by more flexible standards. In the past, total abstinence from drugs was regarded as the only criterion of success in treatment. Today, however, reduced drug use along with improved social functioning is regarded as a degree of success.

The fact remains that no treatment method yet developed has solved, or promises to solve, all of the complex problems involved in drug abuse. There is still confusion and controversy about the nature of drug dependence and how society should deal with it. It is clear, however, that a variety of methods and approaches must be available to help the various types of drug abusers that exist today. The next section of this report briefly describes the major methods of drug abuse treatment in use at the present time.

Present Methods of Treatment

Hospitalization Hospitalization was used to treat drug dependents in the nineteenth century, and the method was continued at the Lexington and Fort Worth clinics established in the 1930s. Treatment began with gradual withdrawal of the drug, by decreasing the dosage over a period of 1 or 2 weeks, until the patient was drug-free. Withdrawal was followed by a period of inpatient care, usually lasting several months, during which the patient remained isolated from his former environment and from drugs, and received psychiatric counseling, psychotherapy, group therapy or work therapy. The third stage of the hospitalization method consisted of a period of outpatient aftercare in which the patient lived in his community but continued to receive counseling, psychotherapy, or vocational rehabilitation.

The California and New York State treatment programs and the Federal NARA program which started in the 1960s used the Lexington model of hospitalization, although they tried to improve it. The precise degree of success or failure of these hospitalization programs is debatable, because followup studies had difficulties with data collection and definition of "success" or "failure" of treatment. Despite the fact that a mental health approach and professional therapy were used, the emphasis on security and isolation of the patients from the community resulted in a prison-like atmosphere in many of the facilities. The term "civil commitment" has often been used to describe the hospitalization method because legal controls have frequently been used to confine patients in hospitals.

Hospitalization is the most expensive method of treatment, and today it is generally believed to be the least effective method, in view of the high relapse rates of most hospitalization programs over the years. For these reasons the Fort Worth clinic has been closed; Lexington is now closed to patients except those participating in research; and the NARA hospitalization programs are presently being phased out.

Methadone Maintenance In recent years, methadone maintenance has been the most widely used method for treating opiate-dependent persons. Most large cities have treatment programs which provide methadone detoxification and maintenance services after a diagnosis of opiate addiction has been made. Methadone maintenance programs have demonstrated the ability to attract and retain in treatment a large number of opiate-dependent persons. In addition, since most methadone maintenance programs offer treatment on an outpatient basis, it is a markedly less expensive method than treatment which involves hospitalization or confinement.

The methadone maintenance technique developed by Dole and Nyswander used methadone in sufficient dosage to create in patients a "blockade effect." In other words, with the use of this technique, patients became tolerant to the euphoric effects of opiates. For example, if a patient used heroin while receiving daily a large oral dose of methadone, he would not experience the usual euphoria that accompanies heroin usage. In many patients this "blockade effect" tended to discourage repeated illicit opiate usage. During the last ten years, however, many investigators have reported similar successful treatment outcomes for patients using smaller daily doses of methadone. This method has a particular advantage in that the patient is less dependent on opiates. For this reason many maintenance programs today use a lower daily dose of methadone, which is sufficient to prevent withdrawal symptoms, although it does not completely "block" the effects of a sufficiently high dose of heroin.

Federal regulations now require that methadone maintenance programs provide additional treatment such as group therapy, family counseling, vocational training, and social services. Eligibility is limited to persons 16 years of age or older who can demonstrate that they are opiate-dependent and have been for at least two years. Persons between the ages of 16 and 18 must have parental consent and must have tried and failed at least two attempts at detoxification. Although the ultimate goal of methadone maintenamce treatment is eventual withdrawal from methadone and elimination of dependence on any drug, for some individuals maintenance may continue for months or years. The general theory behind methadone maintenance is to relieve the craving for heroin while engaging the patient in additional treatment aimed at helping him work out a better way of living.

In addition to maintenance, methadone programs also provide outpatient detoxification. This treatment involves administering decreasing doses of methadone over a period ranging from a few days to a few weeks for the purpose of relieving withdrawal symptoms. Some addicts volunteer for detoxification in an attempt to become drug-free. However, statistics reveal that detoxification alone is usually unsuccessful. Most patients either relapse to heroin use or enter methadone maintenance programs after detoxification has failed.

Critics of the methadone maintenance method point to the fact that methadone does not cure drug dependence but merely transfers dependence from one drug to another. Another criticism is that some patients begin chronic abuse of other drugs such as alcohol, amphetamines, barbiturates, or cocaine while enrolled in methadone maintenance treatment. In view of these deficiencies, current Federal policy emphasizes that entry into methadone maintenance should be voluntary and that drug-free treatment should be offered as an alternative.

Therapeutic Communities Therapeutic communities are residential treatment programs which attempt to deal with the psychological causes of addiction by changing the addict's character and personality. As mentioned earlier, the first therapeutic community for drug addicts was Synanon, founded in 1959. The techniques used were modeled after those of Alcoholics Anonymous, which involved repeated confessions, group interaction, and mutual support among the members. During the late 1950s and early 1960s, the concept of group therapy was growing in popularity throughout the country, and as therapeutic communities developed they adopted it as a major technique. The growth of therapeutic communities also paralleled the growth of communes, and some of the cooperative spirit of the communes was incorporated into the therapeutic communities. The idea of a group of people living and working together for their mutual benefit was, and still is, a basic tenet of the therapeutic community.

Although therapeutic communities are often managed by former addicts, and do not usually have mental health professionals on their staffs, the treatment method is based on two techniques of group psychotherapy. The first technique is confrontation, or encounter group therapy, in which the addict is forced to confess and acknowledge his weakness and immaturity. The second technique is "milieu therapy", in which the addict lives and works within a hierarchial social structure and may progress upward in status as he demonstrates increased responsibility and self-discipline. The principles of behavior modification, or conditioning, are constantly applied within the community in the form of reinforcement of good behavior and punishment of bad behavior. The time period for treatment varies from one therapeutic community to another.

Most therapeutic communities require members to stay 1 or 2 years. The programs also vary in selectivity. The older programs screened applicants rigorously, accepting only the most highly motivated individuals. The older programs also continue to be completely drug-free, whereas some of the newer programs use methadone maintenance or both methadone and drug-free therapy.

The problem with therapeutic communities as a treatment method is that they appear to be suitable for very few people. In fact, about 75 percent of those who enter them drop out within the first month. Members who remain in the communities and seem to respond to the treatment regimen are largely white and from middle-class backgrounds. Some critics feel that the treatment of residents in the demeaning or punitive way, which is characteristic of many communities, goes against the principles of supportive psychotherapy. Because they are residential, therapeutic communities are more expensive to operate than drug-free outpatient programs, even though many are operated entirely by members. In terms of results, however, therapeutic communities do not appear to be more effective than other drug-free methods of treatment.

Drug-Free Outpatient Treatment   The treatment method which offers drug-free services on an entirely outpatient basis is referred to as either drug-free outpatient, ambulatory drug-free, or outpatient abstinence treatment. There are many differences among programs as to the scope or level of treatment they provide, but they usually include some or all of the following services: group or individual psychotherapy, vocational and social counseling, family counseling, vocational training, education, and community outreach. Programs also differ in the degree of patient involvement in treatment. Some programs are social or "rap" centers where patients drop in occasionally. Others are free clinics providing a wide range of health services. Some programs provide structured methadone detoxification and monitor patient drug use by urine analysis throughout treatment. Little evaluation has been done on this method of treatment since program records often omit data on patients who drop out of treatment early. Most experts believe that these programs do help some people but that the attrition rates are very high. It appears that drug-free outpatient treatment may be more effective with youths who are experimenting with drugs than it is with hard-core addicts.

Multi-Modality Treatment   In recent years some treatment programs have adopted a multi-modality approach by providing more than one method of treatment. This approach has the advantage of offering the patient a choice among alternative treatment regimens. Some patients respond better to a particular method of treatment than to others, and in a multimodality program patients may be transferred easily from one type of treatment to another. This approach allows for more choice by patients. The larger multimodality programs may include methadone maintenance, detoxification services, inpatient and outpatient drug-free treatment, and a therapeutic community. The Federal Government today strongly supports the community-based, multi-modality approach to drug dependence treatment.

Treatment for Nonopiate Drug Dependence At the present time, there are no specialized methods for treating dependence on drugs other than opiates or alcohol. There is no chemotherapy, such as methadone maintenance, for treating abuse of the nonopiate drugs which include amphetamines, barbiturates, and hallucinogens. These drugs are often referred to as "soft drugs" as opposed to "hard drugs" (opiates). This term is often misleading in that it implies that these drugs are less harmful. In fact, they are often equally as addictive as hard drugs and in some cases more life-threatening. For example, abrupt withdrawal from barbiturates is much more life-threatening than withdrawal from opiates, and for that reason withdrawal from barbiturates requires hospitalization. Simultaneous use of more than one drug sometimes produces serious adverse reactions, including accidental (or intended) overdose. Individuals who abuse two or more drugs, either simultaneously or alternately, are often referred to as polydrug abusers.

Emergency treatment, usually called crisis intervention, is sometimes required for acute adverse reactions resulting from nonopiate drug use. For example, adverse effects of amphetamines and hallucinogens sometimes result in paranoid or violent behavior. Hospital emergency rooms can provide treatment in such emergencies, as well as in overdose cases. However, during the late 1960s when soft drug use was spreading rapidly, many young drug users were reluctant to go to hospitals, fearing trouble with the authorities or the hospital environment itself. As a result, free clinics were set up in many cities to provide an alternative to emergency room treatment. Since 1967 when the Haight-Ashbury Free Clinic opened in San Francisco, more than 250 free clinics have been established across the country. Staffed by doctors, psychologists and others on a volunteer basis, these clinics provide a variety of general medical and social services in addition to treatment of drug abuse emergencies. For those experiencing adverse psychological reactions to drugs, these centers provide a calm, supportive environment and reassurance, or "talking down," by an experienced staff member. In addition, many crisis intervention programs operate telephone hotline services which provide information, referrals, and counseling on request.

Most crisis clinics have very little followup on patients, since they are primarily concerned with immediate problems. Many of the patients treated are young people experimenting with drugs rather than chronic, heavy users. It is generally believed that crisis centers have little lasting impact on those who are compulsive drug users. In recent years some centers have begun to offer long-term psychotherapy, as well as emergency services, in an attempt to alleviate underlying psychological problems associated with chronic drug use. Some of the larger programs now serve as community mental health centers, providing counseling and therapy for a broader range of social and psychological problems.

Other Treatment Approaches Over the past decade a considerable amount of research effort has been focused on a class of drugs known as narcotic antagonists. These drugs counteract the effects of opiate drugs in the body, including the euphoria, or "high," but, unlike methadone, they do not cause physical dependence. This ability to reverse the effects of opiates has made them useful in treating narcotic overdoses. Research is being conducted on the use of narcotic antagonists in helping addicts to remain abstinent after withdrawal. One problem is that some antagonists have unpleasant or possibly harmful side effects. Another problem is that all of them are relatively short-acting, and must be administered daily. For these reasons, participation in a treatment program using antagonists requires a high degree of motivation. Scientists are attempting to develop a longer-acting antagonist which would be effective for several days or weeks. It is possible that such an antagonist could be very useful in helping the addict who has been rehabilitated while on methadone and is motivated to be detoxified and remain drug-free.

Because no one method of treatment has proved to be the answer to the drug abuse problem, research and experimentation are being conducted on a wide variety of potential treatment methods. Some researchers are working with behavioral techniques such as aversive therapy, or negative conditioning, in which electric shocks or nausea-producing substances are administered simultaneously with narcotics. Others are using bio-feedback techniques to attempt to train people to control internal states and body processes. Transcendental meditation has been investigated as a possible method of reducing soft drug use, particularly among college students. Much attention is currently directed toward developing alternatives to drug abuse, which may include any meaningful activity or pursuits in which young people can become involved instead of resorting to drugs.

The wide diversity of treatment methods reflects the present lack of precise knowledge as to the nature of drug addiction and abuse. Uncertainty still exists regarding the causes, whether or not it is an "illness," and the degree to which the condition is physical or psychological. Policymakers continue to debate these issues while research is attempting to increase our knowledge of this complex social problem. Meanwhile, even though treatment programs across the country are not "curing" some patients of the condition of drug dependence, nonetheless, for the majority, they are providing support and a marked degree of social rehabilitation for better functioning and a better life.

Drug Education The ultimate goal of any drug education program should be the responsible use of potent, and potentially dangerous substances. A secondary goal is the prevention of drug abuse and drug dependency. An added bonus might be the alleviation of some existing alcoholism or other drug dependency. One approach is to use the scare technique, stressing known effects and side effects plus possible long- and short-term effects. To be an effective approach the incidence of side effects should be discussed in relation to the frequency and incidence of use. The approach must include accurate statistics and reproducible research results, not conjecture or quotes taken out of context.

A second technique is the rational, matter-of-fact presentation of scientific fact with the admission that much of our knowledge is incomplete. These presentations should be many sided with emphasis on giving objective evidence and providing a logical basis for decisions. Discussions should include personal and cultural preferences for certain drugs, plus the social, political, legal, and philosophical questions associated with use of various agents. Opposing points of view should be presented and examined with impartiality. Users, exusers, and nonusers can present and discuss their ideas about the various drugs before small groups.

A third technique is to discuss the styles of drug use and the motives involved in this use. Any discussion of motives must include the fact that these motives are similar for adults and youth. Emphasis must be given to the fact that the majority of drug users are not irresponsible, disaffected, alienated, or mentally ill. What should be stressed is that they are all attempting to alter the reality of their existence in one way or another.

A final, infrequently advertised or utilized approach is offering nonchemical alternatives to drug abuse.

Alternatives to Drug Use I don't want to downgrade the real value of accurate information about drug effects—it can be a significant help in decision-making processes. Further, it may serve to bolster the intuition that drugs are harmful and may help justify socially taking a nonchemical route. Educational honesty and credibility must be maximized, in the same way that legislators should make drug use a public health, not criminal, action. But the real promise in education would be to involve educating about alternatives. There is no higher priority and there is no other way to make such a powerful impact minimizing drug-use patterns.

Education about nonchemical alternatives for each level of experience is the best "prevention." It is also the method of choice for moderate experimenters. And finally, the Alternatives Model is the treatment of choice for heavy users (here much stress would be put on the alternative of not using). In the application of the Alternatives Model, it must be realized that there is no one pat alternative for everyone, just as there is no one motive responsible for all drug use. Also, it should be noted that the alternatives of best application are those which are *incompatible* with being high. For example, "listening to recorded music" is not an alternative unless it precludes being stoned while listening. In this particular case, techniques or ways of listening must be sufficiently taught so that chemically-altered awareness gets in the way of the experience. In general, extremely *passive* alternatives must be utilized with a bit more care than alternatives necessitating *action* or work with one's resources. The more active and demanding alternatives most clearly interfere with a drug-taking style.

An Alternatives Model emphasizes causes: and mandates increased attention to the development and communication of alternative attitudes, strategies, techniques, institutional changes, and life-styles which could diminish the desire for using drugs in order to attain legitimate personal aspirations. "Alternative" is *not* just a synonym for "substitute" since it implies an orientation which is *more effective* than drugs for giving the person real satisfaction.

Once we presume that "alternatives" are important, we must expand the model to fit complex variables in all phases of the drug scene. We face questions like: "Which alternative for which drug?" "Which alternative for which motive?" "Which alternative for which person?" It is obvious that motives and relevant alternatives are intimately connected, and that one way of conceptualizing it is in terms of different "levels of experience." Thus, as an illustration refer to Table 1. Each level of experience pertains to certain types of motives leading to drug use or experimentation, examples of which are listed in the Table. Across from each level-motive category are examples of types of alternatives which might replace, ameliorate or prevent drug abuse. The reader can come up with many more motives and an almost infinite addition of alternatives. Of course, there are other ways to conceptualize the different kinds of alternatives—again, this is intended only to serve as an example and stimulation. Needless to say, several levels of experience may operate within a particular individual or subgroup, so categories and motives may be related across levels and should not be taken as mutually exclusive.

There is one alternative not mentioned in the Table because it is so obvious. Yet it deserves some comment. A growingly viable alternative to using drugs is *not using drugs or discontinuing drug use.*

Perhaps the most exciting aspect of the Alternatives Model is that it can be applied to any level of action or reaction to drug use. It is limited only by the imagination and wisdom of the thinker. The positive possibilities seem limitless; while obsession on drug-related symptoms and dangers appears an endless pit of futility.

There are other advantages to the Alternatives Model. Application of provided alternatives to drugs simultaneously provides alternatives to other forms of human difficulties. After all, the need is for truly effective solutions to the problem of "people" and "life." Very possibly, deterioration may be shifted to harmony. Those solutions, applied to every level of experience, should make man's abuse of himself and others fade into a historical remberance of a thankfully transcended cultural psychosis.

The areas which can be offered as alternatives to drug abuse include personal awareness; interpersonal relationships; self-reliance development; vocational skills; creative and esthetic experiences; philosophical existential explorations, social, and political involvement; religious experiences; sexuality; and mind-trips. Two other areas not included, although obviously needed, are meaningful work and meaningful pleasure. Work is too often

TABLE 1. SOME MOTIVES FOR DRUG USE, AND POSSIBLE ALTERNATIVES

Level of Experience	Corresponding Motives (Examples)	Possible Alternatives (Examples)
Physical	Desire for physical satisfaction, physical relaxation, relief from sickness, desire for more energy, maintenance of physical dependency	Athletics, dance, exercise, hiking, diet, health training, carpentry or outdoor work
Sensory	Desire to stimulate sight, sound, touch, taste; need for sensual-sexual stimulation; desire to magnify sensorium	Sensory awareness training, sky diving, experiencing sensory beauty of nature
Emotional	Relief from psychological pain, attempt to solve personal perplexities, relief from bad mood, escape from anxiety, desire for emotional insight, liberation of feeling, emotional relaxation	Competent individual counseling, well-run group therapy, instruction in psychology of personal development
Interpersonal	To gain peer acceptance, to break through interpersonal barriers, to "communicate," especially non-verbally, defiance of authority figures, cement two person relationships, relaxation of interpersonal inhibition, solve interpersonal hangups	Expertly managed sensitivity and encounter groups, well-run group therapy, instruction in social customs, confidence training, social-interpersonal counseling, emphasis on assisting others in distress via education
Social (including socio-cultural and environmental)	To promote social change, to find identifiable subculture, to tune out intolerable environmental conditions, e.g., poverty, changing the awareness of the "masses"	Social service, community action in positive social change, helping the poor, aged, infirm, young, tutoring handicapped, ecology action

Political	To promote political change, to identify with anti-establishment subgroup, to change drug legislation, out of desperation with social-political order, to gain wealth or affluence or power	Political service, political action, non-partisan projects such as ecological lobbying, field work with politicians and public officials
Intellectual	To escape mental boredom, out of intellectual curiosity, to solve cognitive problems, to gain new understanding in the world of ideas, to study better, to research one's own awareness, for science	Intellectual excitement through reading, through discussion, creative games and puzzles, self-hypnosis, training in concentration, synectics—training in intellectual breakthroughs, memory training
Creative-aesthetic	To improve creativity in the arts, to enhance enjoyment of art already produced, e.g., music, to enjoy imaginative mental productions	Non-graded instruction in producing and/or appreciating art, music, drama, crafts, handiwork, cooking, sewing, gardening, writing, singing, etc.
Philosophical	To discover meaningful values, to grasp the nature of the universe, to find meaning in life, to help establish personal identify, to organize a belief structure	Discussions, seminars, courses in the meaning of life; study of ethics, morality, the nature of reality; relevant philosophical literature; guided exploration of value systems
Spiritual-mystical	To transcend orthodox religion, to develop spiritual insights, to reach higher levels of consciousness, to have Divine Visions, to communicate with God, to augment yogic practices, to get a spiritual shortcut, to attain enlightenment, to attain spiritual powers	Exposure to non-chemical methods of spiritual development, study of world religions, introduction to applied mysticism, meditation, yogic techniques

mundane and stifling to the individual worker. To be meaningful, work must be employment which gives the individual some personal satisfaction: pride in his work, a sense of accomplishment or a sense of contribution. Too many mass-production jobs leave the worker without any of these intangible benefits. To change involves emphasizing the quality of the job, providing effective praise and criticism, delegating more responsibility and providing a challenge.

Realities To offer alternatives to drug abuse requires accepting certain, perhaps unpleasant, realities.

Reality I: The use of mood-altering substances is usually pleasurable. People *use* drugs to "feel better" or to "get high." Individuals *experiment* with drugs out of curiosity or hope that the drugs can, in some way, make them feel better. People *abuse* drugs due to personal deficiencies.

Reality II: People start and continue to use (abuse) drugs because they want to do so, not because of some intrinsic nature of the drug.

Reality III: Drugs do not compel behavior. They may lessen inhibitions or interfere with logical thinking, thus allowing unusual behavior. However, drugs do not, of themselves, produce any actions by the person.

Reality IV: Psychological dependence results when the drug effect fills a need or is a people substitute. Any activity or agent which gives pleasure or relieves discomfort may be associated with psychological dependence.

Reality V: Drug users are not necessarily immature, immoral, irresponsible, socially disadvantaged, alienated, rebellious, or mentally ill. Drug use is a part of the continuum of human existence.

Reality VI: All use of illegal or socially disapproved drugs is not necessarily abusive, much less addictive. Some legal drug use is abusive because it produces physical, psychological, or social damage.

Reality VII: The important factor in many forms of pleasure seeking (gratification) behavior is the resultant change in the mood or consciousness of the person.

Reality VIII: Our society appears to stress experience as a prerequisite for maturity. Some drugs are alleged to give experience quickly, painlessly, and effortlessly.

Reality IX: Individuals do not stop using mood-altering substances or pleasure-seeking behavior until they discover something better.

Reality X: The alternatives to drug abuse are also alternatives to the distresses and discomfort which lead to any self-destructive behavior.

Requisites To be acceptable and attractive, any alternatives we offer must be realistic, attainable and meaningful. Any proposed alternative must assist people to find self-understanding, improved self-image, feeling of significance, expanded awareness, or new experiences which they seek through drugs. These alternatives must also meet other criteria:

1. They must contribute to individual identity and independence.
2. They must offer active participation and involvement.
3. They must offer a chance for commitment.
4. They must provide a feeling of identification with some larger body of experience.
5. Some of the alternatives must be in the realm of the noncognitive and the intuitive.

Other alternatives may need to provide a way to transcend day to day routines such as job or education. The ultimate effect is, to quote Herbert Otto, to help the person "discover and make maximum use of his potentialities—the range of his strengths, capacities, and capabilities."

Bibliography

Brecher, Edward, ed.: *Licit and Illicit Drugs.* Mount Vernon, 1972, Consumers Union.

Cornacchia, Smith, Bentel: *Drugs in the Classroom.* St. Louis, 1978, C.V. Mosby Co.

Estes, N. and M. Heinemann: *Alcoholism — Development, Consequences, and Intervention.* St. Louis, 1977, C.V. Mosby Co.

Fuqua, Paul: *Drug Abuse: Investigation and Control.* New York, New York, 1978, McGraw-Hill.

Girdano and Girdano: *Drugs — A Factual Account.* Reading, Mass., 1976, Addison Wesley Publishing Co.

Glatt, M.M.: *A Guide to Addiction and Its Treatment.* New York, New York, 1974, John Wiley & Sons, Inc.

Graedon, Joe: *The People's Pharmacy.* New York, New York, 1976, Avon.

Julien, Robert: *A Primer of Drug Action.* San Francisco, 1978, W.H. Freeman & Co.

Parish, Peter: *The Doctors and Patients Handbook of Medicines and Drugs.* New York, New York, 1977, Alfred A. Knopf.

Ray, O.S.: *Drugs, Society and Human Behavior.* St. Louis, 1978, C.V. Mosby Co.

Weil, Andrew: *The National Mind.* Boston, 1972, Houghton Mifflin Company.

Weil, Andrew: *Drugs of Abuse.* Washington, 1977, Drug Enforcement Administration.

Weil, Andrew: *Fact Sheets.* Washington, 1975, Drug Enforcement Administration.

Weil, Andrew: *Marihuana and Health.* 1975, Rockville, National Institute on Drug Abuse.

Source Book Section

GRADUATE PROGRAMS AND
PROFESSIONAL ASSOCIATIONS,
GOVERNMENTAL AGENCIES AND
VOLUNTARY ORGANIZATIONS

This section includes a listing of graduate programs most interesting to students of the human services. No attempt was made to include all graduate schools which offer human service oriented programs, but rather the most innovative and imaginative degree programs are listed.

For additional information about any program, students need only to call or write to the college or graduate school or to the appropriate professional association listed in the Source Book section below.

Social Work

The following is a representative sample of colleges offering graduate social work programs. For a complete listing of all schools of social work write to:

Council on Social Work Education
345 East 46th Street
New York, New York 10017

Ask for its publication: *Schools of Social Work with Accredited Masters Degree Programs.* It is available free of charge.

University of Connecticut   Degree: M.S.W.
Graduate Admissions Office
Storrs, Connecticut 06268

Atlanta University   Degree: M.S.W.
Graduate School of Social Work
223 Chestnut Street, S.W.
Atlanta, Georgia 30314

Quad Cities Graduate Studies Center   Degree: M.S.W.
639 38th Street
Rock Island, Illinois 61201

University of Kentucky   Degree: M.S.W.
Graduate School Office
Patterson Office Tower
Lexington, Kentucky 40506

Boston University   Degree: M.S.W.
School of Social Work
264 Bay State Road
Boston, Massachusetts 02215

Wayne State University   Degree: M.S.W.
Office for Graduate Admissions
Detroit, Michigan 48202

University of Southern Mississippi   Degree: M.S.W.
Office of Admissions
Box 11, Southern Station
Hattiesburg, Mississippi 39401

Saint Louis University   Degree: M.S.W.
Dean of the Graduate School
221 North Grand Boulevard
St, Louis, Missouri 63103

Rutgers University   Degree: M.S.W.
Office of Graduate and Professional
Admissions
542 George Street
New Brunswick, New Jersey 08903

Fordham University   Degree: M.S.W.
Graduate School of Social Service
New York, New York 10023

State University of New York at Albany   Degree: M.S.W.
Office of Graduate Admissions
School of Social Work
1400 Washington Avenue
Albany, New York 12222

University of North Carolina   Degree: M.S.W.
Dean of the Graduate School
105 Steele Building
Chapel Hill, North Carolina 27514

Case Western Reserve University   Degree: M.S.W.
Graduate Studies Admissions
Cleveland, Ohio 44106

University of Oklahoma   Degree: M.S.W.
The Graduate College
Norman, Oklahoma 73019

Portland State University   Degree: M.S.W.
Office of Graduate Studies
and Research
Portland, Oregon 97207

University of Houston   Degree: M.S.W.
Graduate Admissions
128 Ezekiel Cullen Building
4800 Calhoun
Houston, Texas 77004

West Virginia College of   Degree: M.S.W.
Graduate Studies
Director of Admissions
Institute, West Virginia 25112

Graduate Gerontology Programs

University of Southern California   Degree: M.A. Gerontology
Andrus Gerontology Center
Los Angeles, California 90007

New School for Social Research   Degree: M.P.S.
Graduate School of Management and   Gerrontological
Urban Professions   Services
66 Fifth Avenue   Administration
New York, New York 10011

University of Northern Colorado   Degree: M.A. Gerontology
Greeley, Colorado 80631

University of South Florida   Degree: M.A. Gerontology
Tampa, Florida 33620

Universities which contain Gerontology Centers, and offer programs in Gerontology in conjunction with degree programs in other disciplines include:

University of Michigan
School of Graduate Studies
Ann Arbor, Michigan 48109

Boston University
Gerontology Center
Boston, Massachusetts 02215

Syracuse University
Gerontology Center
Syracuse, New York 13210

Graduate Programs in Alcoholism Studies

University of Arizona
Graduate College
Tucson, Arizona 85721

Degree: M.A.
    Alcoholism
    Studies

Governers State University
Park Forest South
Chicago, Illinois 60466

Degree: M.A.
    Alcoholism
    Science

Graduate Programs in Health

(Community Health, Public Health, Mental Health)

Thomas Jefferson University
Philadelphia, Pennsylvania 19107

Degree: M.S. Community
    Health

University of California at
Los Angeles
Division of Extended Studies
Los Angeles, California 90024

Degree: Masters of
    Public Health

Antioch College/West
3663 Sacramento Street
San Francisco, California 94118

Degree: M.A. Community
    Mental Health

University of Rochester
Associate Dean for Graduate Studies
Rochester, New York 14642

Degree: M.S. Community
    Health

Hunter College CUNY
Office of Graduate Studies
695 Park Avenue
New York, New York 10021

Degree: M.S. Community
    Health

New School for Social Research
Graduate School of Management and
Urban Professions
66 Fifth Avenue
New York, New York 10011

Degree: M.P.S. Health
Services
Administration

Long Island University
Graduate Admissions
University Plaza
Brooklyn, New York 11201

Degree: M.S. Community
Mental Health

University of California at
Berkeley
School of Public Health
19 Earl Warren Health
Berkeley, California 94720

Degree: Masters of
Public Health
(Extended
University
Program)

Graduate Programs in Psychology and Counseling

California State University
800 North Street
Fullerton, California 92631

Degree: M.S. Community
Psychology

University of Northern Colorado
Center for Social and Advanced
Programs
Greeley, Colorado 80631

Degree: Non Resident -
experienced based
Masters in
Psychology,
Human Relations
and Counseling

California State College
Department of Psychology
1861 East Cotati Avenue
Rohnert Park, California 94928

Degree: M.A. Psychology
(Independent
Study Program)

Goddard College
The Graduate Program
Plainfield, Vermont 05677

Degree: M.A. Psychology,
Social Change and
Counseling
(Independent
Study)

Antioch College/West
3663 Sacramento Street
San Francisco, California 94118

Degree: M.A. Community
Psychology

University of Bridgeport
Bridgeport, Connecticut 06602

Degree: M.S. Community
Psychology

Antioch/New England
Graduate School of Education
One Elm Street
Keane, New Hampshire 03431

Degree: M.A. Counseling

New York University
School of Education, Health, Nursing
and Arts Professions
Washington Square, New York 10003

Degree: M.A. Counseling

Federal City College
Dean, School of Graduate Studies
724 9th Street, N.W.
Washington, D.C. 20001

Degree: M.A. Psychology

Ball State University
Dean of Graduate School
Muncie, Indiana 47306

Degree: Masters in
Psychology

Special Graduate Programs

Central Michigan University
Institute for Personal and
Career Development
Mount Pleasant, Michigan 48858

Degree: M.A. Community
Leadership

Antioch College
5829 Banneker Road
Columbia, Maryland 21044

Degree: M.A. Community
Education

The University of Sarasota   Degree: M.A.
Graduate School of Education   Human Services
2080 Ringling Boulevard   (non-resident
Sarasota, Florida 33577   program)

Brandeis University   Degree: M.A.
The Florence Heller Graduate School   Human Services
415 South Street   Management
Waltham, Massachusetts 02154

New York Institute of Technology Degree: M.P.S.
Graduate Admissions   Human Relations
Old Westbury, New York 11568

Graduate Programs in Criminal Justice

Southern Illinois University   Degree: M.S. Admin-
Office of Graduate School   istration of
Carbondale, Illinois 62901   Justice

John Jay College of Criminal Justice Degree: M. S. Admin-
City University of New York   istration of
445 West 59th Street   Criminal Justice
New York, New York 10019

Graduate Programs in Rehabilitation Counseling

University of Arizona   Degree: M.A. Rehabil-
The Rehabilitation Center   itation Counselor
College of Education   Education
Tucson, Arizona 85721

Arkansas State University   Degree: M.A. Rehabil-
Rehabilitation Counselor   itation Counselor
Training Program   Education
College of Education
Box 898
State University, Arkansas 72467

San Francisco State University
Counseling Department
1600 Holloway Avenue
San Francisco, California 94132

Degree: M.A. Rehabil-
itation Counselor
Education

East Carolina University
Rehabilitation Counselor
Training Program, School of
Allied Health and Social Professions
P.O. Box 3248
Greenville, North Carolina 27834

Degree: M.A. Rehabil-
itation Counselor
Education

Florida State University
Rehabilitation Counselor Education
College of Education
902 West Park Avenue
Tallahassee, Florida 32306

Degree: M.A. Rehabil-
itation Counselor
Education

Emporia Kansas State College
Rehabilitation Counselor Education
1200 Commercial Street
Emporia, Kansas 66801

Degree: M.A. Rehabil-
itation Counselor
Education

Oklahoma State University
Rehabilitation Counselor Education
College of Education
Stillwater, Oklahoma 74074

Degree: M.A. Rehabil-
itation Counselor
Education

University of Pittsburgh
Rehabilitation Counseling Program
School of Education
4616 Henry Street
Pittsburgh, Pennsylvania 15260

Degree: M.A. Rehabil-
itation Counselor
Education

Saint Cloud University
Rehabilitation Counselor Education
College of Education
St. Cloud, Minnesota 56301

Degree: M.A. Rehabil-
itation Counselor
Education

Virginia Commonwealth University   Degree: M.A. Rehabil-
School of Rehabilitation Counseling   itation Counselor
901 West Franklin Street   Education
Richmond, Virginia 23220

The University of Wisconsin-   Degree: M.A. Rehabil-
Milwaukee   itation Counselor
Department of Educational Psychology   Education
Enderis Hall, Room 757
Hartford Avenue
Milwaukee, Wisconsin 53201

Reference Material

Sources for reference material contained in this section are of particular interest to human services students. Many professional associations offer student memberships, and publications are available in most fields. For information concerning current research, periodicals, special publications and career information contact the organizations in your interest area.

Addiction Research Center
National Institute of Mental Health
Lexington, Kentucky 40506

Administration for Children, Youth and Family
Department of Health, Education and Welfare
200 Independence Avenue, S.W.
Washington, D.C. 20201

Alcoholics Anonymous
General Service Office
468 Park Avenue South
New York, N.Y. 10017

American Anthropological Association
1703 New Hampshire Avenue, N.W.
Washington, D.C. 20009
Student Memberships Available

American Association of Homes for the
Aging
1050 17th Street, S.W.
Washington, D.C. 20036

American Association of Marriage and Family Counselors, Inc.
225 Yale Avenue
Clairmont, California 91711
Student Memberships Available

American Group Psychotherapy Association
1995 Broadway
New York, N.Y. 10023

American Nursing Association
2420 Pershing Drive
Kansas City, Missouri 64108
Student Memberships Available

American Orthopsychiatric Association
1775 Broadway
New York, N.Y. 10019
Student Memberships Available

American Personnel and Guidance Association
1607 New Hampshire Avenue, N.W.
Washington, D.C. 20009
Student Memberships Available

American Psychological Association
1722 N Street, N.W.
Washington, D.C. 20036
Student Memberships Available

American Public Welfare Association
1313 East 60th Street
Chicago, Illinois 60637

American School Health Association
Kent, Ohio 44240

American Sociological Association
1722 N Street, N.W.
Washington, D.C. 20036
Student Memberships Available

Child Study Association of America, Inc.
50 Madison Avenue
New York, N.Y. 10010

Child Welfare League of America
67 Irving Place
New York, N.Y. 10003

Council on Social Work Education, Inc.
345 East 46th Street
New York, N.Y. 10017
Student Memberships Available

Employment and Training Administration
Department of Labor
601 D Street, N.W.
Washington, D.C. 20213

Family Service Association of America, Inc.
44 East 23rd Street
New York, N.Y. 10010

Hazalden Foundation (Alcoholism Information)
Department of Education
Center City, Minnesota 55012

Mental Health Materials Center, Inc.
419 Park Avenue South
New York, N.Y. 10016

National Association for Retarded Citizens, Inc.
254 West 31st Street
New York, N.Y. 10001

National Association of Social Workers
1425 H Street, N.W.
Washington, D.C. 20005
Student Memberships Available

National Association of Workers for the Blind
1511 K Street, N.W.
Washington, D.C. 20005

National Center for Family Planning Services
Health Services and Mental Health Administration
Department of Health, Education and Welfare
5600 Fishers Lane
Rockville, Maryland 20852

National Clearinghouse for Alcoholism Information
P.O. Box 2345
Rockville, Maryland 20852

National Coalition Against Domestic Violence
Bradley-Engle House
Box 4123
Portland, Oregan 97240

National Council of Senior Citizens
15 K Street, N.W.
Washington, D.C. 20005

National Council on Alcoholism, Inc.
733 Third Avenue
New York, N.Y. 10017

National Council on the Aging
1828 L Street, N.W.
Washington, D.C. 20036

National Directory of Spouse Abuse Prevention Projects
46 Pleasant Street
Cambridge, Massachusetts 02139

National Federation of Settlements and Neighborhood Centers
236 Madison Avenue
New York, N.Y. 10016

National Institute on Alcohol Abuse and Alcoholism
5600 Fishers Lane
Rockville, Maryland 20852

National Rehabilitation Administration
Department of Health, Education and Welfare
200 Independence Avenue, S.W.
Washington, D.C. 20201

National Rehabilitation Association
1522 K Street, N.W.
Washington, D.C. 20005
Student Memberships Available

National Therapeutic Recreation Association
1700 Pennsylvania Avenue
Washington, D.C. 20006

Office of Education
Department of Health, Education and Welfare
400 Maryland Avenue, S.W.
Washington, D.C. 20202

Planned Parenthood Federation of America, Inc.
810 Seventh Avenue
New York, N.Y. 10019

Public Health Service
Department of Health, Education and Welfare
200 Independence Avenue, N.W.
Washington, D.C. 20201

Sex Information and Education Council of the U.S., Inc.
(SIECUS)
84 Fifth Avenue
New York, N.Y. 10011

Social Security Administration
6401 Security Boulevard
Baltimore, Maryland 21235

The Gerontological Society
1 Dupont Circle
Washington, D.C. 20036
Student Memberships Available

The Population Council
245 Park Avenue
New York, N.Y. 10017

U.S. Administration on Aging
HEW South
330 C Street, S.W.
Washington, D.C. 20201

Veterans Administration
810 Vermont Avenue, N.W.
Washington, D.C. 20420